Campaign Dynamics

Campaign Dynamics

The Race for Governor

Thomas M. Carsey

Ann Arbor

THE UNIVERSITY OF MICHIGAN PRESS

Copyright © by the University of Michigan 2000
All rights reserved
Published in the United States of America by
The University of Michigan Press
Manufactured in the United States of America
⊗ Printed on acid-free paper

2003   2002   2001   2000   4   3   2   1

A CIP catalog record for this book is available from the British Library.

Library of Congress Cataloging-in-Publication Data

Carsey, Thomas M., 1966–
     Campaign dynamics : the race for governor / Thomas M. Carsey.
         p.   cm.
     Includes bibliographical references and index.
     ISBN 0-472-11014-4 (cloth : alk. paper)
     1. Governors—United States—Election.   2. Electioneering—
United States—States.   I. Title.

     JK2447 .C37   2000
     324.7'0973—dc21   00-023330

To Dawn, Simon, and Jane, who have sacrificed more than I have over the duration of this project. In fact, the project itself is older than both Simon and Jane. Though they may never read this book—or even want to—it would not have been completed without their love and understanding.

Contents

Preface and Acknowledgments

This book focuses on the interaction between voters and candidates that takes place during campaigns. In this work, I combine ideas from several different theoretical traditions to further the understanding of the electoral process. I show that the salience of factors that predict voting behavior in gubernatorial elections responds to what candidates do and say during their campaigns.

Whereas most studies of campaigns and/or voting behavior examine only one or just a handful of elections, this book includes data from more than one hundred U.S. gubernatorial elections. While the primary goal is to develop a general model of electoral politics, I focus on gubernatorial elections for a variety of reasons. First, compared to presidential and congressional elections, political scientists know relatively little about gubernatorial electoral politics. Second, governors are becoming increasingly important policymakers (Beyle 1990), in part due to the Reagan administration's shifting of responsibilities to the state level (McKay 1989; Williamson 1990). This trend continued in the Republican Party's rhetoric following its historic victory in the 1994 off-year congressional elections. Third, to study empirically the comparative role of campaigns requires observing many of them. There is simply not a large enough sample of modern presidential elections to gain enough observations and sufficient variance on campaign-related factors to evaluate systematically the impact of campaigns. Finally, gubernatorial elections provide several particularly interesting characteristics that facilitate the exploration of direct campaign effects on electoral politics. These characteristics are outlined subsequently.

Rationality serves as the theoretical core of this project for both candidates and voters. Candidates are considered goal-directed individuals whose primary objective, at least in the short run, is electoral success. Voters are assumed rational in the sense that they cast their ballots for their preferred candidate. Thus, the theoretical development pursued in this project draws heavily on spatial voting theory (e.g., Downs 1957; Riker 1990; Enelow and Hinich 1984; Ordeshook 1986; Hinich and Munger 1997).

Assuming rationality does not deny the complexity of the electoral process. Each campaign unfolds within a specific political context involving both the time and place of the election. Both candidates and voters learn over the course of the campaign and from one election to the next. Information asymmetries and uncertainty prevail throughout the electoral process. Finally, the salience of political cleavages may shift from one context to the next. Thus, developing a more complete theory of electoral politics requires incorporating ideas from research on political cleavages, contextual analysis, social learning theory, and social/psychological models of voting behavior.

Testing a general theory of campaigns and elections requires using several complementary methodologies. Specifically, this book presents two case studies using both qualitative and quantitative methods, a content analysis of newspaper coverage of campaigns, and several statistical analyses of pools of thirty-four, fifty-eight, and seventy-one gubernatorial election exit polls.

Chapter 1 presents a more detailed overview of the book, focusing on the project's goals. A literature review highlights what political science knows about campaigns and voting behavior while showing where this project will build on that knowledge. Attention is paid to research on elections in general and gubernatorial elections in particular.

Chapter 2 develops a general theory of elections that places the campaign at the heart of the process. The theory is based on Riker's (1990) notion of heresthetic change, which means change in the structure of the issue space of an election that does not require either candidates or voters to change their views on specific issues. Specifically, I argue that candidates use campaigns to create heresthetic change by changing the relative salience to voters of different issues for a particular election. I draw on several theoretical traditions to embed the theory of heresthetic change in a comprehensive theory of elections that incorporates both voters and candidates. Chapter 2 concludes with several implications of the theory and suggestions for how they might be tested.

Chapter 3 makes explicit the link between the theoretical argument presented in chapter 2 and formal spatial models of elections. The spatial model is presented first in its simple single-dimensional form and then expanded to a multidimensional space. I show that the theory I develop is consistent with the spatial model but that it focuses attention on a component of the model generally left unexamined.

Chapter 4 details the methods used to test the theory. I present a model of the dynamic process of campaigns themselves. The data from the two case studies used to explore this model is also described. I also develop a multilevel model of voting behavior that tests for the influence of campaign strategy. The data used to test this model is described, as is the methodology employed for the content analysis of the newspaper coverage.

Chapters 5 and 6 provide a detailed analysis of the 1993 gubernatorial campaigns in Virginia and New Jersey, respectively. These two chapters illustrate the dynamic process of campaign politics using data gathered from interviews, direct observation, analysis of media content, and public-opinion polls. While the chapters tell good stories, their real value comes from the explicit links made between candidates' and voters' behavior and the theory developed in chapter 2.

Chapter 7 presents the first broad-based empirical test of the theory, focusing on the role played by the abortion issue in the thirty-four gubernatorial elections held in 1990. This chapter demonstrates how the strategies undertaken by candidates in these races influenced the salience of the abortion issue.

Chapter 8 examines the impact that evaluations of the president had on gubernatorial voting behavior in twenty-nine states in 1990 and 1994. Though more closely associated with the GOP congressional campaign effort that year, the Republican Party at all levels worked particularly hard to make evaluations of President Bill Clinton more salient to voters in 1994. This chapter shows that their efforts appear to have succeeded.

Chapter 9 extends the analysis to multiple issues and cleavages for seventy-one gubernatorial elections held from 1982 through 1992. This chapter confirms that voters respond to the strategies adopted by candidates in that the salience of sociodemographic cleavages and partisanship react to the themes stressed by candidates.

Chapter 10 summarizes the findings of the analysis and provides general conclusions, addressing both the strengths and weaknesses of the findings. I explore the implications of this research for thinking about and studying electoral politics. I conclude by outlining a research agenda for the further study of campaign dynamics and elections.

Only my name appears as the author of this work, but it would not have been written without the assistance of many others. This book began as my doctoral dissertation at Indiana University. I thank the members of the IU political science department and the members of my dissertation committee: Gerald Wright (chair), Marjorie Hershey, John Williams, Bob Huckfeldt, and J. Scott Long. They treated me as a colleague and a friend. I learned more in graduate school than I thought possible, but I have also come to know that much more remains to be learned. I thank Jerry Wright specifically for his encouragement and guidance and his expectation that I perform to the best of my ability.

I am grateful to those who provided data for this project: Scott Keeter, Survey Research Lab Director at Virginia Commonwealth University; Louise Seals, *Richmond Times-Dispatch* deputy managing editor; Steve Shaw, director of Media General Research; Edwin Artz III, project manager at Media General; Ken Dautrich, director of the Eagleton Institute of Politics at Rutgers University; the Interuniversity Consortium for Political and Social Research; and, of course, all those who were interviewed.

I also must thank those who provided financial support for this research:

the College of Arts and Sciences at Indiana University; the Office of Research and the University Graduate School at Indiana University; the Goldsmith Awards Program at Harvard University; the Office of Social Science Research at the University of Illinois at Chicago; and the Campus Research Board at the University of Illinois at Chicago. It has also been a pleasure to work with all of the people at the University of Michigan Press.

Finally, a number of colleagues, most particularly Geoff Layman and Barry Rundquist, sat through numerous presentations, served as sounding boards for my ideas, and offered thoughtful comments and criticisms. To all of these people, I am deeply grateful. At this point it is customary to take the blame for all remaining errors and/or misguided ideas. It certainly applies in this case.

CHAPTER 1

Electoral Politics: Background and Review

Elections are the central component of democratic government. No institution plays a more important role in theoretical discussions and real-world manifestations of governments designed to provide representation for citizens. Quite deservedly, elections have been a major focal point for research in political science. However, gaps remain in the knowledge of how voters and candidates interact during the electoral process.

This chapter familiarizes readers with previous research on electoral politics, highlighting areas where this project makes a contribution. This review provides the backdrop for the development of a theory of electoral politics. While theoretical concerns are touched on in this chapter, the task of theory development is left to chapter 2.

The study of individual voters began in earnest with *The American Voter* (Campbell et al. 1960) but has also been strongly influenced by the groundbreaking works of Berelson, Lazarsfeld, and McPhee (1954) and Downs (1957). These three classics spawned volumes of research, which have produced important findings and significant debate regarding the role of party identification, individual ideology, group-level contextual influences, voter perceptions of candidates, economic and noneconomic issues, and the decision-making calculus employed by voters when casting their ballots (for reviews, see Asher 1983; Paul Allen Beck 1986; Niemi and Weisberg 1984, 1993).

While disagreement remains regarding model specification and the relative weight that should be given to these various factors, there is at least a partial list of variables that are generally considered important predictors of individual voting behavior. For example, differences exist regarding the nature of party identification, yet, whether one argues that party identification is a personal psychological attachment or simply a cue to be used as an information shortcut, no one would argue that party identification is not a fundamental predictor of voting behavior.

I do not undertake a complete review of this body of research. Rather, I focus on specific segments of the literature that illustrate where this study makes its contribution. First, I address findings that show that voters respond to factors external to their own psychological attachments and individual situations. This research shows that voters are influenced by the larger political and social environment within which they find themselves, responding to factors that shape the context within which they make choices. I will argue that the campaign itself is part of that context and, as such, also influences voter behavior.

Since V. O. Key (1949), scholars have consistently found a relationship between the racial makeup of a precinct, county, or state and the voting behavior of its residents (Wright 1977; Huckfeldt and Kohfeld 1989; Carsey 1995). Voting behavior also responds to the partisan, ethnic, and social class makeup of neighborhoods (Huckfeldt 1983, 1984; Putnam 1966; Tingsten 1963). Furthermore, political information is received and processed within a social context (Huckfeldt and Sprague 1987, 1995). The point is that voters are shaped by the events that happen around them and the people with whom they interact. They listen to and use information gathered from external sources and are aware of their friends' and neighbors' basic political predispositions.

More specifically, voters respond to the choice of candidates with which they are presented. Stonecash (1989) demonstrates that a more polarized choice between gubernatorial candidates along a particular cleavage produces a more polarized electorate on that same cleavage, a finding also documented in congressional (Wright 1978) and Senate races (Wright and Berkman 1986). Jacobson and Kernell (1983), Squire (1989, 1992), and others show that voters also respond to the quality of the candidates running. More recently, Alvarez presents similar evidence for five presidential elections (Alvarez 1997).

Higher campaign spending has been shown to increase overall turnout (Patterson and Caldeira 1983) and can also increase the vote share of a gubernatorial candidate (Patterson 1982). A large body of literature exists on spending in congressional elections (e.g., Jacobson 1980, 1990, 1992; Green and Krasno 1990; Jackson 1993). While the nature of the influence of spending on voter behavior is still in question, voters are clearly responding in some way to candidates' actions.

Bartels (1993) demonstrates that voters respond to the information on presidential campaigns they receive through newspapers and television news. Franklin (1991) illustrates that the nature of the message sent out by candidates for U.S. Senate affects voters' perceptions of those candidates, while Alvarez (1997) argues that voters are better able to use information about issues when voting for president if they receive sufficient information from the campaign. Finally, Cohen, Crassa, and Hamman (1991) show that presidential campaigning on behalf of U.S. Senate candidates assists those candidates in their quest for office.

To summarize, voters appear to respond to the choice of candidates with which they are presented. Moreover, candidates themselves help to define that choice through what they do and say during the campaign. Some voters certainly are not shaken from their partisan loyalties or ideological commitments by a particular candidate or campaign theme no matter how much money is spent or what the candidates do or say. Factors beyond the short-term control of the candidates remain important. It is critical to remember, however, that there is room for candidates and their campaigns to make a difference.

This book builds a theory that explicitly incorporates candidates' activities, an understanding of how those activities unfold, and how voters respond during that dynamic process called a campaign. Most empirical analyses of electoral politics ignore campaign dynamics, treating the influence of factors such as party identification, demography, or incumbency as exogenous to the campaign itself. Even campaign spending, which is clearly a function of the campaign, is treated only as a dollar amount used as a proxy for candidate legitimacy or ability to mobilize support or as a measure of competitiveness (Jacobson 1980, 1990, 1992; Green and Krasno 1990; Jackson 1993; Patterson and Caldeira 1983; Patterson 1982). Little consideration is given to what messages candidates are trying to push with their spending (but see Bartels 1993; Franklin 1991; Alvarez 1997). Even when factors that are clearly influenced by the campaign, like voter perceptions of candidates or their positions on various issues, are included, the underlying dynamic process producing these variables is often left unaddressed.

Some studies of spending in congressional elections and of presidential primaries deal explicitly with campaign dynamics. Yet recent studies of congressional campaign spending continue to reach conflicting conclusions regarding the importance of incumbent spending (Kenny and McBurrett 1992; Box-Steffensmeier and Lin 1992). Further, several models of presidential primary dynamics raise concerns about the stability of the expression of preference made by the electorate (Bartels 1985, 1987, 1988; Aldrich 1980a, 1980b). Qualitative literature on campaign dynamics provides additional insights into the campaign process but has yet to yield a general theoretical model (for an overview, see Hershey 1984; Salmore and Salmore 1989).

Three ambitious attempts have been made at developing and testing a theory of electoral politics that acknowledges a role for campaigns. Johnston et al. (1992) argue that campaigns give voters reasons why they should vote for or against a particular party. In doing so, campaigns, "'prime' voters to consider the deep seated values which motivate their choice" (Johnston et al. 1992, 4). The cognitive limitations of voters lead candidates/parties to select one or two key issues on which to focus their campaign efforts (Johnston et al. 1992; Popkin 1991; Hinich and Munger 1994). Johnston et al. test their model within the context of the 1988 Canadian national election, uncovering substantial movement in public opinion that they attribute to the campaign.

Gelman and King (1993) argue that for U.S. presidential elections, the campaign serves to inform voters about the weight they should place on what Gelman and King call fundamental variables. During campaigns, voters learn about candidate ideology, the health of the economy, and candidates' stands on important issues. By election day, voters know enough about these fundamental variables to cast a reasonably informed vote. Because voters receive sufficient information about both candidates, the outcome of the election can be predicted with some certainty several months in advance by knowing the values taken on by fundamental variables and the historical weight associated with them. The movement in public-opinion polls over the course of the campaign simply reflects voters' uneven process of learning. In the end, the simple existence of campaigns as vehicles for communicating information to voters is important, but the campaigns' daily content and the day-to-day response of public opinion to campaign events is largely meaningless.

A good recent book on the role of campaigns is Alvarez's (1997) study of presidential elections from 1976 to 1992. Similar to Gelman and King, Alvarez focuses on the information that candidates provide to voters. He differs with Gelman and King, however, on the assumption that presidential campaigns generally provide the same sorts of information from one election to the next. He also suggests that different segments of the electorate respond differently to the information content of presidential campaigns.

More will be said about these three works in chapter 2. For now, it is simply worth noting that these recent efforts to explain the role of campaigns in electoral politics differ in their conclusions regarding whether meaningful change among voters takes place in response to campaigns.

The lack of empirical attention to campaign dynamics is curious given the dynamic nature of electoral politics implied by spatial theories of voting. I borrow heavily from spatial theory, treating candidates as strategic actors operating within a structurally bounded space. Candidates face several constraints beyond their control (outlined in chapter 2), and these constraints limit candidates' options when developing a campaign strategy. The limitations include issues of credibility, the role of party activists, and the simple two-step institutional structure that requires nomination before the general election. Within these constraints, candidates struggle to secure winning coalitions among uncertain voters who have incomplete information. Momentum can shift, and early spending can be countered by the strategic behavior of candidates, but the range of opportunities available to candidates remains bounded by the political environment.

Both formal work on campaigns (e.g., Ordeshook 1986; Enelow and Hinich 1984) and common political wisdom describe the process of a campaign as a series of steps taken by the candidates designed to position themselves for the best possible chance of winning on election day. Candidates plan what they are going to say, where they will go, what to spend, and what to include in advertisements. They do so while continually monitoring the activities of their opponents, the nature of the media coverage, and the response of public opinion. Candidate strategy must adjust and react as the campaign unfolds. Thus, while there is a single general election, candidates take multiple steps to get there. This dynamic is predicted by formal spatial models of elections but needs to be better documented by real-world observation.

In chapters 5 and 6, I explore the dynamic process that results in campaigns influencing voting behavior using case studies of the 1993 gubernatorial elections in Virginia and New Jersey. Case studies of individual candidates or specific campaigns are not new to political science. Fenno's (1978) development of the concept of home style has had a dramatic impact on the understanding of candidates and campaigns. The richness and depth of our understanding of politics is greatly enhanced by the case-study approach (Diesing 1971).

The case-study component of this project benefits greatly from being part of a larger study of the electoral process. In chapters 7, 8, and 9, I use data on the behavior of candidates and voters in more than one hundred other gubernatorial elections to test the generalizability of the findings derived from the two cases.

Another contribution of this book results from the context in which the analysis is carried out: U.S. gubernatorial elections. Relative to other areas of research in electoral politics, scholars know little about gubernatorial elections. Further, much of the evidence that exists is sketchy at best and contradictory at worst. Models designed to predict gubernatorial election outcomes have not fared well (Erikson, Wright, and McIver 1993), and some controversy remains regarding what factors influence gubernatorial electoral politics.

Stein (1990) argues that incumbent governors escape much of the blame for a state's economic troubles unless they belong to the same party as the current president. Peltzman (1987) agrees, saying that members of the president's party, not the gubernatorial candidates themselves, pay the electoral price for economic downturns or benefit from upswings. In contrast, Howell and Vanderleeuw (1990) and Carsey and Wright (1998) find that evaluations of the state economy predict evaluations of gubernatorial job performance, while Chubb (1988) uncovers a significant relationship between state-level changes in the economy and the gubernatorial vote. Kenney (1983) finds no consistent relationship between state-level changes in unemployment and the cost of living and gubernatorial voting.

Chubb's (1988) analysis does point to a much stronger influence of shifts in the national economy on gubernatorial elections, a finding shared by Holbrook-Provow (1987). Yet others find that evaluations of the national economy do not affect gubernatorial job performance evaluations (Howell and Vanderleeuw 1990) or voting in gubernatorial elections (Carsey and Wright 1998). In addition, Simon (1989) shows that presidential popularity influences the voting behavior of independents and independent leaners, particularly in gubernatorial elections.

The question raised by these inconsistencies is the degree to which gubernatorial elections are driven by state versus national factors. Typically, the question becomes to what degree gubernatorial politics is linked with presidential politics. Stein (1990) and Carsey and Wright (1998) argue that such a link exists. Yet this contention does not deny the potential importance of state-specific factors.

A number of studies indicate that gubernatorial elections are becoming increasingly independent of presidential politics. The correlation between state-level presidential voting returns and gubernatorial voting returns declined from 1900 to 1969, both in the South and elsewhere (Turett 1971). More recent studies (Tompkins 1988; Chubb 1988; Jewell and Olson 1988) find a continued decline in the importance of presidential coattails, and Cohen (1983) links gubernatorial popularity to evaluations of state government rather than to presidential popularity.

Thus, while presidential politics and the national economy may influence gubernatorial elections, it seems clear that gubernatorial elections turn on state-specific events (Jewell and Olson 1988). In recounting an analysis of newspaper coverage positing reasons for a candidate's success or failure, Jewell and Olson (1988) find that party conflict is mentioned 40 percent of the time, personal characteristics of the candidates another 40 percent, and the record of the incumbent (mostly related to tax issues) is mentioned 75 percent of the time. Tompkins (1988) finds that gubernatorial elections are increasingly a function of short-term forces not derived from national political or economic factors. Erikson, Wright, and McIver (1993) conclude that, looking at voting behavior on a state-by-state basis, gubernatorial voting is more subject to campaign-specific factors than is presidential voting.

The one factor that receives almost universal support regarding its importance in predicting gubernatorial electoral behavior is incumbency (Erikson, Wright, and McIver 1993; Tompkins 1984; Pieneson 1977; Cowart 1973; Holbrook-Provow 1987; Jewell and Olson 1988; but see Chubb 1988). Furthermore, incumbency may be becoming more important as gubernatorial campaigns become less connected with national partisan politics (Tompkins 1984). Incumbent governors are no more vulnerable than in the past (Turett 1971; Jewell and Olson 1988), but they are much more visible to voters (Turett 1971; Squire and Fastnow 1992).

It may be that the candidates' campaigns account for much of these election-specific idiosyncrasies. As mentioned earlier, Stonecash (1989) illustrates how different combinations of gubernatorial candidates produce different electoral bases of support. Patterson and Caldeira (1983) find that campaign activism (spending) produces a higher turnout, and Patterson (1982) finds that higher relative spending increases the vote share for both incumbents and challengers. Sigelman (1989) demonstrates that gubernatorial activism can change the salience of short-term cleavages, and Cook, Jelen, and Wilcox (1992) provide evidence that positions taken by gubernatorial candidates on the abortion issue in ten states in 1990 influenced voter behavior.

Sitting governors have the opportunity to influence upcoming elections through their policy actions (Beyle 1990; Pomper 1968; Eismeier 1979; Kone and Winters 1993). Incumbent governors are highly visible to voters, and voters have more information about governors than they do about U.S. Senators (Turett 1971; Squire and Fastnow 1992). In particular, Wright (1974) finds that voters have much more policy-related information about gubernatorial candidates than they do about candidates for the U.S. Senate.

Governors are becoming increasingly important policymakers. The governor's office has been strengthened institutionally and has been occupied by an increasing number of "quality" individuals (Sabato 1983). With increased institutional resources, sufficient levels of media coverage, policy-related information available to voters, an expanded policy-making role, and the declining influence of national party and economic factors, strategic gubernatorial candidates have increased incentives and opportunities to structure their campaigns in an attempt to influence voters. Thus, gubernatorial elections provide an ideal setting in which to test a theory of elections that focuses on the role of campaigns.

To summarize, political science has focused a substantial amount of attention on the study of elections. Campaigns unfold in a dynamic process. However, while an extensive formal literature deals with candidate behavior in response to electoral pressures and how it shapes voting behavior, there is relatively little empirical knowledge of that process. Finally, I have shown that what is known about gubernatorial elections is sketchy at best and contradictory at worst. This project offers and tests a general theory of campaigns and elections that takes some initial steps toward filling these gaps.

What follows is, to my knowledge, the most extensive analysis of gubernatorial elections ever undertaken. Given the inconsistencies of previous research and the wealth of information to be considered, one could easily get lost in a maze of data. Avoiding this pitfall requires the development of a clear theoretical framework. Chapter 2 presents such a framework.

CHAPTER 2

Campaigns and Candidates:
What Should We Expect?

More than anything else, an election campaign is a learning process for both candidates and voters. Voters receive information about the candidates from the media, neighbors and coworkers, and directly from the candidates themselves. Voters also learn about the electorate as a whole through the publication of public-opinion polls. Candidates gather information about potential supporters through polls, focus groups, and coffee-shop discussions as they hit the campaign trail. Candidates also learn more about each other during the campaign.

Central to the unfolding of a campaign is the struggle between candidates to provide new information to voters. Candidates shape the informational context within which voters make their decisions by battling to influence what is salient to voters when they cast their ballots. Through this process, the content of campaigns influences voting behavior. To reach this conclusion, I blend into a single theoretical framework the motivations of voters, party activists, and candidates, the basic institutional structure of the electoral process, and a contextual view of voting behavior.

Gubernatorial candidates are goal-seeking individuals. Like other political actors, they may be driven by the commitment to enact specific policies, the desire to obtain power or prestige, or the ambition to use an elective office as a stepping-stone along a particular career path. Regardless of which is paramount, the achievement of any of these goals by elected officials depends first and foremost on getting elected. Thus, this study begins with the same assumption with which Downs (1957) began: that candidates' primary goal is winning elections.

Voters are also goal oriented. Specifically, voters in a two-candidate race are assumed to vote for their more preferred candidate. To understand voting behavior, those factors that shape the preferences of voters and thus their voting behavior must be discovered. I am not concerned here with the psychological process by which voters synthesize information, predispositions, and past behavior into preferences. Instead, I focus on how the content of a gubernatorial campaign influences the relative importance of factors linked with a voter's preference for one candidate over another.

Candidates and voters interact under these basic assumptions. The bulk of that interaction process takes place during the campaign, and it culminates on election day.[1] Voters know that candidates want to win, candidates know that voters want to vote for their preferred candidate, and candidates know that their opponents also want to win. Thus, each participant has a basic understanding of the motivations of everyone involved in the process.

In a world of complete and costless information, candidates and voters would reveal their preferences honestly. Candidates would choose which policy positions to advocate, and casting ballots would be free of costs. Political science has produced simple yet elegant theories based on such a model, but alas, gubernatorial elections do not take place in such a world. This situation makes theory building more complicated and analysis more cumbersome, but it also makes both processes more interesting and more fun.

First, the assumption of complete and cost-free information is untenable. When pressed, it is difficult to define exactly what would constitute complete information, but both logic and observation suggest that it is not necessary to do so. Voters do not have complete information about candidates or other voters, and candidates, try as they may, never seem to have enough information about the electorate or each other. The simple fact of incomplete information alters the campaign process markedly, particularly for candidates.

Incomplete information leads in part to uncertainty, and uncertainty encourages candidates to behave strategically during the campaign. Under complete information, candidates may attempt to misrepresent their strategy to their opponents or their policy stances to voters during the course of the campaign. Thus, some strategic behavior may take place. However, if voters have full information, they realize that candidates engage in such behavior, and voters will wait until candidates make their "last moves" before making a decision (Ordeshook 1992). If the policy choices open to a candidate fall on a single dimension (an assumption addressed later), and there are only two candidates, such strategic plays by the candidates will not alter the outcome of the election if voters have complete information: the median voter theorem articulated by Downs (1957) holds.

In response to uncertainty, candidates test various campaign themes and alter their approaches to accommodate new information. They react to changes in the behavior of their opponents as well as to shifts in public opinion. Incomplete information and uncertainty among voters also leave open the opportunity for public opinion to shift as more information is provided. Strategic candidates try to provide voters with additional information in attempts and counterattempts to sway the public's mood. Because information is incomplete, the campaign becomes a learning process for both the candidates and voters.

Thus, the dynamic nature of campaigns becomes a struggle to reduce uncertainty.

While information is incomplete, both voters and candidates do not start from scratch with each election. Candidates learn from past campaigns and from their state's voting history that certain patterns can be anticipated. This process has been facilitated by the increase in professional consultants who work for multiple campaigns in numerous settings. When looking at historical patterns, candidates tend to view electorates in terms of groups or geographic regions: blacks, the panhandle, farmers, suburban middle-class married women, and so forth. Such categorization simplifies the process for candidates and meshes well with Feld and Grofman's (1988) finding that groups of voters tend to reveal single-peaked preferences for candidates, even if individuals do not. In other words, groups of voters behave in more predictable ways than do individual voters.

Voters also use information shortcuts. Partisanship may be the single most important cue that voters use, but, as outlined in chapter 1, voters' behavior is also influenced by social interaction and the sociodemographic makeup of their neighborhoods. Building on earlier work by Lazarsfeld, Berelson, and Gaudet (1944), Converse (1990) argues that an informational division of labor develops among voters. Opinion leaders gather a disproportionate amount of information, and other voters look to these leaders for cues on how to cast ballots. Converse posits that this situation gives opinion leaders an exaggerated influence on electoral politics, but Putnam (1966) suggests that such persons will accurately represent the values of the community in which they have become leaders because of their high level of integration into that community. The point is that voters use a variety of external information sources when deciding for whom to vote, which implies that their behavior on election day may be influenced by the strategic decisions made by candidates as manifest in the information their campaigns provide.

In analyzing the 1980 presidential election, Bartels (1993) finds that voters' information prior to the New Hampshire primary influenced their voting behavior in November. One can imagine a similar process taking place in gubernatorial elections. This phenomenon suggests that prior information and the predispositions of voters consistently influence voter evaluations of candidates over the course of the campaign and will influence voting behavior. Most party identifiers surely knew which party they preferred long before any specific gubernatorial campaign began, which will no doubt influence who they support. Furthermore, both Knight (1985) and Inglehart (1985) suggest that ideological self-placement is nearly as stable as partisanship.

To summarize, the information voters have prior to the beginning of a campaign will influence their voting behavior. Yet voters do not possess complete information. Thus, the importance of prior information does not negate the potential for new information provided over the course of the campaign to influence who voters choose on election day. Incomplete information creates uncertainty in the electoral process, and candidates try to reduce that uncertainty by providing additional information to voters over the course of a campaign.

The second overly restrictive basic assumption made by Downs (1957) and employed most recently by Alvarez (1997) is that voters' views on political issues fall on a single ideological dimension. Conover and Feldman (1984) argue that voters organize their systems of beliefs multidimensionally. Even partisanship has been argued to exist for voters in a multidimensional way (Weisberg 1984). Finally, formal spatial theory now commonly adopts a view of the issue space or policy dimensions of an election as multidimensional (Ordeshook 1986; Enelow and Hinich 1984; Hinich and Munger 1997). This perspective does not necessarily mean that there is not a median point or at least a critical central region in that issue space (Enelow and Hinich 1984). Thus, the concept of the median voter remains important. Still, viewing the electorate as divided along several dimensions has strong theoretical and empirical support. The importance of viewing the issue space of an election as multidimensional will be made clear in the following sections.

If the issue space defining an electorate is multidimensional, and both voters and candidates face uncertainty due to incomplete information, then all rational candidates wanting to win elections must make a choice regarding the information they try to communicate to voters: should candidates try to change their own positions on a dimension already salient to voters by moving toward the median voter on that dimension, should candidates try to convert voters to candidates' positions on an already salient dimension, or should candidates seek to alter the focus of the election away from one dimension and toward another that appears more beneficial to them? I argue that candidates are limited in their ability to shift their own locations in a multidimensional issue space. Further, I suggest that rational candidates would attempt to shift the focus of the election to an alternate dimension or set of dimensions rather than attempt to convert voters along a dimension on which the candidate is currently at a disadvantage with voters.

I began by adopting Downs's (1957) assumptions that candidates seek to win and voters seek to elect those candidates who advocate policies closest to voters' own preferences. Downs shows that this situation encourages candidates to converge toward the median voter. The underlying assumption is that, over the course of an election, voters' preferences are fixed, while the positions offered by candidates can change. However, several important theoretical developments and empirical observations suggest that candidates are not as free to move as the original model suggests.

Hirshman (1970) suggests that Downs focuses only on the opportunity for voters in the middle of the issue space to switch from one candidate to the other as one candidate moves closer to them. Voters on the extreme can only continue to support the candidate closest to them, even if that candidate is moving away from their ideal point in an attempt to secure the support of the median voter. Thus, voters on the fringes of the political space are held captive.

In contrast, Hirshman asserts that voters on the extreme have other options available to them. They can complain if their candidate moves too far toward the center. They can reduce their efforts on behalf of the candidate, contribute less money, fail to work to mobilize support, or simply not vote. In the extreme, they could form a new party and run a more acceptable candidate. Aldrich and McGinnis (1989) show that candidates who depend in part on the resources of activists will not converge to the median voter. Thus, the first important critique of the simple spatial theory is that candidates are not completely free to move to the center of the issue space. Moving in some direction in the political space of the election in an effort to attract new voters risks alienating current supporters.

The critique just outlined casts doubt on the assumption of rational voters as originally framed by Downs and on the idea that candidates are strictly election-oriented. If rational voters are given a choice, says Downs, they should vote for their preferred candidate, even if that candidate has moved away from their ideal point. Looking at a single election, opting out is not rational because it may cause the preferred candidate to lose.[2] Conversely, candidates wanting to win should not care about losing support on the margins if it can be offset with enough support from the vast majority of voters located closer to the center. Several factors, however, allow the elaboration of the assumptions of rationality for candidates and voters while building a more realistic theory that incorporates Hirshman's critique.

A number of studies show that party activists have clear policy preferences (see Miller and Jennings 1986; Erikson, Wright, and McIver 1993; Wittman 1983). Activists do not adopt a win-at-all-costs approach. Winning elections is a mechanism that allows for the adoption of preferred policies. If the party had to abandon its policy views to win, the victory would be hollow. Party elites and political activists can accept losing for a cause over winning without one, at least occasionally.

While any one election has a clear beginning and ending, voters and party activists realize that the next election is just around the corner. Thus, not participating in any one election does not mean completely opting out of electoral politics. Activists may sit out one election, even if it jeopardizes their preferred candidate's chance of winning, to send a message to future party candidates. Thus, as any one election can be viewed as a dynamic two-candidate game with multiple plays over the course of the campaign, the larger realm of sequential elections can also be viewed as a game with multiple plays. Under such a structure, it may be perfectly rational for some voters to sit out of a single election as part of a long-term strategy to keep future candidates from moving too far away from their ideal points.

Another factor that prevents general-election candidates from moving to the median voter is that candidates must win the support of their partisans to compete in the general election, whether through a convention or a primary election.[3] Party identifiers in general and primary voters in particular have policy preferences distinct from those of the general electorate. Because candidates must first receive the approval of this subset of the electorate before going before the general electorate, and because incumbents seeking reelection may face a challenge at the primary level, candidates must appeal to some voter other than the general-election median voter if they hope to even reach the general election as a party nominee.

Several scholars have studied this institutional component of the American electoral system, while others have focused more generally on the role played by party activists over the course of several elections (Erikson, Wright, and McIver 1993; Chappell and Keech 1986; Miller and Jennings 1986; Wright 1993b; Coleman 1972; Aldrich and McGinnis 1989). Whether discussed as simply an institutional structure or as candidates having to represent multiple constituencies, the result is the same: candidates are not free to move about the issue space of any one election without paying a cost. Viewed in this light, it may be more rational for a candidate to not move. Why risk alienating an existing supporter for only the chance to win over a voter who is closer to the median?

Finally, it is unclear just how successful candidates can expect to be in attempting to relocate themselves in the issue space of an electorate. Sellers (1994) and Austen-Smith and Banks (1989) show that candidates have difficulty maintaining credibility when campaigning on an issue position that they have newly adopted, especially if that position is contrary to a lengthy history of political activity. Furthermore, partisanship likely plays a role in defining those issues on which a candidate can and cannot credibly focus a campaign. Simply put, voters supporting abortion rights will find it hard to believe a candidate with a history of opposing abortion rights who suddenly switches positions just before an election campaign. The traditional spatial model assumes that voters will believe candidates when they change their positions on issues as they converge toward the middle. However, the critique presented here suggests that candidates should only risk such moves if they are believable.

To summarize, rational candidates are limited in their ability to move about the issue space defined by an electorate. Candidates certainly feel pulled toward the median voter (Erikson, Wright, and McIver 1993; Wright and Berkman 1986; Wright 1993b; Kuklinski 1978). Yet rational candidates are considerably restricted in their ability to exploit relocation as a strategy to win an election. Doing so risks alienating historically loyal supporters. Voters, knowing that the next election is just around the corner, have several options at their disposal with which to limit the movement of candidates. The institutional structure of preelection nominating helps party activists keep their candidates from looking too much like the opposition. Finally, a candidate's relocation is limited by the need to maintain credibility. In fact, Johnston et al. (1992) suggest that candidates must demonstrate clear differences between themselves and their opponents simply to mobilize their own partisans. In this sense, candidates must do more than avoid converging to the median on all issues: they must actively campaign at some point away from the median that allows them to distinguish themselves from their opponents. Most rational candidates will probably ultimately conclude that some strategy other than trying to relocate themselves in the voter-defined policy space of a given election is more likely to produce a victory.

Having decided that changing locations in the issue space of an election is often not a viable alternative, a candidate might instead attempt to manipulate the location of voters. If more voters adopted ideal points closer to the candidate's ideological location, that candidate could expect a better showing at the polls. As noted earlier, most of the work on spatial theories of voting assumes that the preferences of voters remain constant and that if anyone can move, it is the candidates. The one body of research that does address the conversion of voters is the realignment literature (see, e.g., Sundquist 1983; P. Beck 1979; Dalton, Flanagan, and Beck 1984; Erikson and Tedin 1981; Carmines and Stimson 1989). However, this work focuses on a few critical presidential elections and the process by which they did or did not produce significant shifts in partisan attachment rather than on changes in issue preferences (but see Layman and Carsey 1998). Most elections are not realigning elections, and major shifts in voter allegiance do not appear to happen in the normal course of events in presidential electoral politics, let alone at the state level.

Riker (1990) presents a microlevel view of voters that supports the idea that voter conversion is unlikely during typical elections. He argues that asking voters to change their opinions on an issue demands a great deal of them. Asking voters to make such a conversion requires that they at least implicitly admit that their previous view was wrong, which may be particularly difficult if candidates ask voters to change their minds on issues deemed important enough to be the basis on which ballots should be cast. In addition, voters being asked to change may have the option of supporting an opponent who shares their current views.

Thus, it seems unlikely that a candidate can readily induce voters to switch their position on some issue that would bring them closer to that candidate, particularly given that voters, at least in gubernatorial elections, generally have a viable alternative candidate to consider. A candidate can try to convert voters by presenting new information, but that new information will be viewed through the perceptual screen of voters' current beliefs and will often be countered by an opponent. There might, however, be some room to induce voters to convert on issues that are relatively new to the political landscape.

A third strategy candidates might adopt is to attempt to alter the dimensions on which the election takes place. For example, a candidate with a long history of supporting tax increases cannot credibly adopt an antitax position, and it is unlikely that voters can be induced during a campaign to change their opinions on taxes. However, a candidate can manipulate how much emphasis is placed on the tax issue during the campaign with an eye toward influencing the salience of the tax issue to voters in that particular election. In this example, candidates do not try to convert voters to the candidates' position on taxes. Rather, candidates must decide whether to emphasize taxes during the campaign, hoping that the salience of the tax issue for voters for that specific election responds in kind.

This argument requires that candidates have the opportunity to induce such changes. I offer three points. First, Inglehart (1985) argues that any one survey may not detect the stability he argues is present in voter ideological self-placement or even specific issue positions because not every issue is equally salient at any point in time. Second, Zaller (1992) suggests that this volatility in salience responds not only to the survey instrument but also to broader political stimuli to which voters are exposed, including campaigns. Third, Conover and Feldman (1984) suggest that voters organize their belief systems in a multidimensional way. Taken together, I argue that the short-term salience of issues among voters is volatile and that volatility results from a shift in attention given by voters to different policy dimensions. Thus, candidates can create a short-term influence on voting behavior if they can alter the salience of particular dimensions at the time of the election by shifting voters' attention to different issues.

Riker (1990) describes this strategy as attempting to induce heresthetic change. *Heresthetic change* means changing the nature of the issue space for voters so they are encouraged to change which candidate they support. Heresthetic change does not mean that candidates change their stands on issues, as the traditional spatial model implies, or that voters convert on issues, which Riker labels *rhetorical change* or *persuasion*. Instead, this strategy leads each candidate to find a dimension that, if made sufficiently salient relative to other dimensions, improves that candidate's chance of winning. Candidates use their campaigns to try to create this shift. Thus, the campaign becomes a struggle between candidates providing information to voters as they try to define for voters the important issues in that particular election. One candidate might focus on economic concerns while the other stresses social issues. Which candidate wins will depend in part on who is better able to make their campaign theme more salient for voters.

Riker (1990) describes a similar process in economics. He argues that marketing research searches for products that fit the preexisting tastes of consumers rather than for ways to change their tastes. It is easier to develop a new product than it is to develop new tastes among consumers for an existing product. Tastes may be latent, and discovering a latent taste is of great benefit to a company, but the basic assumption is that it is not possible to sell something that people do not want, and it is hard to convince them to want it if they do not.

In politics, developing a new product is not as easy. Candidates for governor typically come to the electoral arena with a significant political history, and I have already argued that candidates are not free to remake themselves. However, they are free to present those aspects of their political views that should appeal to the widest array of voters. No one would argue that rational candidates would do anything other than put what they think is their best foot forward. In doing so, candidates hope to make those issues on which they agree with a substantial number of voters the politically salient issues for those voters, at least for the upcoming election. Candidates need not make one factor more or less important for voters than another in general. Rather, they only need to focus the terms of the debate for the immediate election on one or more factors on which candidates believe that they have an advantage.

In general, cleavages first exist in society and then become politicized (Zuckerman 1975). Politicized cleavages may emerge from key political events or crises, but the decisions made by political elites are also critical. "Strategic politicians play the most obvious and perhaps most influential role in determining the relative competition among political issues" (Carmines and Stimson 1989, 6). In fact, Riker (1982) argues that political elites constantly search for dimensions in the voting public that can be exploited for electoral gain. In so doing, elites determine, at least in part, the context within which electoral battles are fought.

To link this view back to the traditional spatial model, candidates do appeal to what might be called a median voter because they still need to mobilize a majority. However, candidates struggle over the definition of that median or, rather, over which median is important, by battling over which dimension or dimensions within the electorate will be salient for that election.

Rabinowitz and Macdonald (1989) note that most candidates do not campaign at the median of the general electorate. Instead, candidates take clear, though not too extreme, stands on issues. Rabinowitz and Macdonald develop a directional theory of voting out of this beginning, but I believe that something different is happening. Candidates take clear positions to become identified with views that they feel appeal to a majority of voters along a particular dimension. Candidates are not concerned with the direction of voter preference; rather, they are focusing on the dimension that they wish to make salient. Rational candidates cannot expect to induce heresthetic change by taking anything other than a clear stand.

Again, shifting the focus of a campaign to a dimension on which a candidate has an advantage is not the same as the candidate moving toward a median voter. I have already outlined the various factors that restrict a candidate's ability to relocate in the issue space of the electorate. Candidates are also not trying to change where voters locate themselves in the issue space of an election. Inducing heresthetic change means shifting the attention of the electorate to a dimension on which one candidate holds a more preferable position than does the opponent.

For example, suppose in a particular electorate, the only salient political cleavage is social class, and Candidate A holds a more preferred position on that dimension than does Candidate B. Candidate A can win if all voters cast their ballots based on social class. By appealing to that dimension during the campaign, Candidate A will appear to be more mainstream than Candidate B in terms of political views. Next, suppose that Candidate B successfully shifts the focus of the electorate to a racial division among voters, so that all voters make their choices based on race rather than social class. Further suppose that the reason Candidate B did so is because Candidate B holds a more preferred position on this dimension than does Candidate A. Candidate B will now be viewed as more mainstream politically than Candidate A not because the candidates altered their positions or because voters altered their preferences on these dimensions but because Candidate B induced voters to change the criteria used to assess the candidates. The significance of this particular hypothetical for understanding class- and race-based politics in the United States is obvious.

The existence of most potentially salient dimensions in any one election is typically beyond the control of the candidates involved. The party of the president, the policies already adopted by the incumbent, and the sociodemographic makeup of the electorate are all exogenous to the heresthetic process. These factors exist and will play some role in shaping voting behavior. A Republican gubernatorial candidate running in 1990 could not change the fact that President George Bush reneged on his "Read my lips" pledge to not raise taxes any more than a Democratic gubernatorial candidate running in 1984 could alter the reality of President Ronald Reagan's popularity.

Still, the salience of such factors relative to other issues facing the electorate is open to some manipulation by candidates. The popularity of a president often influences voting in gubernatorial contests. However, I argue that the relative magnitude of that effect is subject to strategic manipulation by candidates.

Chapter 1 outlined the importance of the sociodemographic and geographic context within which voters find themselves. I argue that the themes stressed by candidates during the campaign also shape the context within which an election takes place. The sociodemographic makeup of a neighborhood and the social interaction that takes place there influence voters because they provide information that voters use when casting their ballots. Campaigns also provide information (Alvarez 1997), both directly and through opinion leaders (Converse 1990), that informs voters' decisions. In other words, sociodemographics, social interaction, and the campaign itself all contribute to the informational context of the election.

Finally, even in an issue space that theoretically has an infinite number of dimensions, the cognitive limitations of voters and their desire to simplify the voting calculus suggest that candidates could expect success in producing heresthetic change regarding only one or a few specific dimensions for any one election (Popkin 1991; Hinich and Munger 1994). Candidates hoping to create heresthetic change should limit their campaigns to only one or a few dominant themes. This limitation places a constraint on campaigns. However, the fact that only a limited number of dimensions will be salient to voters creates the opportunity to induce heresthetic change.

Johnston et al. (1992) describe a similar process in their analysis of the 1988 Canadian national election. They argue that the salience of a free-trade agreement with the United States responded to appeals made by party leaders during the campaign. In one sense, their description of the campaign process is more limited that what I am describing. They stress the need to take clear stands simply to mobilize core supporters, while I argue that the broader goal is to mobilize a winning majority. In another respect, Johnston et al.'s argument goes beyond heresthetic change, suggesting that real conversion took place among voters regarding their attitudes toward economic relations with the United States and their evaluations of party leaders. These authors describe the process as "priming" voters with information about the critical issues of the election.

It is ultimately not exactly clear what Johnston and his coauthors are describing. They criticize the heresthetic argument, mistakenly claiming that it does not allow for the content of the campaign to influence voting behavior. Riker (1990) distinguishes between rhetorical persuasion and heresthetic change in the issue space. However, implicit in Riker's model—and explicit in mine—is that communication between candidates and voters is essential. Not only the heresthetic argument but all spatial theories of voting come crashing down if parties or candidates do not communicate their locations in the issue space to voters. Communication is an assumption of spatial models, thus requiring the content of campaigns to matter.

Johnston et al. do have a point, however, when they suggest that spatial theories of voting are not concerned with the source of voters' information. The works cited previously in this chapter and in chapter 1 demonstrate that the source of a message matters. The impact of a message depends on the credibility of its source (Sellers 1994), as does whether a message clarifies or obfuscates voters' views of elected officials (Franklin 1991). Finally, selective perception of and exposure to messages likely produces asymmetry in who hears a message, which may lead to asymmetries in who responds and how (Johnston et al. 1992). Thus, which candidate stresses a theme may influence the nature of voters' reaction to that particular theme.[4]

Johnston et al.'s (1992) distinction between priming and heresthetic change is unclear. They argue that priming and heresthetic change are not the same thing. At one point they describe heresthetic change as functionally equivalent to setting the campaign agenda, yet, they also say that priming "is the electoral manifestation of the elite struggle for control of the agenda" (212). They also argue that even if these two processes are conceptually different, it may be impossible to disentangle them empirically, concluding that some of both happened in the 1988 Canadian election. The first task is to disentangle the concepts theoretically and then assess empirically their influence on voting behavior.

The distinction is between altering the salience of a particular issue or dimension for voters in a given election (heresthetic change) and converting some meaningful portion of voters on that issue or dimension (what I and Riker [1990] call persuasion and Johnston et al. [1992] appear to mean by *priming*). Using this distinction, each process leads to distinct empirical predictions about the response of voters to campaign appeals, which are presented in chapter 4.

A significant challenge to the theory developed in this book is presented by Gelman and King (1993). They argue that campaigns are important for democratic government because they communicate to voters important information about candidates. In that regard, they and I agree that campaigns shape the informational context of an election. However, Gelman and King argue that rational candidates will run the best campaigns possible. Assuming sufficient or relatively equal resources, the candidates will provide voters with essential information about themselves and their opponents. In so doing, however, the actual events of the campaigns will cancel each other out by the time voters reach the polls.

Gelman and King base their conclusions on an analysis of public-opinion data and election outcomes in U.S. presidential elections. They conclude that the volatility in public-opinion polls illustrates an uneven learning process for voters. Yet by election day, public opinion reaches an aggregate level that can be predicted months in advance based on what Gelman and King call "fundamental variables" and the relative weights voters would likely attach to these fundamental variables when casting ballots. These relative weights, or the salience of each fundamental variable, reflect long-standing patterns within the electorate and can be predicted from past elections. Gelman and King suggest that movement in public opinion over the course of the campaign simply represents a gradual correction back to a mean produced by voters refocusing their attention on politics as election day approaches.

In fact, much of the shift in attitudes Johnston et al. (1992) show in the

Canadian electorate is consistent with the kind of process Gelman and King (1993) describe. Gelman and King say that such apparent conversion supposedly created by campaigns is expected. Rational candidates have no choice but to push fundamental variables such as party identification back to their means. Thus, what looks like attitudinal conversion during a campaign is really just different groups of voters reapplying their normal weights to fundamental variables at different rates.

Even if Gelman and King are right concerning presidential elections, there are several reasons why their model may not apply to subpresidential elections in general and to gubernatorial elections in particular. Gelman and King's "fundamental variables" include party identification, economic health, presidential popularity, race, and a variety of election-specific dummies to fit past elections more closely.[5] That public opinion returns to the level predicted by these variables suggests that presidential elections are determined by them—that phenomenon is what makes these variables fundamental. The reason public opinion returns to the level predicted by these fundamental variables is that, in presidential elections, neither side is hypothesized to have an advantage in money or expertise, and both campaigns produce sufficient levels of information for voters to learn about the candidates and their positions relative to these fundamental variables.

The most obvious problem with applying Gelman and King's model to gubernatorial elections is that political science, as shown in chapter 1, has yet to develop a set of fundamental variables and normal weights for gubernatorial elections. Either these variables and weights do not exist, or they have yet to be discovered. It may also be that the learning achieved in presidential elections is not achieved at subpresidential levels, a situation complicated by the lack of exact equality in financial resources and expertise among candidates running in subpresidential races. These issues are explored in later chapters, particularly in the discussion of the 1993 gubernatorial elections in Virginia and New Jersey.

Finally, for the eleven presidential elections studied by Gelman and King (1993), aggregating across a series of variables does produce a mean level of importance for each of them. Yet even for this set of elections, the salience of various dimensions differed from one election to the next in response to the choice presented to voters. The importance of religious affiliation in 1960 may be the most obvious example. Aggregating to a mean ignores information that describes the nature of the vote choice for any one election. By extension, it mutes a discussion of the impact a campaign might have on the outcome of any one election. Gelman and King's assertion that the importance or salience of fundamental variables in determining voting behavior is constant ultimately serves as the null hypothesis tested in this book.

The most recent contribution to theories of campaigns and voting behavior comes from Alvarez's (1997) study of five presidential elections. He argues that voters' issue preferences can affect their voting behavior only when the candidates differ from each other and voters have enough information about this difference to reduce their uncertainty about the policy positions of the candidates. Like the theory developed here, Alvarez argues that campaigns influence voting behavior by shaping the informational context of the election. However, he limits his view to a general consideration of policy preferences, failing to consider the specific issues candidates stress during their campaigns. This limitation stems from Alvarez basing his models on the assumption of a single-dimension issue space, an assumption I criticized earlier.

Alvarez's approach also results from his interest in the role of nonpolicy factors that often become part of one or both candidate's campaign strategy. The character issue, of primary importance to George Bush's campaigns for president in 1988 and 1992, appears in various forms at the subnational level as well. Scandals in the personal lives of candidates can become major campaign issues, as can alleged wrongdoing while in office.[6] Thus, a candidate's integrity, honesty, leadership and management ability, and experience are all factors that may come into play. Like any other issue, candidates may focus on one or more of these nonpolicy factors if they believe that making such a factor salient to voters improves the candidates' chances of winning.

It is not clear how these types of factors might align on one or more dimensions among voters. For example, it is difficult to predict which candidate would typically have an advantage on a factor like honesty or how to represent the distribution of voters' evaluations of candidate honesty along a dimension. Incumbents might be expected to focus on leadership and experience more than would challengers, and in open-seat races, the more experienced candidate may opt for a similar strategy. Still, it is unclear if any sociodemographic or political cleavage would generally be made salient by these types of appeals.

In that uncertainty, however, may lie at least one prediction about campaigns that focus on nonpolicy factors: appeals made on a nonpolicy basis may cut across policy dimensions, thus reducing the relative salience of all policy-related cleavages. This contention is similar to Alvarez's (1997) claim, which is weakly supported, that voting in presidential elections is increasingly influenced by party identification when voters have relatively little information about issues. Supporters and opponents of abortion both want honest leadership, as do identifiers of both parties. Thus, a focus on nonpolicy factors should blur the lines of distinction along issue-based cleavages. This book touches on nonpolicy factors, particularly in the two case studies that are presented. However, I focus on the policy content of campaign themes and the resulting response of various divisions within the electorate.

Finally, Hammond and Humes (1993) make an initial attempt to formalize a model of heresthetic change. Having agreed with Riker (1990) that candidates are limited in their ability to shift their locations on issues and that voters are limited regarding how much information they can use, Hammond and Humes argue that campaigns are about defining the issues on which voters evaluate candidates. In their view, candidates try to present issues to voters on which they have an advantaged position in terms of their closeness to the majority of voters. For example, Candidate A might stress Issue 1, while Candidate B stresses Issue 2, because each is closer to the majority of voters on that respective issue. Hammond and Humes suggest that voters will then choose to support Candidate A if Candidate A is closer to them on Issue 1 than is Candidate B on Issue 2. In other words, these authors argue that voters do not evaluate both candidates on the same issues because Candidate B, seeing that he is disadvantaged on Issue 1, will not provide voters with any information about his position on Issue 1. Similarly, Candidate A will conceal her position on Issue 2. Thus, voters will not have sufficient information regarding Candidate B's position on Issue 1 or Candidate A's position on Issue 2 with which to evaluate them on those issues.

Hammond and Humes's approach fails to acknowledge the role of others in providing information to voters about candidates' stands on issues even if the candidates would prefer that such information not be shared. For Candidate A to make Issue 1 salient and to make it clear that she holds a preferred position on that issue compared to Candidate B, Candidate A must provide information to voters about both candidates' positions. Just because Candidate B might not want to talk about Issue 1 does not mean voters will not receive information about Candidate B's stance on that issue. In fact, the incentive for Candidate B to avoid talking about Issue 1 is exactly the same incentive that Candidate A has for making sure that voters know about Candidate B's position: Candidate A holds an advantage on that issue. Thus, while I share Hammond and Humes's focus on candidates' efforts to shift the salience of different issues, I disagree with their argument about how heresthetic change takes place. I consider Hammond and Humes's argument again in the next chapter, where I illustrate the implications for the formal spatial model of voting of the theory of heresthetic change for which I argue here.

The theory presented here may also be extended to understanding the mobilization of party loyalists for an election. Hirshman's (1970) exit option for voters, which I posit makes sense for voters who view elections as a series of related events (or plays in a game), suggests that candidates must choose strategies that mobilize their core supporters while reaching out to additional voters to form a winning coalition. Johnston et al. (1992) call this process the fundamental tension in electoral politics, and I agree. Thus, campaigns may produce heresthetic change by altering the makeup of the electorate through mobilization or the failure to mobilize supporters. While theoretically important and consistent with the research here, the empirical analysis of campaign themes and voter mobilization is left for future research.

To summarize, candidates and voters are goal-directed individuals. They interact through campaigns, which take place within the larger institutional structure of electoral politics. That structure combines with incomplete information to provide candidates with the opportunity and the incentive to behave strategically during a campaign. Candidates have three basic strategies from which to choose: changing their location in the issue space of an election, converting voters toward their ideal point on issues, or altering the nature of the issue space by changing the salience of dimensions along which the election is structured. Rational candidates seem most able to pursue this third option. Attempting to induce heresthetic change boils down to a struggle between candidates over the terms of the campaign debate. Candidates take clear stands and try to manipulate the salience of different dimensions, battling to influence which factors voters will use to evaluate the candidates on election day. Thus, campaigns shape the informational context of the election and can alter the short-term relative salience of divisions within the electorate. Many of the factors that constitute a political environment are beyond the control of the candidates. However, the relative importance of these factors to voters in any one election is subject, at least in part, to manipulation. In a competitive race, that motivation is all a candidate needs.

CHAPTER 3

A Spatial Model of Issue Salience
in Voting Behavior

In this chapter, I present a formal representation of the theory described in chapter 2.[1] In chapter 2, I argued that candidates compete with each other to influence the relative salience to voters of various issues or cleavages by providing information. In doing so, candidates attempt to create what Riker (1990) calls heresthetic change in the issue space of the election. Voters are assumed to vote for the candidate who most closely reflects their policy preferences. Candidates are assumed to be motivated, first and foremost, to win elections. While the issue space of an election may have any number of dimensions, in practice candidates can highlight only a few during any one campaign.

Though the theory calls for a multidimensional model, I begin by reviewing the spatial model of voting for a single dimension. The simple spatial model places all policy preferences on a single dimension, generally expressed as a liberal-conservative dimension. The model assumes that preferences are ordered, single peaked, and symmetric and that voters vote sincerely (for their preferred alternative). By "preferred," spatial theorists generally mean the alternative that is closest to the voter's ideal point.[2] Figure 3.1 illustrates this model. In each panel of figure 3.1, Voter X's ideal point on the liberal-conservative dimension is closer to the position advocated by Candidate A than that advocated by Candidate B. Thus, in each circumstance, Voter X would cast her ballot for Candidate A. The importance of the proximity to the ideal point of each voter combined with the aggregation of the preferences of individual voters into a distribution of preferences for the entire electorate leads to the now famous median voter theorem (Downs 1957; Black 1958). A fundamental prediction of the median voter theorem is that parties (or candidates) will converge toward the median voter's ideal point on the liberal-conservative policy dimension because they need to win a majority of votes on election day.

The next step is to be explicit about measuring the distance between Voter X's ideal point and the locations of the two candidates. These distances can be

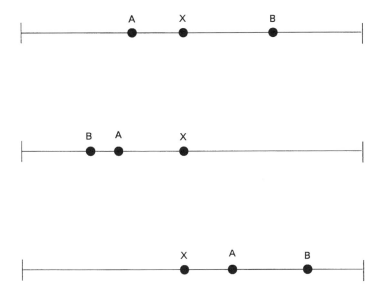

Liberal-Conservative Policy Dimension

Fig. 3.1.   Single-dimension spatial model for Voter X and Candidates A and B

measured as the squared distance between the voter's ideal point and the position advocated by a candidate.[3] Let

> x = Voter X's ideal point on the liberal-conservative dimension[4]
> a = Candidate A's location on the liberal-conservative dimension
> b = Candidate B's location on the liberal-conservative dimension

Thus, the distance between Voter X's ideal point and the location of Candidate A = $(a - x)^2$. For Candidate B, the distance = $(b - x)^2$. From this, we conclude that Voter X will prefer Candidate A when $(a - x)^2 < (b - x)^2$, or when Candidate A is located closer to Voter X's ideal point than Candidate B, which brings us back to where we started in figure 3.1. From the median voter theorem, the outcome of the election depends on how close the two candidates are to the median voter's ideal point.

Of fundamental importance to the basic spatial model is that voters actually know where Candidates A and B are located on the liberal-conservative dimension. If voters do not have this information, they cannot calculate their preferences for the two candidates. In the extreme, it does not matter what position the candidates take if voters are completely uninformed. In the real world, voters are somewhere in between having complete information, as traditionally assumed in the development of spatial models, and being completely uninformed. In fact, the theory developed in chapter 2 describes campaigns as struggles between candidates to provide additional information to voters.

Because of the uncertainty resulting from incomplete information, the voter's perception of the location of the two candidates is used in calculating that voter's relative preference for one candidate over the other. Alvarez (1997) defines that perception as

$$P_{xa} = p_a + v_{xa}$$

where:

P_{xa} = Voter X's perception of the location of Candidate A
p_a = Candidate A's actual location
v_{xa} = Voter X's perceptual uncertainty of Candidate A's actual location

In Voter X's mind, the distance between his ideal point and Candidate A $= (x - P_{xa})^2$. Through substitution, this distance can also be expressed as $(x - (p_a + v_{xa}))^2$, or ultimately as $(x - p_a)^2 + v_{xa}^2$.[5] In this final expression, v_{xa}^2 can be interpreted as the variance, or uncertainty, that Voter X has around his estimate of Candidate A's actual location along the liberal-conservative policy dimension. The same specification applies to Candidate B, such that Voter X now prefers Candidate A over Candidate B only if $(x - p_a)^2 + v_{xa}^2 < (x - p_b)^2 + v_{xb}^2$. This raises a number of implications for the campaign strategies of the two candidates.[6]

Most generally, this model suggests that voters prefer candidates for whom there is a relatively higher degree of certainty regarding the policies they advocate. For example, when both candidates are an equal distance from Voter X's ideal point, such that $(x - p_a)^2 = (x - p_b)^2$, Voter X will prefer Candidate A to Candidate B only if $v_{xa}^2 < v_{xb}^2$. In other words, Voter X will prefer the candidate of whose location on the liberal-conservative policy dimension Voter X is more certain. This action is consistent with the common assertion that voters are risk averse—when everything else is equal, voters prefer the devil (or angel) they know over the one they do not know.

From the candidates' perspective, the model implies that they could improve their chances of winning by taking clear stands on issues. At the same time, gains could also be made by confusing voters regarding the policy positions advocated by the opposing candidate.

Alvarez, borrowing from Enelow and Hinich (1984), extends the model by incorporating a term for nonpolicy factors that influence voting behavior. Alvarez defines the utility Voter X would receive from supporting Candidate A as a function of these nonpolicy factors minus Candidate A's perceived distance from Voter X's ideal point, such that:

$$U(A) = c_{xa} - (x - p_a)^2 - v_{xa}^2$$

where c_{xa} = nonpolicy factors Voter X uses to evaluate Candidate A. Alvarez then adds a weight term that captures the relative importance of policy versus nonpolicy factors in determining voting behavior. The model then becomes:

$$U(A) = c_{xa} - w_{xa}(x - p_a)^2 - v_{xa}^2$$

where w_{xa} = the weight Voter X places on the distance between her policy ideal point and Candidate A's policy location.

Alvarez asserts that w_{xa} is proportional to Voter X's uncertainty about Candidate A's location, and he constrains w_{xa} to be between 0 and 1. Thus, when Voter X is more uncertain about Candidate A's location, v_{xa}^2 gets larger and w_{xa} gets smaller. The first situation means that Voter X is less able to evaluate Candidate A on issues, while the latter means that Voter X is less willing to use that issue-based evaluation in determining whether to support Candidate A. Of course, the same elaboration can be made for Candidate B.

The strategic implications for candidates are clear. If a candidate is closer to a voter's ideal point on the liberal-conservative policy dimension than is his opponent, that candidate should strive to reduce voter uncertainty about the policy locations of both candidates, thereby increasing the importance of policy considerations to the voter in question. In contrast, the candidate located further away could benefit by raising the level of uncertainty regarding the policies each candidate advocates, thereby shifting relatively more weight to nonpolicy factors.

There are two links between Alvarez's model and the theory I developed in chapter 2. First, Alvarez explicitly models voter uncertainty that results from having incomplete information about candidates. The conclusions based on his model suggest that candidates may benefit from influencing the nature of the additional information gathered by voters. This fits well at a general level with my argument that campaigns impact voters through the provision of information.

Second, Alvarez argues that the weight voters place on their evaluations of candidate issue positions, or the salience of issues, varies as a function of the information voters have. Since campaigns provide this type of information, voting behavior depends in part on what candidates do and say. Alvarez rightly describes elections as an interaction between the content of campaigns and voters. This view resembles my argument that the issue content of campaigns interacts with various cleavages among voters to make issues more or less salient for a particular election.

However, Alvarez's model is limited by assuming a single policy dimension. He can argue that voters' quantity and quality of information influences the role of policy evaluations in voting behavior, but this thesis ignores the content of that information. For Alvarez, a campaign focusing on abortion could provide the same amount of policy information as a campaign focusing on tax policy.

The solution is to allow for multiple policy dimensions. The logic of his model approaches this solution if one considers nonpolicy factors as a second dimension. Recall that the strategic implications of Alvarez's model suggest that candidates will adopt strategies to make either policy or nonpolicy factors relatively more important for voters. This contention parallels the strategy of heresthetic change described in chapter 2 and formalized later in this chapter in the multidimensional model, but Alvarez does not make that extension.

Extending the model to multiple policy dimensions is essential to accurately represent the theory of electoral politics developed in chapter 2. The model presented here will be described in terms of two dimensions but is generalizable to multiple dimensions.[7]

Adding a second dimension to the issue space of an election raises two considerations: whether voter preferences on the two dimensions are separable and whether voters must choose between proposals on the two dimensions sequentially or simultaneously. If preferences are separable, then the expected outcome of a choice on one dimension has no effect on the voters' preferences on the other dimension. An example of separable preferences might be a voter's preferred level of a state's income tax and support for state restrictions on abortion. One's support or opposition to abortion likely is not influenced by the expected level of a state's income tax, and vice versa. An example of nonseparable preferences would be spending on two programs like health care and education under a fixed budget. If preferences are nonseparable, how much someone wants to spend on health care will be influenced by how much that person expects to be spent on education, and vice versa.

If preferences are separable and voting along two dimensions is sequential, then the expected outcome for each policy is the same as if we simply applied the single-dimension model separately to each dimension (e.g., tax rates, then abortion). This may be a useful way to model voting behavior in an election containing several single-issue ballot initiatives if voters hold separable preferences on those issues. However, voting for a candidate represents voting simultaneously for a bundle of issues.[8]

If voters must make a choice that simultaneously involves two issue dimensions, then the relative salience of each dimension must be considered. The salience of a dimension refers to the influence of the distance between the voter and a candidate on one dimension (tax policy) on that voter's preference for that candidate relative to the distance between the voter and the same candidate on the second dimension (abortion). The relative salience of each dimension, generally assumed away in most treatments of spatial theories, lies at the heart of heresthetic change. However, before I can examine the question of salience, I must present the basic two-dimensional spatial model.

The critical factor in the two-dimensional model remains the distance between a voter's ideal point and that voter's perception of where the two candidates are located. The only new wrinkle is that the overall distance between the voter's ideal point and a candidate's location is the combination of the distances between the two on both dimensions. For example, assume that we have two dimensions, numbered 1 and 2, two candidates, labeled A and B, and a single voter, labeled X. Furthermore, define Voter X's ideal point, x, equal to (x_1, x_2), where x_1 represents Voter X's ideal point on the first dimension and x_2 represents Voter X's ideal point on the second dimension.[9] Thus, (x_1, x_2) equals Voter X's coordinates, or location, in the two-dimensional issue space. Similarly, Candidate A's and Candidate B's locations in the two-dimensional issue space, a and b, are defined by the coordinates (a_1, a_2) and (b_1, b_2), respectively. Figure 3.2 illustrates the distance between Voter X and Candidate A in a two-dimensional space. In this example, Candidate A differs from Voter X on both dimensions. On the horizontal dimension, Dimension 1, the distance between Voter X and Candidate A is labeled f. On the vertical dimension, Dimension 2, the distance between Voter X and Candidate A is labeled g. However, the distance between Voter X and Candidate A in the two-dimensional issue space is a function of both f and g and is labeled h.

The Pythagorean theorem can be used to compute h. The Pythagorean theorem states that for any right triangle, the sum of the squares of the two sides equals the square of the hypotenuse. In this case, $h^2 = f^2 + g^2$. Solving for h, the distance between Voter X and Candidate A, the result is:

$$h = [f^2 + g^2]^{1/2}$$

where the superscript ½ indicates the square root of the term inside the brackets. This distance captured by h is referred to as the Euclidean distance. This is the most common method of measuring distances in multidimensional space. Given these definitions, the Euclidian distance (ED) between Voter X's ideal point, x, and the Candidate A's location, a, is:

$$ED(x - a) = [(x_1 - a_1)^2 + (x_2 - a_2)^2]^{1/2}$$

Similarly, for Candidate B:

$$ED(x - b) = [(x_1 - b_1)^2 + (x_2 - b_2)^2]^{1/2}$$

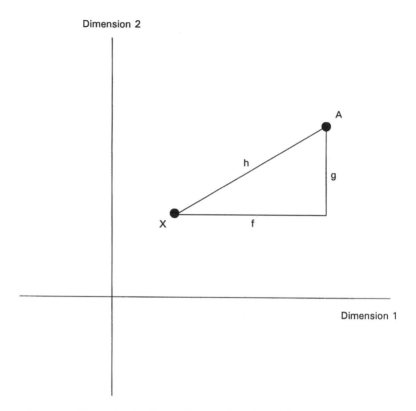

Fig. 3.2.   Measuring the distance between Voter X and Candidate A in a two-dimensional space

As a result, Voter X prefers Candidate A over Candidate B if:

$$[(x_1 - a_1)^2 + (x_2 - a_2)^2]^{1/2} < [(x_1 - b_1)^2 + (x_2 - b_2)^2]^{1/2}$$

In other words, Voter X prefers Candidate A to Candidate B when Candidate A is located more closely to Voter X's ideal point than is Candidate B.

As presented, this measure of Euclidian distance assumes that preferences on the two dimensions are separable and that both dimensions are equally salient to Voter X. Under these restrictions, the preferences of Voter X over the two policy dimensions can be represented graphically as a set of circular indifference curves (Enelow and Hinich 1984). Indifference curves represent those sets of points in the two-dimensional space that correspond to locations that candidates might occupy that are equally appealing to Voter X because all

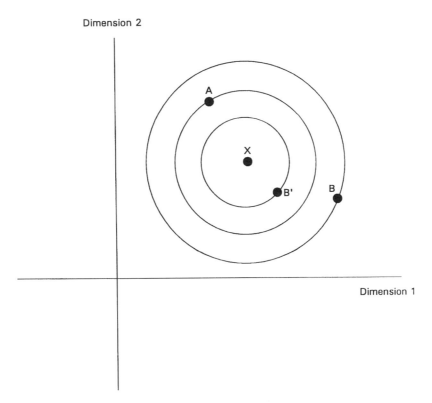

Fig. 3.3. Indifference curves for Voter X in a two-dimensional space with separable preferences and equal salience among dimensions

points on a single indifference curve are the same Euclidian distance from Voter X's ideal point. Because Voter X prefers candidates that are closest to his ideal point, Voter X prefers the candidate who is closest in terms of Euclidian distance—or, in other words, falls on the indifference curve closest to his ideal point. Figure 3.3 illustrates this situation for a single voter, X, and Candidates A and B.

In figure 3.3, we see that Candidate A falls on an indifference curve closer to X's ideal point than does Candidate B. Thus, even without measuring the exact Euclidian difference, we conclude that Voter X will prefer Candidate A to Candidate B. However, if Candidate B were to be located instead at B', Voter X would prefer Candidate B to Candidate A.

Following the logic of the model illustrated in figure 3.3, one way Candidate B can hope to defeat Candidate A is to change locations in the issue space.

This type of candidate relocation is generally predicted based on spatial models. Candidate B could also try to convince Voter X to change her ideal point, which would require Voter X to change her preferences. Of course, I suggested in chapter 2 that a candidate's ability to exploit these two options is limited. I argued instead for a third alternative: changing the salience of different dimensions in the issue space without either candidates or voters changing their locations. This factor can be incorporated into the spatial model by modifying the calculation of the distance between Voter X's ideal point and the locations of the two candidates.

In the initial calculation of the Euclidian distance between a voter and a candidate, $(x_1 - a_1)^2$ and $(x_2 - a_2)^2$ contribute equally—that is, both dimensions are treated as equally salient to the voter. What if the salience of the two dimensions is not equal? What if a voter cares more about one dimension, for example, abortion, than about another dimension, tax policy? Such a voter would place a different level of importance, or a different weight, on how far away a candidate is from his ideal point on each of the two dimensions. This situation can be modeled by using a weighted Euclidian distance as the measure, which simply adds weight parameters to the measure of Euclidian distance outlined earlier. If we represent the weighted Euclidian distance between Candidate A and Voter X as WED($x - a$), the new measure of the distance between Voter X and Candidate A becomes:

$$WED(x - a) = [z_{11}(x_1 - a_1)^2 + z_{22}(x_2 - a_2)^2]^{1/2}$$

where $z_{11} > 0$ and $z_{22} > 0$. These two parameters, z_{11} and z_{22}, represent the weight Voter X places on the first and second dimensions, respectively.[10] When they are both equal to 1, the measure simplifies to the simple Euclidian distance previously defined. The same modification should be made regarding Candidate B using the same values for z_{11} and z_{22} used to calculate the distance between Vote X and Candidate A, such that:

$$WED(x - b) = [z_{11}(x_1 - b_1)^2 + z_{22}(x_2 - b_2)^2]^{1/2}$$

If Dimension 1 is more important to Voter X in terms of selecting a candidate in the upcoming election than is Dimension 2, then $z_{11} > z_{22}$. This situation means that the relative proximity of the candidates to Voter X on the first dimension is more important to Voter X than is the relative proximity of the two candidates to Voter X on the second dimension.[11] At the election level, the implication is that the attitudes and characteristics associated with the more salient Dimension 1 will, on average, be better predictors of voting behavior than will voter attitudes and characteristics associated with Dimension 2, everything else being equal. For example, if abortion is made more salient to voters, the atti-

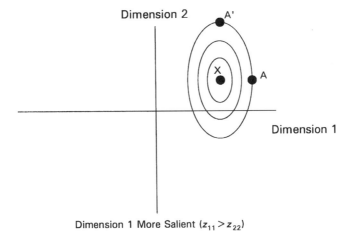

Dimension 1 More Salient ($z_{11} > z_{22}$)

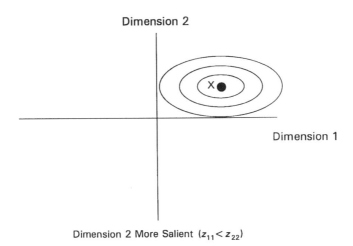

Dimension 2 More Salient ($z_{11} < z_{22}$)

Fig. 3.4. Indifference curves for Voter X in a two-dimensional space with separable preferences and unequal salience among dimensions

tudes voters hold on the abortion issue, along with characteristics such as gender and religious affiliation, should play a more prominent role in determining vote choice than they would have had abortion not been made a salient issue.[12]

Figure 3.4 illustrates the changes in Voter X's indifference curves that result when $z_{11} > z_{22}$ and when $z_{11} < z_{22}$. The upper panel of figure 3.4 shows that, when Dimension 1 is more salient ($z_{11} > z_{22}$), the indifference curves are compressed along the first dimension relative to the second. Conversely, the

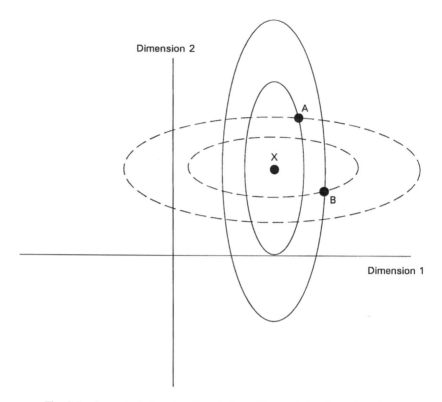

Fig. 3.5.   Impact of changing the relative salience of the dimensions in a two-dimensional space for Voter X's candidate preferences

lower panel of figure 3.4 shows that, when Dimension 2 is more important to Voter X ($z_{11} < z_{22}$), the indifference curves are compressed along the second dimension relative to the first. The two panels of figure 3.4 show that it no longer takes an equal shift on either dimension alone to reach a new indifference curve. Consider the two possible locations of Candidate A in the upper panel of figure 3.4, labeled A and A'. Both locations are on the same indifference curve for Voter X, meaning that Voter X would have equivalent preferences for Candidate A if she located at either of these two positions. However, the linear distance between X and A on Dimension 1 is less than the linear distance between X and A' on Dimension 2. In this case, Candidate A can be further away from Voter X's ideal point on Dimension 2 than on Dimension 1 and still be equally preferred by Voter X because Dimension 1 is more salient.

Figure 3.5 illustrates the implications of allowing the salience of different dimensions to vary in response to the campaign themes stressed by candidates.

This figure presents two sets of indifference curves for Voter X. The solid curves show the results if Dimension 1 is more salient, while the dashed curves show what happens if Dimension 2 is more salient. Recall that Voter X's support of a candidate depends on which candidate lies on the indifference curve closest to X's ideal point. Figure 3.5 shows that if Dimension 1 is more salient than Dimension 2 (the solid curves), Voter X will prefer Candidate A over Candidate B because Candidate A is located on an indifference curve that is closer to Voter X's ideal point. Conversely, if Dimension 2 is more salient than Dimension 1 (the dashed curves), Voter X will prefer Candidate B. Thus, strategic candidates have a third option besides trying to relocate themselves in the issue space or trying to convince voters to change their preferences: candidates can attempt to alter the salience of different dimensions to improve the chances of winning.

Consider again the full inequality that Voter X evaluates when determining which candidate to support:

$$[z_{11}(x_1 - a_1)^2 + z_{22}(x_2 - a_2)^2]^{1/2} < [z_{11}(x_1 - b_1)^2 + z_{22}(x_2 - b_2)^2]^{1/2}$$

which can be simplified by writing:

$$\text{WED}(x - a) < \text{WED}(x - b)$$

Voter X prefers Candidate A over Candidate B if this inequality holds, which means that Candidate A is closer as measured by a weighted Euclidian distance to Voter X's ideal point than is Candidate B.

As noted in chapter 2, traditional applications of spatial models to campaigns have focused on candidates relocating in the issue space of the election (e.g., Downs 1957; Enelow and Hinich 1984) or in providing additional information so that voters are more sure of the candidates' locations (e.g., Alvarez 1997). In terms of the model presented, these examinations imply that the campaign is about candidates attempting to alter a_1, a_2, b_1, and/or b_2. Rhetorical interpretations of campaigns (described by Riker 1990; advocated by Johnston et al. 1992) designed to persuade voters to accept a new view of an issue—or, in other words, to change their ideal points—implies that campaigns are candidates' efforts to alter x_1 and/or x_2. I argued in chapter 2 that both of these approaches face substantial limitations in most circumstances. Largely ignored in explicit treatments of the spatial model, though described by Riker's heresthetic argument, are attempts by candidates to alter the relative salience of those factors that voters might consider when picking a candidate. This hypothesis suggests that campaigns consist of efforts by candidates to alter z_{11} and z_{22}. Figure 3.5 makes it clear that for Voter X to change her candidate preference, candidates do not have to change their stances on issues and Voter X does not have to alter her ideal point. This is exactly the kind of change in the issue space that

I argue can result from the content of a typical campaign. The empirical tests that follow in later chapters are tests of whether the content of campaigns did in fact alter z_{11}, z_{22}, up to z_{nn} in an n-dimensional space—the weights placed on, or salience of, voters' various attitudes and characteristics that influence voting behavior.

At this point, I will return briefly to the question of the separability of preferences across dimensions. The weighted Euclidian distance defined earlier still assumes that preferences on the two dimensions are separable, though the model is easily expanded to allow for nonseparable preferences. The resulting measure of the distance between Voter X and Candidate A when preferences on the two dimensions depend in part on each other is:

$$\text{WED}(x - a) = [z_{11}(x_1 - a_1)^2 + 2z_{12}(x_1 - a_1)(x_2 - a_2) + z_{22}(x_2 - a_2)^2]^{1/2}$$

where $z_{11} > 0$, $z_{22} > 0$, and $z_{12}^2 < (z_{11} \times z_{22})$. This results in all $\text{WED}(x - a)$ being greater than 0 unless $x = a$. The parameter z_{12} measures the degree to which preferences on the two dimensions are separable. Thus, when $z_{12} = 0$, preferences are completely separable.

I will not fully explore the question of separability here because the following empirical analysis does not test for it. The implications of nonseparability when the salience of the dimensions differs can be illustrated rather simply, however. The result is that the oblong sets of indifference curves presented in figure 3.5 will be tilted, the direction and magnitude of which depends on the sign and magnitude of z_{12}.[13] Figure 3.6 illustrates one possibility. In figure 3.6, the solid curves indicate the indifference curves for Voter X regarding the two dimensions when preferences are separable and Dimension 2 is more salient. The dashed curves indicate the resulting tilt if z_{12} is positive. Now consider the location of the two candidates relative to Voter X in figure 3.6. If Voter X's preferences are separable, Candidate A lies on an indifference curve (solid) closer to X's ideal point than does Candidate B, so Voter X will prefer Candidate A to Candidate B. If, however, Voter X's preferences on the two dimensions are not separable such that z_{12} is positive, then Candidate B lies on a closer indifference curve (dashed) to Voter X's ideal point than does Candidate A. The implied campaign strategy for Candidate B in this case is to link in voters' minds their views on the two dimensions, particularly in terms of how they evaluate the two candidates. This linkage might be accomplished simply by reminding voters that when voting for Candidate A, they must take Candidate A's entire platform into consideration.

In the previous chapter, I noted that Hammond and Humes (1993) present an initial effort to formalize a model of heresthetic change, illustrating their model with a two-dimensional example. They argue, as do I, that the dimen-

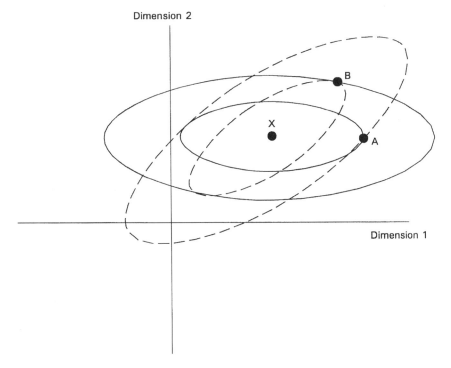

Fig. 3.6. Impact of change in separability of preferences in a two-dimensional space on Voter X's candidate preferences when Dimension 2 is more salient and z_{12} is positive

sions that will be salient to voters depend in part on which dimensions (issues) the candidates choose to stress during their campaigns. Hammond and Humes argue that, given fixed locations for a voter and both candidates in a multidimensional issue space, each candidate will focus on that dimension on which the voter's location is closest to their own. In the simplest case, the candidates will stress their best dimensions. For example, Candidate A might stress Dimension 1, while Candidate B stresses Dimension 2. Hammond and Humes then argue that the voter in question will vote for Candidate A over Candidate B if the voter is closer to Candidate A on Dimension 1 than to Candidate B on Dimension 2. In other words, the candidates are evaluated only in terms of the dimensions they stress during the campaign.

Critical to Hammond and Humes's argument is their assumption that voters only gather information about the locations of candidates on these dimensions from the candidates themselves. Voters do not know Candidate B's location on Dimension 1 because Candidate B does not tell them. As noted in chapter 2, this view fails to acknowledge that voters can and will receive information about Candidate B's location on Dimension 1 from Candidate A (as well as the media, interest groups, and others). Candidate A stresses Dimension 1 because Candidate A has a competitive advantage. This advantage is presumably why Candidate B wants to avoid making this dimension salient but is exactly why Candidate A has an incentive to make sure that voters know where both candidates are located on that dimension. To make a dimension more salient, candidates have the incentive to draw sharp contrasts between themselves and their opponents, which means that candidates can be expected to point out their opponents' weaknesses as readily as they point out their own strengths.

If one accepts that voters will generally have information about each candidates' location on both dimensions, Hammond and Humes's model breaks down. And given their assumption of circular indifference curves, their model is simply the traditional two-dimensional spatial model discussed previously. If voters evaluate both candidates on both dimensions, then the battle over which dimension is more salient centers on changing the shape of the indifference curves, which is equivalent to changing the relative weights placed on each dimension. Their approach has the advantage of not forcing the two dimensions introduced by the two candidates to be orthogonal (perpendicular in the two-dimensional case) to each other. However, this situation is easily captured by allowing preferences to be nonseparable, as described earlier.

Finally, the role of uncertainty resulting from incomplete information described at the beginning of this chapter regarding Alvarez's (1997) model can be incorporated into everything that has been presented here regarding the multidimensional model. One way of illustrating the role of such uncertainty is to imagine drawing something like a confidence interval around the indifference curves presented in the figures in this chapter. This is essentially what Alvarez does in the single-dimension case. However, the fact that voting behavior, the efforts of candidates, and the resulting outcomes of elections are characterized by uncertainty and, thus, as probabilistic, does not detract from the analytical power of the spatial model described here. As I have argued, voter uncertainty resulting in part from incomplete information provides the opportunity and the incentive for candidates to attempt to create heresthetic change.

To summarize, this chapter provides a formal representation of a spatial model of voting directly implied by the theory presented in chapter 2. I illustrated the strategic option of attempting to alter the salience of different issues or factors to voters over the course of the campaign. Campaigns have their effect on voting behavior by providing voters with information. That information interacts with voter attitudes and characteristics that largely existed before the campaign began, resulting in changing the relative salience of these factors for voters for this particular election. This change is captured formally in the weights assigned by voters to the distance between their ideal points and the locations of the candidates on the various dimensions of the issue space of the election.

CHAPTER 4

Data and Methods

In this chapter, I describe the data and methods used to evaluate predictions about both candidates and voters generated by the theory presented in chapters 2 and 3. The analysis that follows consists of two case studies along with data spanning more than one hundred gubernatorial elections held from 1982 to 1994.

I have argued that as a general strategy, candidates try to induce heresthetic change in the electorate by shifting the focus of the campaign to different issues, thus altering the relative salience of various divisions among voters. As a result, a campaign is a struggle to define the nature of the election: a battle between the candidates to raise and/or lower the relative salience of particular issues or cleavages for voters. Thus, the interaction between the candidates themselves and with the voters that takes place during the campaign influences the behavior of both the candidates and voters.

If the theory guiding this book is correct, we should observe candidates linking the themes they stress with target populations as the candidates develop their campaign strategies. Candidates and their staffs should discuss the campaign in terms of setting the agenda or defining the choice for voters. Given the voters' limitations outlined in chapter 2, candidates should focus on a limited number of issues and generally take clear stands on those issues. We should also see campaign strategies evolving as candidates learn more about their opponents and the electorate.

Furthermore, if the theory presented is correct, the salience of various determinants of voting behavior should respond to the themes candidates stress. The particular characteristics that respond to the themes stressed by candidates depend on the choice of theme. For example, if candidates in one race stress the abortion issue, voter attitudes on abortion should be stronger predictors of voting behavior in that election relative to an election in which the candidates did not stress abortion.

The complexity of the campaign process requires a research design that incorporates data on individual and aggregate-level factors that influence voting behavior as well as data on the themes candidates stress during elections. The research design should also examine the dynamic process of campaigns. Most important, the design must isolate the interaction between the campaign themes adopted by candidates and the salience of various divisions among voters.

Case Studies

Does the characterization of the campaign process presented in chapters 2 and 3 fit real-world examples of statewide campaigns? Do candidates and voters respond in the dynamic way predicted? I seek to answer these questions first through a detailed examination of two gubernatorial campaigns, the 1993 races in Virginia and New Jersey. Both races received some national attention, were highly competitive, and witnessed dramatic shifts in public opinion regarding candidate support over the course of the campaign. While no two elections could be considered representative of all gubernatorial elections, these two contests dramatically illustrate the dynamics of gubernatorial campaigns and the voters' responsiveness to them. Before I discuss the data gathering process for these two cases, I will say a bit about a statistical model of campaigns implied by the theory developed in chapters 2 and 3.

One can model the dynamic process of a campaign as a system of simultaneous equations that captures the interaction between the strategies of the two candidates and the salience of various cleavages among voters. The media plays the key role of linking these elements together by providing everyone involved with information about each other. The process is dynamic because the previous behavior of candidates and voters influences the current behavior of both candidates and voters. For those who are interested, a more detailed specification of such a model is presented in appendix A.

Before any campaign begins, we know that certain individual-level voter characteristics, election-level factors, and national-level factors characterize the current political environment. From this initial position, candidates develop their campaign strategies. For example, the partisan makeup of a state and the role of partisanship in previous elections serves as an initial value for the potential salience of such a cleavage. Candidate strategy is assumed to influence the salience of such factors but not their existence.

This preexisting political context can be treated as exogenous to the dynamic process of the campaign. The political context provides the bounds for the campaign. It presents specific opportunities and obstacles, and strategic candidates choose how to respond to them. The choices candidates make and how well they are able to capitalize on their strategic opportunities will influence what is salient to voters and, because of the volatility of gubernatorial elections, may be critical in determining who wins.

One way to exam the dynamics of campaigns is to conduct in-depth case studies. Chapters 5 and 6 present such studies of the gubernatorial campaigns in Virginia and New Jersey, respectively. For each case, I obtained several public-opinion polls. I also conducted extensive interviews with campaign managers, campaign staff members, party officials, volunteers, convention delegates, and members of the press. I subscribed to newspapers from each state and traveled to each state several times to observe the candidates in action. I received regular mailings from some of the campaigns and made an effort to gather samples of their campaign literature. Thus, in the tradition of Fenno (1978), I engaged in extensive "soaking and poking," supplemented by survey data and newspaper coverage.

I gathered information about the strategies and themes the candidates developed during these two campaigns from numerous sources. I subscribed to the *Richmond Times-Dispatch* from June 1 through the election and to the *Trentonian* from August 1 through late November. I also read many articles about these campaigns from the *New York Times,* the *Washington Post,* and *Star-Ledger* (Newark, N.J.). I also received a number of mailings from the campaigns. This information allowed me to track the daily proceedings of both campaigns and provided background information for interview questions.

The personal interviews I conducted with members of each candidate's campaign staff, political reporters, state party officials, and campaign volunteers are a critical part of this portion of the analysis. I began making contacts in February 1993 and maintained contact with each campaign through the election. I maintained detailed notes from each interview and, after each interview was over, I made a point of adding to my notes any information I was unable to fully record during the conversation. I assured every person that I interviewed that I would maintain confidentiality, and no information presented in this study gathered through the interview process is attributed directly to anyone. I have used the pronoun *he* to refer to all sources quoted anonymously, but it should not be inferred that all my contacts were male.

I traveled to each state several times to conduct interviews and to observe the campaigns and candidates in action. I attended both party conventions in Virginia and traveled to New Jersey to follow up immediately after the primaries. I returned over the Labor Day weekend and traveled with campaign staff members to public appearances made by each candidate in both states. I returned to both states for a final trip that included election day to observe local media coverage of the election and to conduct follow-up interviews. Again, I kept detailed notes of each interview and event.

The success of the case-study portion of this project depended on maintaining the trust of the individuals interviewed and protecting their confidentiality. Several factors improved my ability to do so. First, the early contacts over the phone and during my spring trips were critical. Even in February, campaign staff workers are very busy, and spending a half hour or more on the telephone with someone who cannot vote in the election and is not making a substantial financial contribution is not high on their list of priorities. The first step is to get past the person answering the phone and get the name of someone in the campaign for whom one can ask. Even talking to an assistant is a start. To make progress, I needed at least one worker in each campaign who was willing to be my contact person over the course of the election. Phone messages from an unknown researcher at an out-of-state institution often go unreturned. Persistence is a requirement.

Once I developed contacts in each campaign, developing and maintaining their trust was critical. Doing so was important because it allowed them to provide me with better information and made them feel more secure in setting up interviews for me with other staff and party insiders. Four factors assisted me in developing this trust.

First, I provided information about myself and my research, along with several references, to assure each person that I was not really a spy from an opposing campaign. Two of the campaign organizations were initially somewhat worried about this possibility, but I did not encounter any serious problems.

Second, I made it clear that I believed that these workers had a unique insight into the campaign process. Even though I am a political scientist, I wanted them to know that I was there to learn from their expertise. Frankly, most of my contacts were somewhat skeptical of political science and its "theories" that do not fit the "real world," even though many had some background in political science, typically as undergraduates. In general, these staff members believed that political science oversimplifies the electoral process and fails to grasp the importance and subtleties of campaign strategy. I told each contact that my research focused on uncovering and documenting the role of campaigns in determining electoral outcomes, thereby playing off of their skepticism and making them feel more comfortable. In short, I did my best to make them feel like the experts and that I was there to listen and learn rather than to lecture—which was true.

Third, I made it clear right from the beginning that I was following both candidates in each race and interviewing people from both campaign staffs. However, when conducting each interview, it often helped to respond in a manner that implied that I might be somewhat more sympathetic on a personal level to their particular candidate, their party, and the particular role they served in the organization of the campaign. While I had some very lively discussions regarding their views of electoral politics and campaigns, I avoided arguments. The best strategy was to let them dominate conversations. However, some interaction is necessary to facilitate discussion and to increase their level of comfort. Staff members believe in what they are doing and for whom they are working, and they seem more willing to share their views if they believe the interviewer has a sympathetic ear (Dexter 1970).

Finally, while interviews often involved discussions of the opposing campaign, I was very careful not to relate any information I personally gathered from one campaign to individuals working for the opposing campaign. When talking about the opposing campaign, I referred only to factors already reported in the state's press. Had I shared information obtained from an opposing campaign, I would not only have violated the trust placed in me by that campaign but also have lost all credibility with the other campaign, whose staff members would have had no reason to believe that I would keep confidential anything they told me.

From a scientific theory standpoint, had I shared information across campaigns that would otherwise not have been shared, I would have artificially altered the process I was studying, making any findings based on that analysis suspect. Only once did a staff member ask me a potentially compromising question about what I had learned from staff members in the opponent's campaign. I simply replied that I could not answer, and I pointed out that the staffer would not want me to answer the same question if someone on the other side had asked it. The person agreed and apologized, and we moved on.

To summarize, I found gathering data via interviews and direct observation to be critical for testing a theory of heresthetic change during an election. Gaining access to campaign organizations can be difficult. Although I believe I gained sufficient entry to each campaign, I was more successful in some than in others. Early and regular contacts were required. Face-to-face meetings were key to establishing trust. In addition, walking the fine line between presenting an image of objectivity yet some degree of sympathy to the views being expressed was central to creating an atmosphere in which the interviewee felt comfortable enough to share honest views about the process.

The extensive data gathering for these two case studies is consistent with the recommendations of King, Keohane, and Verba (1994) regarding case-study methods. Traditional views of case-study research characterize them as small N studies—studies with few observations. The implication is that the ability to generalize beyond these cases is limited. However, as King, Keohane, and Verba point out, scholars can make multiple observations within each case. In a sense, researchers increase their N size every time they explore another piece of evidence within the case at hand. Thus, every interview I conducted, campaign speech I witnessed, convention I attended, or newspaper story or press release I read adds to the number of observations. In this project, I searched for as many such observations as I could find from as many different sources as I could identify with an eye toward what proportion of these observations fit with the theory guiding this book.

Comparative State Analysis

While the two case studies provide a unique opportunity to explore the dynamics of campaigns, they are limited in their ability to support general statements about voter response to campaign themes applicable across elections. To test the theory presented in this book more generally, chapters 7 through 9 expand the number of elections considered. In each of these chapters, the principal sources of data are election-day exit polls and newspaper articles reporting the issue content of each campaign. Again, before commenting on the data in more detail, I present a statistical model designed to test the response of various cleavages among voters to the themes stressed by candidates. A more detailed development of the model is presented in appendix B.

A model capable of testing whether heresthetic change takes place must isolate the interaction between what candidates stress during their campaigns and the relative salience of factors that predict voting behavior. If the heresthetic argument presented in chapters 2 and 3 is correct, the effect of campaign themes on voting behavior is not direct. Instead, campaigns indirectly influence voting behavior by altering the relative weight voters place on certain factors when deciding for whom to vote.

Fortunately, once this indirect interactive process is understood, a relatively straightforward statistical model can be developed. In short, I build a statistical model that allows for the direct influence of some factor on voting behavior, the direct influence of campaign themes, and the interaction between the two. That interaction is captured by a multiplicative interaction term, which is simply a new variable created by multiplying two existing variables together. For example, chapter 7 examines the response of voters in gubernatorial elections to appeals on the abortion issue. A statistical model that fails to consider the content of a campaign might express voting behavior as a function of a respondent's view on the abortion issue along with other control variables. Excluding those other controls, such an equation might look like:

$$\text{VOTE}_{ij} = \beta_0 + \beta_1(\text{ABORTION}_{ij}) + e_{ij} \tag{4.1}$$

Equation 4.1 expresses the voting behavior of voter i in election j as a function of that voter's attitudes on abortion (I excluded other control variables at this point to keep the presentation of the example clear) plus a constant. The coefficient β_1 captures the average relationship between the views voters hold on abortion and their voting behavior. As it stands, equation 4.1 assumes that the effect of abortion attitudes on voting behavior is constant across elections or at least that any variation in that relationship from voter to voter or election to election is random. The heresthetic argument, however, says that the effect of abortion attitudes on voting behavior should vary as a function of whether abortion is stressed during a campaign. In other words, the heresthetic argument assumes that β_1 varies systematically as a function of another variable—in this case, whether abortion was stressed during a campaign. Thus, equation 4.1 should be expanded as follows:

$$\text{VOTE}_{ij} = \beta_0 + \beta_1(\text{ABORTION}_{ij}) + \beta_2(\text{STRESS ABORTION}_j)$$
$$+ \beta_3(\text{ABORTION}_{ij} \times \text{STRESS ABORTION}_j) + e_{ij} \qquad (4.2)$$

In equation 4.2, I have added a dummy variable[1] (STRESS ABORTION) that measures whether the abortion issue was stressed during election j and a multiplicative interaction term created by multiplying individual voter attitudes on abortion by whether the abortion issue was stressed during a campaign.[2] In equation 4.2, β_1 captures the effect of individual attitudes regarding abortion on voting behavior when the abortion issue is not stressed. The coefficient β_3 measures whether that base relationship between abortion attitudes and voting behavior differs between races where abortion is stressed and those contests when it is not. If β_3 is statistically significant, it would constitute evidence that the salience of voters' views on abortion responds to whether the issue is stressed during the campaign. In other words, β_3 measures the presence or absence of heresthetic change. In chapters 7, 8 and 9, I examine these sorts of interaction terms regarding the role of abortion in thirty-four elections held in 1990, the influence of presidential job approval in the 1990 and 1994 elections in twenty-nine states, and the response of several individual-level factors to a variety of campaign themes across seventy-one gubernatorial campaigns held from 1982 through 1992.

Data on individual voting behavior for these elections come from election-day exit polls conducted by CBS/*New York Times* and by Voter Research and Surveys.[3] Table 4.1 lists the states included for each year and the number of respondents in each exit poll. For each poll, state samples were selected by the polling agency in two stages. First, a sample of voting precincts was selected with a probability proportionate to the number of voters in each precinct. Thus, all voters had equal probabilities of their precincts being selected, except for some oversampling of precincts with large minority populations. Within each precinct, individual voters were randomly selected.

Using poll or survey data is necessary because the dependent variable in equation 4.2 is individual vote choice. The exit polls also provide measures on individual-level characteristics that influence voting behavior. The only other source of individual voter behavior and attitudes in gubernatorial elections is the American National Election Study (ANES) series. However, exit-poll data have two clear advantages over the ANES. First, the exit polls provide larger samples from each state, which results in more efficient parameter estimates and provides the additional degrees of freedom necessary for more complicated models. Furthermore, the cluster-sampling technique employed by the ANES is designed to provide a representative sample of the country but not necessarily a representative sample for each state.[4] Second, the ANES seriously misreports the vote in gubernatorial elections to such a degree that reliable tests of models of gubernatorial voting behavior cannot be achieved using the ANES

TABLE 4.1. CBS/*New York Times* and Voter Research and Surveys Exit Polls and Sample Sizes for States with Gubernatorial Elections, 1982–92

State	1982	1984	1986	1988	1990	1992	Total
AL	1,773				1,038		2,811
AZ					1,426		1,426
AR	790				1,580		2,370
CA	3,054		2,544		3,313		8,911
CO			1,233		1,557		2,790
CT	2,070		892				2,926
FL			1,449		1,897		3,346
GA			646		1,490		2,136
ID					1,550		1,550
IL	1,541		1,088		3,144		5,773
IN				1,201			1,201
IA	1,094				1,781		2,875
KS					1,635		1,635
ME	1,532				1,422		2,954
MD			912		918		1,830
MA	2,938				2,302		5,240
MI	864				2,244		3,108
MN	1,203				1,844		3,047
MO				1,285		1,335	2,620
NE	1,252				1,354		2,606
NV	1,158		1,048		1,125		3,331
NH		652			1,301	1,342	3,295
NM	1,161				980		2,141
NY	2,423		1,438		1,889		5,750
NC		1,948		1,505		1,573	5,026
ND						767	767
OH	985				1,994		2,979
OK					1,329		1,329
OR			790		1,029		1,819
PA			1,407		1,763		3,170
RI	1,286				1,595		2,881
SC					1,875		1,875
SD					787		787
TN	850				1,012		1,862
TX	2,044		1,481		2,832		6,357
VT	1,092	956			1,143		3,191
WA				1,128		1,549	2,677
WI					1,606		1,606
WY	893				873		1,766
Totals	30,003	3,556	14,036	5,119	53,628	5,799	112,141

(Wright 1993a; Carsey and Wright 1998). This misreporting favors the winning candidate, but the cause of the problem is not clear. It does not appear to be related to the time of the interview, and it is not tied to the wording of questions (Wright 1993a). Exit polls avoid the misreporting problem because they are conducted as the election is taking place.

Of course, no data set is perfect. Exit polls typically lack detailed questions regarding voters' positions on issues. When issue-related questions are asked, the content of the questions often varies from poll to poll. However, there is a sufficient number of common questions across the polls to test models based on equation 4.2. Finally, exit polls tend to overrepresent large states with competitive races. However, the analysis in chapter 7 on the abortion issue includes thirty-four of the thirty-six gubernatorial elections held in 1990.[5] Chapter 8 includes twenty-nine states that held gubernatorial elections in both 1990 and 1994. Thus, these two chapters include a near census of gubernatorial campaigns. Finally, chapter 9 contains data from seventy-one races held in thirty-seven states from every region of the country. Thus, while not a random sample, each chapter does contain a large and diverse set of gubernatorial elections.

I pool the exit polls to provide variance on election-level and national-level variables expected to influence voting behavior in gubernatorial elections. Doing so is necessary because the key variable in this analysis—the themes stressed by candidates—only varies at the election level. An additional advantage of combining these elections into a single model is that the analysis can control for other election-level factors, such as incumbency, campaign spending, and whether it is a presidential election year.

However, pooling data from several separate polls does have its problems. While each poll contains a random sample of voters, combining a set of random samples into one data set does not necessarily result in a data set that can be treated as a random sample. The observations within each exit poll will likely be correlated with each other relative to the observations across the pools, and the variance in voting behavior will probably not be constant across all elections. Thus, pooling data presents a number of statistical problems.[6]

The largest pool of elections analyzed in chapter 9 contains more than one hundred thousand individual voters in the data set. Yet, it is important to remember that this group still includes only seventy-one elections over a ten-year span. Because several hundred to a few thousand individuals are associated with each candidate-level or state-level measure, the effect of moving a state from one category and into another is magnified.

For example, New York in 1990 had a Democratic incumbent, Mario Cuomo, running for reelection. Thus, all 1,889 respondents in that election are assigned to the category of having a Democratic incumbent present in the race, and they bring with them every other idiosyncratic factor of the 1990 New York election not captured in other measures included in the model as well as the measurement error of that particular exit poll. The same is true for each state for every election-level variable, potentially producing strange mixes of state-specific idiosyncracies and measurement error.

This phenomenon does not prevent equation 4.2 from producing unbiased estimates of β_1 or β_3. However, this situation does raise serious questions about the standard errors associated with those estimates. Thus, for the models estimated in chapters 7, 8, and 9, I calculate robust standard errors based on Huber's (1967) and White's (1980) approach that accounts for the clustered nature of the pooled data.

Most of the election-level and national-level measures included as control variables, including candidate incumbency and state and national economic conditions, are taken from the *Book of the States, Statistical Abstracts,* and *Congressional Quarterly Weekly Reports.* Campaign-spending data for each election have been graciously provided by Professor Thad Beyle. Two measures of state political context were also examined: state political ideology (Erikson, Wright, and McIver 1993) and a dummy variable for the South. The specific measurement of the independent variables ultimately included in each analysis is discussed in the relevant chapters.

Measures of campaign themes are based on a content analysis of the newspaper coverage of each election along with election summaries found in *Congressional Quarterly Weekly Reports* and the *Almanac of American Politics.*[7] For each election, I reviewed one major newspaper from each state and read every article dealing with the gubernatorial election. Table 4.2 provides a list of newspapers used for each state.[8] Each paper was selected primarily based on the size of its daily circulation and its availability, though in some cases, a paper from a state's capital city was selected even if its circulation was slightly smaller than that of the state's largest newspaper. Each newspaper was reviewed from October 1 through election day. From this review, I created a series of dummy variables that report whether a particular issue was stressed by either candidate during the election.

These measures are not based on a mechanical process of counting mentions of a topic or paragraphs dealing with a topic. Rather, they rely on the interpretations of reporters assigned specifically to cover the campaigns along with the people they interviewed. I use the newspaper coverage more as an informant than as a raw data set. Newspaper coverage reports the views of candidates, consultants, party officials, other reporters, and even scholars regarding gubernatorial campaigns. The coverage also reports on the candidate's speeches and advertising efforts, and it typically reports the results of public-opinion polls. In short, newspapers report much of the same information that scholars look for when conducting their own case studies. Scholars would no doubt gather somewhat different and possibly more information than do re-

TABLE 4.2.   Newspapers Reviewed

State	Newspaper
AL	*Birmingham News* (1990); *Montgomery Advertiser* (1982)
AZ	*Arizona Republic*
AR	*Arkansas Democrat* (1982); *Arkansas Gazette* (1990)
CA	*Los Angeles Times*
CO	*Denver Post*
CT	*Hartford Courant*
FL	*Miami Herald*
GA	*Atlanta Journal-Constitution*
HI	*Honolulu Star-Bulletin*
ID	*Idaho Statesman*
IL	*Chicago Tribune*
IN	*Indianapolis Star*
IA	*Des Moines Register*
KS	*Wichita Eagle*
ME	*Bangor Daily News*
MD	*Baltimore Sun*
MA	*Boston Globe*
MI	*Detroit News*
MN	*Minneapolis Star-Tribune*
MO	*St. Louis Post-Dispatch*
NE	*Omaha World-Herald*
NV	*Las Vegas Review-Journal*
NH	*Union Leader* (Manchester)
NM	*Albuquerque Journal*
NY	*New York Times*
NC	*Raleigh News and Observer*
OH	*Columbus Dispatch*
OK	*Daily Oklahoman* (Oklahoma City)
OR	*Oregonian* (Portland)
PA	*Philadelphia Inquirer*
RI	*Providence Journal-Bulletin*
SC	*The State* (Columbia)
SD	*Argus Leader* (Sioux Falls)
TN	*Tennessean* (Nashville) (1982); *Commercial Appeal* (Memphis) (1990)
TX	*Houston Chronicle*
VT	*Burlington Free Press*
WA	*Seattle Post-Intelliger*
WI	*Milwaukee Journal*
WY	*Casper Star-Tribune*

porters. However, I am not trying to conduct a full case study of each of these races. I only need to be able to reliably measure the basic issues stressed by each candidate in each campaign.

The variables are coded as dummy variables for several substantive reasons. The literature reviewed in chapters 2 and 3 suggests that voters cannot pay attention to more than a few simple messages at any one time. Also, the theory presented here and in many other studies asserts that candidates campaign on limited and simplified issue agendas. Candidates identify themselves as either for or against something—they take clear stands and do not campaign in the middle (Rabinowitz and Macdonald 1989; Johnston et al. 1992). Voters tend to boil campaign messages down to agreement or disagreement with a candidate, creating an "us" versus "them" view of politics. This information suggests that campaigns unfold in a dichotomous way.

Identifying the major themes of candidates' campaigns proved to be fairly straightforward. Stories about candidates' stump speeches frequently used language such as "Candidate Smith today continued to stress her views on taxes." Such descriptions point to the issues that are consistent themes of a candidate's campaign. Also, many recent elections include coverage of the content of candidates' television advertising, which again points out the themes a candidate is trying to stress. Debate coverage also proved to be quite useful in this regard. Many such stories could have been—and often were—given headlines like "Gubernatorial Debate Breaks No New Ground: Common Themes Repeated." Finally, the newspaper coverage of gubernatorial campaigns consistently quotes senior campaign staff members, party leaders, and the candidates themselves, which provides more direct information on the messages campaigns are trying to convey.

I considered a more traditional content analysis coding scheme early in the research, but it became apparent that such an approach was not appropriate for the purposes of this analysis. The problem with a counting approach stems largely from the variation in the nature of campaign coverage from newspaper to newspaper and from year to year. Some newspapers focus on descriptive stories (What did the candidates do yesterday? To whom did they speak? What did they say?). Others provide more analysis. A newspaper might report once that an issue looks to be important for this campaign but then not mention that issue again for the remainder of the campaign. In contrast, some papers report whatever a candidate says each day, even if the candidate says the same thing every day. Also, the nature of campaign coverage seemed to evolve over time. In particular, coverage of more recent elections focused more on candidates' television advertising.

An example illustrates the problems caused by a coding scheme based on counting paragraphs. Cook, Jelen, and Wilcox (1992) and I argue that abortion was an important issue in the gubernatorial races in Texas and Kansas in 1990.

In contrast, I assert that abortion was not stressed in Maryland in 1990, while Cook, Jelen, and Wilcox do not comment on that race, presumably because they also believed that abortion was not stressed.

In Kansas, the Republican incumbent, Mike Hayden, was viewed as vulnerable in large part due to unpopular tax policies. His Democratic opponent, State Treasurer Joan Finney, had developed a populist appeal. Hayden was prochoice on abortion, while Finney held a rather extreme prolife position. As part of a general strategy to define Finney as unfit and potentially dangerous, Hayden regularly attacked her on abortion in speeches and television advertisements. Finney tried to downplay the issue, saying she would not actively seek restrictions on abortion. However, she did indicate that she would sign them if passed, and at one point she implied that she did not favor access to abortion even in cases of rape or incest.

Of the 699 paragraphs in the *Wichita Eagle* that dealt with this election from October 1 through election day, only thirty-two (4.6 percent) dealt with abortion in any way.[9] The longest single section in any one article that dealt with abortion was six paragraphs and reviewed the voters' positions on abortion according to a public-opinion poll. This level of coverage occurred in spite of a poll released on October 21 that reported that voters ranked abortion as the campaign's second-most important issue (behind taxes). Abortion was a major part of Hayden's campaign and an important issue for voters, yet mentions of the issue constituted less than 5 percent of the newspaper coverage of the campaign. In comparison, just over 20 percent (141 paragraphs) of the newspaper coverage was devoted to taxes, a percentage that would be larger if more general references to balancing budgets and spending were included.

In Texas, Democratic State Treasurer Ann Richards made abortion rights a central part of her campaign against Republican businessman Clayton Williams. She advocated her prochoice stance as part of a general strategy to define Williams as out of touch and unsympathetic to women. Williams did not back away from his prolife stance, although abortion was somewhat less central to his campaign. Of the 1,089 paragraphs about this campaign of the *Houston Chronicle,* only twenty-one (1.9 percent) dealt with abortion, thirteen of them in a single story.

In Maryland, incumbent Democrat William Schaefer and his challenger, Republican William Shepard, devoted very little attention to abortion, and neither candidate stressed it during their campaigns, even though they disagreed sharply. Interest groups on both sides of the issue endorsed candidates but focused on state legislative races. In short, abortion was not an issue debated by the candidates or by anyone else during this gubernatorial campaign. Yet of the 422 paragraphs about the race in the *Baltimore Sun,* twenty-nine (6.9 percent) dealt with abortion, eleven of them in one article.

The total number of paragraphs devoted to abortion was higher in Maryland than it was in Texas, and the percentage of the coverage devoted to abortion was larger in Maryland than in either Kansas or Texas. Thus, a measure based strictly on paragraph counts would mistakenly code the abortion issue as being stressed more in Maryland than in Texas or Kansas.

In this particular case, the problem may stem from two sources. First, abortion is what Carmines and Stimson (1989) call an easy issue. Voters can readily understand candidates' positions on abortion, and those positions are reasonably clear and nontechnical. Thus, it may not be news to report on a daily basis that one candidate is prochoice and the other is prolife. Second, simply counting paragraphs dedicated to a particular topic fails to consider the content of those paragraphs. Six paragraphs about each candidate's views on abortion and how the candidates focus on abortion in speeches gets counted the same as six paragraphs pointing out that the candidates differ on abortion but are not emphasizing that difference in the campaign. One could attempt to incorporate this information in a more elaborate coding scheme, but the development and implementation of such a scheme would require at least as much subjective interpretation of the content of the coverage as does the approach I undertook, and it would continue to introduce measurement error.

The measure I employ may appear to be more subjective than would be a measure based on a simple counting procedure. However, by letting the newspaper coverage report what issues are stressed, I am relying on the expertise and experience of reporters, who typically have a history of covering statewide elections, as well as the academics, party officials, and longtime observers of state politics whom the reporters interview. Counting-based coding would also incorporate measurement error into a variable designed to capture the strategies adopted by campaigns by inadvertently including differences in the style of coverage into the measure.

Given that coding campaign themes using dummy variables is justified, I need to report more fully how that process was completed. I read every available article from October 1 through election day for each race. As I read this information, I took extensive notes, which I then used to code whether each candidate stressed any of the following during their campaigns: taxes, education, the environment, economic development and job creation, state spending and the budget, crime, abortion, traditional class-based appeals (rich versus poor), and appeals to "stay the course," which tend to be made by incumbents and candidates of the incumbents' parties when the incumbent stepping down remains popular with voters. Chapters 7 and 9 report which candidates stress which issues. After more than six hundred hours of experience, I am convinced that boiling the thirty to one hundred articles that typically appear during the final weeks of a gubernatorial campaign down to a handful of issues stressed by each candidate is valid and reliable, in large part because candidates want voters to be able to boil down this information for themselves by election day.

TABLE 4.3.   Frequency of Issues Stressed
by Gubernatorial Candidates 1982–92

Issue	Democrats (%)	Republicans (%)
Gun control	1	4
Taxes	35	48
Education	31	14
Environment	15	3
Economy/jobs	34	35
Budget/spending	20	23
Crime	8	24
Abortion	18	10
Class-based appeals	24	7
"Stay the course"	21	25

To provide some background information to the chapters that follow, table 4.3 presents the frequency of each issue being stressed by the Democratic and Republican candidates for governor in the seventy-five elections examined in chapter 7 and/or 9. Candidates from both parties most frequently made taxes the central part of their campaigns. This supports Jewell and Olson's (1988) finding regarding the importance of state tax policy in gubernatorial elections. After taxes, Republican candidates tended to stress jobs and the economy, crime, and budgetary concerns. Democrats also focused on jobs and the economy but were more likely to make education and class-based appeals.

The differences between candidates of the two parties reflect the differences in their traditional constituencies as well as a pattern of focus on different cleavages: Democrats focus on a class-based cleavage while Republicans focus on crime, which chapter 9 will show to be related to a racial division among voters.

In this chapter, I described the data and methods used to analyze the heresthetic change resulting from campaigns. These data and methods allow for the examination of the dynamics of campaigns, the comparison of multiple campaigns, and the exploration of the interaction that takes place between campaigns and voters that culminates on election day. It is now time to turn to the actual analysis of heresthetic change in gubernatorial campaigns.

CHAPTER 5

Virginia's 1993 Gubernatorial Campaign

"The campaign must talk about those issues that matter to people, but you can't stray away from what the candidate has a background on. You must meld together the voters' concerns and the candidate's qualities. You need to be credible on the issues you discuss."

> Terry campaign staff member

"No candidate runs a campaign strictly based on the polls. We use the polls to tell us what to stress, or how to package things, but they don't tell us whether or not we are for or against something."

> Allen campaign staff member

"You don't pick issues based just on polls, but, rather, you blend candidate strengths with voter concerns."

> Terry campaign staff member

"Polls tell you how to sell a message, not what message to sell. Polls will tell on which issues you have an exploitable advantage. Candidates don't move themselves around; they just try to shift the focus of the election and try to define the election in terms beneficial to themselves."

> Allen campaign staff member

"We will win or lose based on whose views get accepted by the voters."

> Terry campaign staff member

Campaigns are dynamic events that unfold over time. The themes candidates stress may shift and flow as the campaign unfolds, and all the while the electorate learns more about the candidates. Chapters 7, 8, and 9 will demonstrate that this process culminates on election day with voters responding to the dominant themes stressed by candidates during their campaigns. But first, this chapter and chapter 6 illustrate how the dynamics of campaigns unfold. This chapter focuses on the 1993 gubernatorial election in Virginia, while chapter 6 explores the 1993 gubernatorial election in New Jersey.[1]

These two case studies will show how voters respond to the choice candidates present. Evidence of candidates trying to alter the salience of different issues and/or cleavages in the electorate is presented. These two examples also show that voters and candidates learn about and respond to each other as the campaign unfolds.

Overall, these two elections provide excellent opportunities to study campaign dynamics at the gubernatorial level. Gubernatorial elections have been competitive in New Jersey for most of the state's history, and a truly competitive two-party system has emerged in Virginia.[2] Neither party in either state enjoys a significant advantage in party identifiers. Finally, the office being sought is a powerful one in each state's politics.

These two elections obviously do not constitute a representative sample of gubernatorial elections. The specific opportunities and obstacles faced by candidates depend on who they are, who they run against, and in what state they are running. However, the dynamic process of developing campaign strategy over the course of an election in response to these factors and the way voters can be expected to respond are similar across contexts.

Mary Sue Terry, a Democrat, opposed George Allen, a Republican, for the governorship in Virginia in 1993. Both lawyers, each had served in the Virginia state legislature. Terry had also served seven years as the state's attorney general, resigning to devote more time to her gubernatorial campaign. After winning a special election in the Seventh District, Allen spent one year in the U.S. House of Representatives. He decided to run for governor after redistricting placed him and popular GOP incumbent Thomas Bliley Jr. in the same district.

It is said that military generals develop strategies based on the previous war, not the next. The theory guiding this book suggests that candidates begin campaigns using a similar approach. They look to what they believe has worked and not worked in the past. Terry and Allen began their campaigns in this way.

Republican success in winning Virginia state races in the 1970s depended in part on raising the specter of liberal Democrats (Atkinson 1992). There is also strong precedent for Democratic presidential candidates to be unpopular in Virginia, at least since 1952, a situation that has provided Virginia Republicans with something to run against. Virginia Democrats, conversely, had success in statewide elections before the 1970s by maintaining a coalition of moderates and conservatives while charging that Republican candidates like Ted Dalton were too liberal (Atkinson 1992). In the 1980s, Democrats recaptured the governorship by regaining the support of many white moderates and, in the latter part of the decade, by raising the specter of the radical Right in the GOP. Thus, history suggests that contemporary swing voters in Virginia are moderate to conservative on fiscal matters yet moderate to liberal on social and cultural issues and that successful gubernatorial candidates avoid the label of *extremist* on either the liberal or conservative side.

Many of these swing voters live in the Washington, D.C., suburbs of

Northern Virginia. In fact, a senior staff member in the campaign of Republican Earl Williams, an Allen challenger for the Republican nomination, called Northern Virginia the "eight hundred pound gorilla in Virginia politics. . . . You can't lose badly in the north suburbs and expect to win the state."

Though incumbent governors cannot seek a second successive term in Virginia, Terry entered the race in the eyes of many as the de facto incumbent. She had twice won the attorney general's office and in 1989 received more than one million votes—the first candidate for statewide office to ever do so in Virginia.[3] She was well known, well liked, and well financed. She had strong ties in the business community, having developed a reputation as fiscally conservative and supportive of economic development. Finally, she faced no opposition within her party for the gubernatorial nomination. Early polls had her well ahead of any GOP competitor, and some commentators were calling the race over before it started.

Her campaign faced some potential problems, however. President Bill Clinton, U.S. Senator Charles Robb, and then Governor Doug Wilder, all Democrats, were widely unpopular in Virginia in 1993. Second, politicos from both parties sensed a desire for change among the voters, and Democrats had controlled state government for the previous twelve years. Finally, some perceived Terry as an overly cautious politician to the point that political considerations weighed too heavily in her decision making both as attorney general and as a candidate for governor.

Allen entered the race for the GOP nomination largely unknown outside of his own congressional district, even among Republicans. Unlike Terry, Allen faced two other candidates for his party's nomination. When he received the nomination, however, Allen appeared to have an organizational advantage over Terry.[4] He also had Terry's weaknesses on which to build. However, entering the general election in June, he faced three serious obstacles. First, he was not well known. Second, his campaign was at a tremendous financial disadvantage. Finally, Allen was the most conservative of the three GOP gubernatorial contenders, had open support from the National Rifle Association (NRA) and Christian Coalition founder Pat Robertson, and was saddled with a staunchly conservative lieutenant governor nominee in Michael Farris. Thus, he was in danger of being labeled a right-wing extremist. Conversely, Allen had previously waffled on his position on abortion, and failing to appear conservative enough, especially with Farris on the ticket, might alienate some of the fiercely conservative activists in the GOP.

Both parties used conventions instead of primaries to nominate their candidates for statewide office. Conventions place an increased importance on party activists in the nomination process (Jewell 1984). Chapter 2 noted that dependence on activists limits the ability of candidates to use relocation in the issue space as an electoral strategy.

In discussing the presidential nomination process, Aldrich (1980a) argues that candidates who secure early nominations have an advantage going into the general election because they can shift their focus sooner to the issues that will dominate the general election. Terry clearly had this advantage. She had effectively been the Democratic Party's 1993 gubernatorial nominee since she passed on the opportunity to contest Wilder for the nomination four years earlier.

The mood among the Democratic convention delegates at the convention on May 7–8 could best be described as artificial enthusiasm. Most people whom I interviewed felt comfortable with Terry's early lead in the polls and felt confident that she would win. Reporters covering the convention described her as a centrist who was a safe noncontroversial selection for the Democrats. Those same reporters were hard-pressed to point to one or two issues that they thought would dominate during the general election.

When asked about the best strategy for the Terry campaign to adopt, a member of Wilder's gubernatorial staff who worked for his campaign four years earlier said, "Keep it boring. Don't get [voters] too excited or thinking that this is a critical election. Just let them vote for someone they are comfortable with." Given her advantage in name recognition, her generally favorable rating among voters, and her enormous early lead in both the polls and fund-raising, the Terry campaign in fact initially adopted this strategy.

The lead story in the *Richmond Times-Dispatch* after the first day of the Democratic convention focused not on Terry's nomination but on the public feud between Wilder and Robb (Whitley 1993o, 1). Both Robb and Wilder spoke on the first night, and both called for party unity. However, immediately after his speech, Wilder held a press conference on the convention floor during which he attacked Robb's service in the U.S. Senate. Mention of Terry was relegated to the final few paragraphs of the newspaper's story.[5]

The candidates were nominated and spoke on the second night. Terry presented a policy agenda in which she said she would focus on jobs, education, health care, and crime. She walked a fine line during the speech between crediting the three previous Democratic governors for their accomplishments and suggesting that she represented change. In particular, she discussed being tough on crime. This tension in her speech reflected disagreement within the Terry campaign regarding the focus of her message. The question was whether she should defend the previous Democratic accomplishments, including her own, or campaign strictly on her agenda for the future. Staff members connected with the Virginia Democratic Party argued that Terry should campaign on her record. One senior staff member said in early May that "Even though Mary Sue is not an incumbent governor, she is part of the incumbent administration and has her own record as attorney general. She must be able to run on that. She can't run away from it."

In contrast, consultants hired from outside the Virginia Democratic Party wanted Terry to distance herself from unpopular Democrats like Clinton, Robb, and Wilder. One outside consultant said in April that he expected the Republican nominee, whoever it turned out to be, to campaign against twelve years of Democratic control of state government. This consultant believed that Terry could survive such an attack because she was not closely tied to Wilder or Robb and had managed to keep herself out their conflicts. The implication, however, is that this consultant did not want Terry to do or say anything during the campaign that would tie her more closely with these unpopular Democrats. This information shows that candidates develop their initial strategies based on their beliefs about what their opponents will do.

The Allen campaign was pleased by Terry's speech. A senior Allen campaign staff member, speaking after the Democratic convention, said that Terry could not sell herself as an agent for change: "If the election is based on change, then we win."

The Republican nomination process differed from the Democrats' in many respects. There were hotly contested battles for the nomination for all three offices (governor, lieutenant governor, and attorney general). As a result, the GOP convention, held on June 4–5, was much more alive with energy and interest among the delegates and reporters. Because each nomination was contested, however, the Republicans also faced the increased potential for serious and long-lasting splits to develop in their party. Without a preordained ticket like the Democrats, the more than fourteen thousand GOP delegates had the clear chance to shape the direction of their party and the course of the general election.

Allen ran against Clint Miller, a longtime member of the state legislature and late entry into the race, and Earl Williams, a wealthy businessman from Northern Virginia who had never before sought political office. Williams ran as a moderate, focusing on his business skills. Allen was clearly more conservative. Miller entered the race late as a moderate compromise candidate.

The Republican Party, and in particular the Allen campaign, encouraged a large number of delegates to attend the convention. They viewed the mobilization of delegates as a precursor to developing a statewide volunteer organization for the general election. One Allen staff member said, "The organizational effort for the Democrats is through unions, teachers, and environmental groups. [Republicans] don't have that organizational base, so we created it."

It was clear at the Republican convention, however, that the NRA and various antiabortion groups associated with the Christian Coalition were playing a major role in the party's fortunes. Both of Allen's opponents attacked him for allowing the NRA to funnel money into his campaign. The overwhelming presence of the Christian Right was obvious as its workers staffed numerous information booths and distributed literature. A booth set up by a group of prochoice Republicans was relegated to a far corner of the auditorium, rarely visited by convention goers, and several delegates told the booth's staffers that they were at the wrong convention. Several delegates I spoke with expressed concern that the convention might go too far to the right, but as the result of the convention indicates, they were outnumbered.

The Allen campaign began contacting unit party chairpersons more than a year before the convention to line up early endorsements and develop a statewide volunteer organization. Allen's staffers arrived at the convention believing that about 60 percent of the 14,565 delegates were firmly committed to their candidate. The Allen camp flexed its muscle on the first day by easily defeating several attempts to alter the convention rules, and Allen easily secured the nomination the following day.

Two additional events occurred during the convention that influenced the dynamics of the campaign that followed. First, instead of a written document, the Resolutions Committee released as its "report" a fifteen- to twenty-minute video. This decision was unpopular with some of the conservative delegates but was supported by the Allen campaign to avoid rifts in the party over language in the platform. The video focused on the perceived failings of the Robb-Wilder-Terry Democrats. It presented the GOP approach to education, welfare reform, economic development, and crime, to which it paid particular attention. However, the delegates' favorite segment of the video dealt with abortion: a young mother said something to the effect of, "You know, my daughter can't even get an aspirin at school without a parental-consent form. Shouldn't we go at least that far on abortion, too?" When asked, a senior Allen staff member confirmed that the goal was to avoid a fight as well as to avoid extremist language in any written resolutions, adding, "It was a nice touch wasn't it?"

The second significant development was the nomination of an extreme conservative, Farris, for lieutenant governor. The governor, lieutenant governor, and attorney general run for their respective offices separately in Virginia. In other words, voters can split their tickets between these offices. Farris's views on social issues, including abortion, concerned members of the Allen campaign staff and many party officials, who thought Farris's nomination might take the party too far to the right and give the Democrats an issue. At the convention, Farris, not Allen, generated the most enthusiastic responses among delegates, and the Allen campaign hoped to benefit from the conservatives Farris mobilized. However, the Allen campaign also planned to avoid the social agenda supported by that wing of the party. Shortly after the Republican convention, a senior Allen staff member said flatly, "If abortion is the critical [campaign] issue, we lose. We want people to vote instead on the issues of political reform, crime, education, and workfare."

The press coverage of the Republican convention, even in the fairly conservative *Richmond Times-Dispatch,* focused on the conservative nature of the GOP's ticket. If fact, the first line of the paper's June 6 lead story on the convention read, "Ignoring cries for moderation, Virginia Republicans yesterday assembled their most conservative ticket in memory" (Schapiro and Hardy 1993, 1). In the same story, political scientist Mark Rozell said, "This is the image the Democrats wanted: of a Republican party beholden to an ideological faction not representative of mainstream voters." Three days earlier, the *Times-Dispatch* quoted political scientist Larry Sabato as saying, "Even after three statewide defeats, [the Virginia GOP] would rather be right than govern" (Whitley 1993d, B1).

Results of an independent poll conducted June 8–10, just after the GOP convention, gave Terry an eighteen-point lead over Allen, at 49 percent to 31 percent (Whitley 1993l, B5). Thus, coming out of the nomination process, Terry had a big lead in the polls, a big lead in name recognition, high favorability ratings, and $2.3 million in the bank, while Allen was being described as leading an extreme right-wing ticket, was not well known across the state, and had spent virtually all his funds to secure the nomination.

The Allen campaign expected the Democrats to attack their candidate as a right-wing extremist. However, my early discussions with members of the Terry campaign suggested that she did not intend to attack unless attacked first or the election got too close. The Allen campaign, however, knew it had to attack Terry. "We will need to attack her because she has no strong negative evaluations right now," said a staff member in early May. "She will be attacked for her management of the attorney general's office. We want to show her as an old-style political crony."

Given Terry's early lead in the polls and her huge financial advantage, her campaign decided to play it safe and try to spend Allen out of the campaign. For Allen, the strategy was to generate name recognition, try to raise money, to avoid the label of intolerant right-winger, and to increase voters' negative evaluations of Terry by focusing on crime and on her tenure as attorney general.

Terry's one bold new proposal was to announce her support for a law requiring a five-day waiting period for the purchase of a handgun. She had opposed such measures in the past but now said it was time to adopt such a law. An Allen campaign staffer believed this switch was an attempt to preempt the Allen campaign on crime policy by supporting an issue that had widespread public support. While this is likely the case, the Terry campaign also hoped that this strategy would draw attention to the NRA's support of Allen.

The Allen campaign welcomed the early focus on crime. "We were thrilled that they decided to start their campaign on the crime issue," said a senior Allen staff member. During the GOP convention, Allen had attacked Virginia's rising crime rate while Terry was attorney general and had planned to stress crime during the campaign. The focus of his crime package—and what turned out to be the defining issue of his campaign—was abolishing parole for violent offenders.

Even by late August, Terry's staffers believed that stressing the crime issue was a winning tactic for them. One Terry worker said, "Allen's stance against parole is just a scare tactic, while Mary Sue's support for a five-day waiting period and tougher sentencing is good policy." Terry had good reason to believe that supporting a five-day waiting period would help her campaign, as an independent poll reported in the June 16 *Richmond Times-Dispatch* that 88 percent of Virginians supported the proposal (Johnson 1993, B12). In the same article, Tom King, a consultant to the Terry campaign, was quoted as saying, "[even] Ronald Reagan supports a 5-day waiting period."

The Allen campaign also felt that crime was a winning issue for its candidate. In August, a senior Allen staff member said that they had used polls to test the crime issue after the GOP convention and found "that it works well for us, particularly in the suburbs." When asked later to describe how the issue was tested, the same worker said that polling indicated broad support for both a five-day waiting period and abolishing parole. However, a consultant for the Allen campaign realized that voters were being presented with a choice between the two. Thus, Allen's pollster asked potential voters to choose one policy over the other, and the results favored abolishing parole by about four to one.

The early and sustained focus on crime also made it easier for Allen to focus attention on what his campaign presented as the increasing crime rate while Terry was attorney general. A repeated theme of the Allen campaign centered on the question, "If Terry has such good ideas on crime, why didn't she do something about it while she was Attorney General?" Another line used by the Allen campaign to defuse the five-day-waiting-period issue and raise questions about Terry's years as attorney general was, "Virginia has had a seven-year waiting period [on crime]." By focusing early on the five-day waiting period specifically and on the crime issue more generally, Terry made it easier for Allen to make the abolition of parole and Terry's record as part of past Democratic administrations more salient to voters. Both candidates believed that their positions on crime put them on the winning side, so they both strived to make crime a salient issue.[6]

Terry began her "play it safe and spend" strategy on June 7 with two television advertisements. They were positive policy-related spots that provided viewers with a toll-free number to call to receive Terry's pamphlet, "Agenda for Action." The advertisements did not talk about her record as attorney general or mention the accomplishments of former Democratic governors: the ads were about as politically safe as they could be. After seeing the Terry ads, Michael Cornfield, a political scientist, said, "I don't think there's anything in either one of them that either David Duke or Jesse Jackson would disagree with" (Allen 1993b, B5). By running advertisements early, Terry forced Allen to spend money he did not have to keep up with her. By running safe advertisements, she was hoping to avoid conflict and any association with unpopular Democrats.

Although the Allen campaign said publicly that it had enough money to wage a campaign, privately there were real concerns. Terry had tapped a number of moderate business leaders who felt early on that she was the likely victor, and Terry staffers worked hard to keep the fund-raising issue in the press throughout the summer. Even a senior member of the Allen campaign admitted that Terry's staff had done a good job of getting the money issue in the press.

Both sides knew that a candidate's ability to raise money is seen as an indication of that candidate's legitimacy (Salmore and Salmore 1989). Candidates who cannot raise money are viewed as unlikely to win elections, which compounds the inability to raise funds.

Allen began running television advertisements on June 22 because his campaign felt compelled to keep pace with Terry. The ads contained mostly biographical information, including numerous shots of his family. The commercials were designed to build name recognition and define Allen as a conservative but not a dangerous right-wing extremist. Both campaigns pulled their television advertisements by early July. Financial disclosure reports filed July 15 revealed that the Allen campaign had taken out a loan for one hundred thousand dollars and that the Terry campaign had a ten-to-one advantage in cash on hand. In a July 17 *Richmond Times-Dispatch* interview, Sabato stated what Allen staff members were saying privately: that Allen needed a "legitimate [i.e., independent] poll that shows him closing the gap on Ms. Terry" to help him raise funds (Whitley 1993a, B7).

One week later, Terry called for the candidates to file additional financial disclosure reports. State law did not require another report until October 15, but Terry said she planned to file additional reports on September 1 and October 1 "for the public interest," and she called on Allen to do the same. She clearly intended to continue drawing attention to Allen's financial troubles. As would be expected, the Allen campaign did not capitulate.

Terry resumed statewide television advertising at the end of July. The Allen campaign, pressed into spending limited resources, again felt obligated to keep pace and went back on the air a week later. A senior Allen staff member later confessed that the Terry strategy nearly worked. Even in early August, the Allen camp was concerned about whether it could raise enough money to mount a full campaign in October.

The financial situation of the two campaigns was a major issue in the press throughout the month of August, picking up on the theme of campaign contributions as an indicator of legitimacy. A headline in the August 7 *Richmond Times-Dispatch* said, "Allen Seen as Having Difficulty in Raising Money" (Whitley 1993b, B5). In the article that followed, a prominent GOP contributor, John Hazel, said that most of the Virginia business community felt comfortable with Terry and that Allen did not have an issue he could use to pry away their financial support. One week later, Terry held a press conference to distribute a list of one hundred business leaders supporting her candidacy. On August

18, Allen halted his television advertising. The stated reason was that voters were not that interested in the race in August, but the press treated it as another indication of the campaign's financial troubles. According to all the Allen staff members I talked with, the media was right.

At the same time, however, indications that Terry had paid a price by adopting a "play it safe and spend" strategy began to appear. On August 20, the *Times-Dispatch* reported that some Terry supporters believed that her campaign was faltering and that Allen might be developing some momentum (Schapiro 1993d, B6). Criticisms of Terry's limited public appearances and focus on fund-raising appeared, and the paper reported that Terry's repudiation of President Clinton "apparently is alienating some Democrats in Northern Virginia."[7]

On the following day, the results of a poll funded by GOP favorite and later U.S. Senate candidate Oliver North claimed that the governor's race was even (Whitley 1993g, B6). GOP officials played up these results, but Allen insiders said that because the poll was not conducted by an independent firm, its results did not provide the credibility needed to improve their fund-raising efforts.

Several events occurred in the final week in August that proved critical for the remainder of the campaign. On August 23, when introducing Allen before a speech, a supporter suggested that Allen, because he was married and had a family, would be more in touch with the concerns of families as governor than would Terry, who was single. The Allen campaign had gone to great lengths to avoid the perception of right-wing intolerance, but now a supporter had raised that specter.

On the same day, Terry released a new television advertisement that claimed that she was the only candidate for governor who "supports the death penalty and a five-day waiting period for the purchase of handguns." In fact, Allen did support the death penalty, but since he did not support the waiting period, the advertisement was technically correct. The ad was intended to show Terry's toughness on crime, but because of its obviously misleading nature, it opened Terry to the criticism of negative and misleading campaign tactics. These two events provided potential openings for each candidate to exploit. The Democrats misplayed their chance, while the Republicans capitalized.

Terry said little about the comments regarding her and Allen's marital status, but several surrogates spoke harshly on the subject. Unfortunately for Terry, one of her surrogates went on to suggest that Terry, because she was single, would have more time and energy to devote to the job of governor. Thus, one inappropriate remark about the marital status of the two candidates was countered with an equally inappropriate one. Both the Allen and Terry surrogates looked bad, the press criticized both comments, and Terry and her surrogates were left unable to use this incident as evidence of GOP intolerance.

In contrast, the Allen campaign attacked the Terry ad on the death penalty and support for a five-day waiting period as intentionally misleading. The incident helped Allen characterize Terry as a politician willing to bend the facts to get elected, thereby helping Allen draw a contrast between Terry as an old-style politician and himself as a populist agent for change.

On August 27, the third major event of the week was reported. Governor Wilder (who is African-American) said that Terry was not doing enough public campaigning and that she was relying too heavily on paid advertising. In the same *Richmond Times-Dispatch* story, another African-American community leader said that Terry appeared to be taking the African-American vote for granted (Schapiro 1993f, B6). Terry had hoped to maintain strong African-American support, but she had also hoped to remain at a distance from Wilder. These press reports put Terry in the position of either responding to Wilder's suggestions and even seeking his help to restore her support among African-Americans or rejecting his advice and risking further erosion of support.

Along similar lines, an August 28 story in the *Times-Dispatch* reiterated that while the Virginia AFL-CIO had endorsed the Democratic nominees for lieutenant governor and attorney general, it had withheld its endorsement from Terry (Whitley 1993p, B5). The original announcement, made on June 28, was viewed at the time as a positive sign of Terry's support among business leaders, won through her support of such policies as Virginia's right-to-work laws. However, by late August, it was reported instead as another sign of the erosion of support for Terry among the traditional Democratic base.

The fourth event of this week occurred on August 30, when Allen received the endorsement of the Fraternal Order of Police (FOP), which both candidates had actively sought. Allen staff members indicated that this endorsement lent credibility to Allen's plan to abolish parole. The Allen campaign also reminded voters that the FOP had endorsed Terry for attorney general in 1985 and 1989. While some commentators downplayed the endorsement, Allen advisers felt it was very important (Whitley 1993h, B1).

The next day saw the fifth and clearly most important development of the week: an independent poll, reported in the press on September 1, found that Terry's lead over Allen had slipped to just 6 percentage points (46 percent to 40 percent). This development provided legitimacy to Allen's candidacy, which, according to advisers, produced a new wave of financial contributions. The poll also appeared to confirm Wilder's and others' criticisms of Terry's campaign. The news coverage quickly switched from why Allen could not raise money to what Terry had done to blow her big lead.

Finally, Terry had run a safe campaign during the summer, limiting her public appearances and avoiding any attacks on her opponent. By doing so, Terry allowed Allen to define himself to the electorate, which turned out to be a mistake. Now, any change in Terry's strategy, especially more activity or direct attacks on Allen, could appear as a panicked response to the new closeness of the race and/or the recent criticisms voiced by Wilder and others. In fact, the

Allen campaign characterized everything Terry did during the remainder of the campaign in precisely these terms. The Terry campaign had planned all along to increase its activities, starting with a Labor Day tour focusing on education. However, the fact that this increased activity came on the heels of this independent poll tarnished the image the Terry camp had hoped to create.

Terry responded to the race's changing environment by attacking Allen as untrustworthy. She argued that Allen's policy proposals, while promising not to raise general taxes, did not add up. She attacked the NRA's support of Allen and its television ads asserting that Terry's support for a five-day waiting period was politically motivated. Also, on September 14 a new Terry ad began running that called Allen "reckless on guns." While not the first ad to draw a contrast between the candidates, both the Allen campaign and the press called it the first negative attack ad of the campaign. Thus, Terry was labeled as starting the attacks, and the Allen camp said she was doing so because of her deteriorating standing in the polls.[8]

Additional independent polls released during the first two weeks of September suggested that the race was now a dead heat. Allen launched a full attack on Terry with a new television ad on September 22 saying that as attorney general, Terry presided over "the largest increase in violent crime [in Virginia] in history." In a quote in the *Richmond Times-Dispatch* on September 23, Terry argued that the increase in violent crime in Virginia was only half that of the national average during the same period (Whitley 1993m, B8). However, that point did not become a focus of the Terry campaign, leaving Allen to continue defining Terry's record in negative terms.

The remainder of the campaign saw Allen pound away on abolishing parole and growing crime rates under Terry's tenure in office. Allen also began to raise questions about Terry's ethics while serving as attorney general. He suggested that she took campaign contributions from people who received favorable rulings from her office (Whitley 1993i, B5), repeated attacks that she failed to intervene in a coal strike in 1989 because of union pressure (Whitley 1993e, 1), and continued to refer to himself as an agent of change away from the failed policies of the Robb-Wilder-Terry legacy. In October, Allen ran an ad saying that Terry gave out $1.5 million in no-bid contracts to political friends while serving as attorney general.

Terry's first line of attack focused on Allen's integrity. She accused Allen of flip-flopping on issues (Allen 1993a, B1), suggested that Allen was tied closely to the NRA (Whitley 1993k, B5), declared that he was making false campaign promises for which he could not pay (Hardy 1993, B1), and accused the Allen campaign of stealing a tape of a Terry television commercial (Whitley 1993i, B5).

Later, Terry began labeling Allen as an agent of the extreme right-wing element of the Republican Party. The Democratic Party chairman attacked the

GOP ticket as "extreme" (Wilkerson 1993, B5), and Terry began claiming that Allen, if governor, would take Virginia, "back and to the right" (Whitley 1993c, 1). In an October 14 *Richmond Times-Dispatch* interview, she said, "When businesses come to the state, they want an environment where the freedoms and liberties of their employees will be respected" (Whitley 1993j, 1). In the same article, Mark Warner, Virginia Democratic Party chairman, said, "The ticket we are opposing is the most extremist, most far right-wing that this state has seen in 30 years. I'm afraid of what this ticket offers." Finally, Terry began running a television ad on October 14 saying that Allen was against "protecting choice for women." The commercial included a picture of Pat Robertson in an attempt to associate Allen with him.

Amidst this flurry of activity, the *Richmond Times-Dispatch* reported that Allen's lead had ballooned to 17 percentage points (Schapiro 1993a, 1). The same poll reported that Allen was viewed as more trustworthy than Terry and that he was also seen as more of an agent of change. A poll released two days later had Allen's lead at what was probably a more realistic 7 percentage points (Schapiro 1993c, B1).[9]

The campaign concluded with Allen spending much of his time helping state legislative candidates while Terry scrambled just to secure her political base. Commentators who had all but anointed Terry in June were now suggesting that she never had a chance. Sabato suggested that the demand for change overwhelmed the Terry campaign and that maybe Terry had hit a "glass ceiling" in Virginia politics that prevented a woman from reaching the governor's office (Schapiro 1993e, 1).

Ironically, the Allen campaign ended up with more money at the end of the campaign than it knew what to do with. A senior staff member said, "This is the first campaign that I have worked on where [staff] got paid during the final month. We were buying all the signs, TV time and anything else we could find to spend the money on."

Allen ended up with a dominating win, 58 percent to 41 percent. He won eighty-nine of ninety-five counties and thirty-one of forty-one cities, including all of the southwestern part of the state, Terry's home area. Allen made significant gains among African-Americans and dominated among the 40 percent of white voters who identified themselves as evangelical, born-again Christians (Billingsley 1993, 1). Figure 5.1 presents the levels of support enjoyed by each candidate over the course of the campaign. A member of the Allen campaign produced this illustration for me, and it is based on the campaign's internal polls.

The number of explanations for the outcome of the election reported in the media equaled the number of people who were interviewed. Terry suggested that the unpopularity of Democrats Robb and Wilder hurt her chances. "I run far better as 'Mary Sue Terry' than 'Robb-Wilder-Terry,'" adding that she was

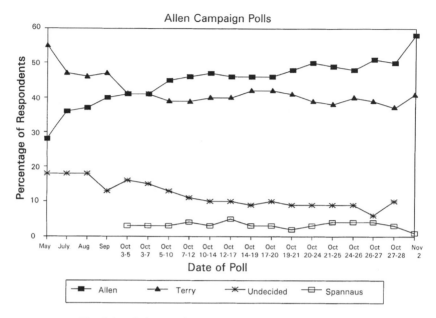

Fig. 5.1.   Gubernatorial candidate support, Virginia, 1993

swamped by a "tidal wave for change. To analyze it drop by drop is of no use" (Schapiro 1993b, 10). Wilder blamed Terry for the loss, saying that she failed to make personal contact with voters and that she should have defended his and other Democratic governors' records. He also suggested that she took the support of African-Americans for granted. Others credited Allen with "trumping" Terry on the five-day waiting period by proposing to abolish parole.

Terry's campaign advisers were also blamed for the loss. Reports of mismanagement and disagreement in the focus of the campaign were widely reported after the election. One story was offered as typical of the mistakes that were made (Whitley 1993f, 1). On the Sunday before the election, Terry campaigned in southwest Virginia instead of the vote-rich Northern Virginia suburbs of Washington, D.C. When asked about this decision, an aide said that because the Washington Redskins football team gets so much attention in the D.C. area on game days, the campaign decided that it would have a better chance of generating media interest if they waited until Monday to campaign in that area. The problem: the Redskins played on Monday that week.

A senior member of the Allen staff described the campaign in terms more expressly consistent with the theoretical argument guiding this book, saying, "The candidate [who] controls the terms of the debate will most often win the election. The single most important factor [in a campaign] is controlling the agenda, and we were able to do that." He said that Allen decided in June to focus on abolishing parole, to call for change, and to attack Terry's record as attorney general. "We stuck to our message and let many of the attacks [on Allen] go by so we wouldn't get off track. We did not want to get into a debate about abortion or drunk driving. . . . That's why we responded to [Terry's] attacks by saying that they were just attempts to distract voters away from the real issues and from her record."

According to a staffer, Allen's polling data revealed that his campaign succeeded in altering the importance, or salience, of some issues to voters during the campaign. In other words, Allen's supporters believed they created heresthetic change as described in this book and by Riker (1990). "Our polling showed that when asked what were the most important issues facing Virginians, government spending was always number one. However, crime was second, and it climbed in importance over the course of the campaign."

The same staff member suggested that Terry should have attacked Allen early as an extremist and part of a ticket that could not win. As I noted earlier, the press, political commentators, and many Democratic leaders did so during and immediately after the Republican convention. However, that effort was not sustained, surfacing again in a substantial way only during the last month of the campaign.

"One of the things we wanted to do early in the campaign was to make George cool and hip in Chesterfield and Fairfax Counties. We wanted to get yard signs up in middle- and upper-class neighborhoods, especially yuppie subdivisions, to make it acceptable to vote for him. We needed to make sure that George was not seen as a Pat Robertson clone in the Northern Virginia suburbs, or we would lose them." By failing to maintain an attack on Allen as a right-wing extremist, Terry and the Democrats allowed Allen to accomplish this goal.

Terry also erred, according to an Allen aide, in assuming that voters accepted her as a moderate. This staffer argued that Terry's initial popularity was based on name recognition and that most voters did not have a clear view of her ideology. Terry "ended up defining herself more as a liberal by talking about gun control, education, and bashing the Christian Right. With these issues, she unconsciously moved herself to the left."

Thus, it appears that this campaign turned on how voters defined the candidates based in part on the campaigns they ran and the issues they helped to make most salient. The next step is to examine more closely the movement in public support that took place during the campaign. Before doing so, I will briefly summarize the nature of the electoral coalition Terry had mobilized four years earlier in her successful bid to become attorney general.

Analysis of an exit poll conducted during the 1989 election reveals that Terry's base of support extended well beyond that of Wilder, the successful Democratic gubernatorial candidate.[10] She received significantly more support from Republicans, conservatives, those claiming to have voted for George Bush for president in the previous year, those with higher educations, and whites. Terry also did somewhat better among those who were prolife on abortion and those who felt crime was an important issue. At the same time, Terry held onto support among Democrats, liberals, and African-Americans at the same rate as did Wilder. Thus, entering the 1993 gubernatorial race, Terry had reason to believe that she had a broad base of support that encompassed the traditional base of her party but that also extended into traditionally Republican groups.

Table 5.1 presents an empirical look at voter behavior during Virginia's 1993 gubernatorial campaign. The table presents a base model predicting support for Allen and Terry as a function of sociodemographic characteristics and partisanship tested on five different polls conducted by two separate independent organizations.[11] The dependent variable for each model is the response to the question, "If the election were held today, who would you vote for?" In each poll, voters indicated whether they intended to vote for Allen, Terry, or someone else or were undecided. Those saying they would vote for someone else, a relatively small proportion of voters, were dropped from the analysis to simplify the presentation of findings. However, a more substantial portion of the respondents indicated that they were undecided. Because they constitute an important group of potential voters, they are not dropped from the analysis. Thus, the dependent variable is coded with three categories that do not necessarily follow a clear order. As a result, I estimate each model using multinomial logit.

The independent variables in each model are a series of dummy variables indicating whether the respondent is a Democrat, a Republican, female, and black. The three *Richmond Times-Dispatch* polls also contain dummy variables for whether the respondent lives in a city or in a rural area, with suburbs the excluded category. Each model also includes categorical measures of the respondent's age, level of formal education, and family income.

Table 5.1 presents logit coefficients comparing respondents supporting Terry versus those supporting Allen and logit coefficients comparing respondents supporting Terry versus those who were undecided. Comparing coefficients from similar models across different data sets should be done with caution, but doing so allows the emergence of a picture of the flow of support from Terry to Allen over the final two months of the campaign. Although inferences regarding the movement of groups of respondents over time will be made, the polls in table 5.1 do not represent a longitudinal analysis of a single set of respondents but rather five different cross sections. The last poll in the series was completed several days before the election. Ideally, an exit poll would be included, but one was not available. However, the final poll does approximate the outcome of the election.

As a check on the ability of these five polls to reflect changes in public opinion during the campaign, the predicted probability of a respondent supporting Allen, supporting Terry, or being undecided is calculated based on the

TABLE 5.1. Multinomial Logit Models of Factors Predicting Voter Intentions
for the 1993 Virginia Gubernatorial Election

Independent Variable	Comparison	Poll 1	Poll 2	Poll 3	Poll 4	Poll 5
Constant	T v A	0.897	−0.248	−3.183*	−2.204*	−1.481*
	T v U	0.898	1.295*	−1.442	−1.630*	−0.409
Female	T v A	0.465*	0.595*	0.879*	0.571*	0.536*
	T v U	0.132	−0.011	−0.252	−0.004	0.042
Democrat	T v A	2.227*	2.237*	1.938*	1.970*	2.005*
	T v U	1.219*	1.141*	1.081*	1.754*	1.469*
Republican	T v A	−1.681*	−1.774*	−1.697*	−2.052*	−1.714*
	T v U	−0.199	−0.345	−0.542	−0.817	−0.929*
City resident	T v A	0.126		0.469		−0.172
	T v U	−0.341		−0.137		−0.079
Rural resident	T v A	0.044		−0.221		−0.401
	T v U	0.262		0.067		−0.063
Age	T v A	−0.242*	−0.101	0.232*	0.031	0.035
	T v U	−0.150*	−0.302*	0.193*	−0.051	0.054
Level of education	T v A	0.097	0.172	0.607*	0.315*	0.258*
	T v U	0.199	0.014	0.412*	0.271*	0.120
Family income	T v A	−0.291*	−0.098	−0.053	0.034	0.027
	T v U	−0.359*	−0.117	0.289	0.299*	0.392*
Black	T v A	1.104*	1.136*	1.589*	1.619*	1.356*
	T v U	0.713*	0.322	0.203	0.020	−0.319
Chi-square		264.8*	164.0*	225.2*	308.1*	241.8*
Percentage correctly predicted		63.1%	60.1%	68.9%	63.6%	69.3%
Sample size		643	427	498	686	638

Note: T = Supports Terry for Governor
  U = Undecided
  A = Supports Allen for Governor
Poll 1: *Richmond Times-Dispatch,* September 3–8
Poll 2: Virginia Commonwealth University, September 9–15
Poll 3: *Richmond Times-Dispatch,* October 11–14
Poll 4: Virginia Commonwealth University, October 18–24
Poll 5: *Richmond Times-Dispatch,* October 25–28
*Significant at $p < .05$

estimates reported in table 5.1. Those predicted probabilities are presented in figure 5.2 and are based on holding each variable in each model constant at its mean. Comparing figure 5.2 to figure 5.1 shows that these polls appear to capture the same dynamic measured by the Allen campaign's polling.[12]

All five polls report that women had a significantly higher probability than

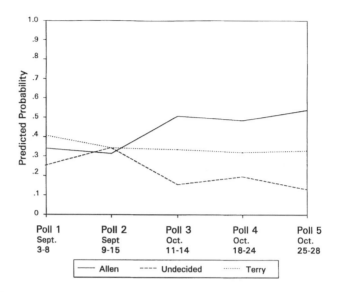

Fig. 5.2.   Mean predicted level of support for Allen or Terry for governor

did men of supporting Terry over Allen. Gender was never a statistically significant predictor of the difference between Terry supporters and those who were undecided. However, a statistically significant advantage among women relative to men does not mean an absolute advantage. Simple cross-tabulations not shown here demonstrate that Terry's overall level of support among both men and women declined during this two-month period so that even among women, Allen eventually gained an advantage. Comparing the coefficients for gender in poll 1 and poll 5 in table 5.1 suggests that the drop-off rate in support for Terry was roughly equal for both men and women. However, the noticeably larger coefficients on the gender variable in the intervening polls, particularly poll 3, suggest that Terry first lost support among men. In other words, the larger gap between women and men in poll 3 results from Terry losing support among men faster than among women rather than from Terry expanding her support dramatically among women.

Figure 5.3 demonstrates this finding more clearly. It presents the predicted probability of men and women supporting either candidate while holding all other variables in table 5.1 constant at their means.[13] Figure 5.3 shows that Terry's advantage among women did not diminish completely until the second week in October. However, while nearly equal to Allen in the support garnered among men in early September, a gap of nearly 40 percentage points between the probability that a male voter would support Terry or Allen had opened by the time poll 3 was taken. Figure 5.3 shows female voters gradually shifting to-

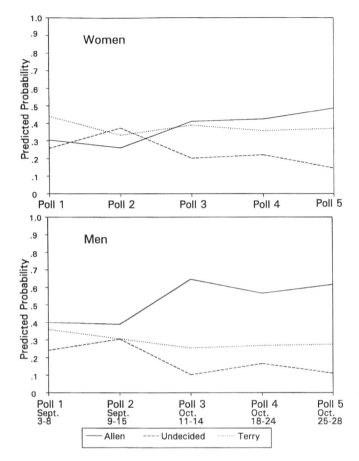

Fig. 5.3. Predicted level of support for Allen or Terry for governor, by gender

ward Allen over the course of the campaign, whereas male voters moved sharply toward Allen between mid-September and mid-October.

Table 5.1 reports that Democrats demonstrated a clear and sustained preference for Terry over Allen. The coefficients comparing Terry voters to undecided voters based on partisanship also indicate that Democrats were more likely to indicate support for Terry than to be undecided. Similarly, Republicans consistently indicated support for Allen over Terry. However, the comparison of Terry supporters against those who were undecided suggests that in early September, Republicans who did not support Allen were equally likely to be either undecided or supporting Terry, controlling for other factors.

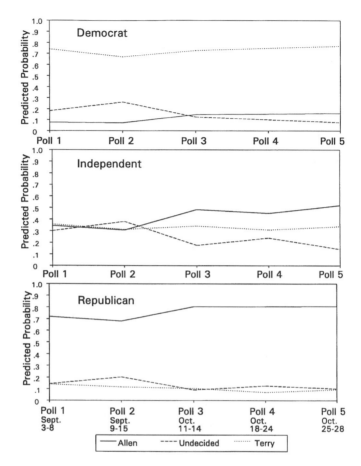

Fig. 5.4.   Predicted level of support for Allen or Terry for governor, by party identification

The coefficients in table 5.1 do not clearly reveal the behavior of independents, but figure 5.4 plots the predicted probability of Democrats, Republicans, and independents supporting each candidate, holding all other factors in table 5.1 constant at their means. Figure 5.4 shows that Terry's support among her own partisans remained strong. However, the slight movement among Democrats from the undecided to the Allen categories suggests that Allen ultimately won over many Democrats initially unwilling to support Terry.

Among Republicans, Allen's support also remained steady. In contrast, however, it appears that Terry did less well at capturing the support of Republicans who had not decided earlier to support Allen. Both candidates clearly held onto their partisans at reasonably high rates. Yet it appears that Allen may have made more headway cutting into Terry's base than Terry did in cutting into Allen's.

Figure 5.4 shows that in early September, independents were about equally likely to support Allen or Terry or to be undecided. In mid-September a plurality of independents remained undecided, but by the second week in October, they had clearly broken for Allen.

Whether respondents lived in cities, suburbs, or rural areas was asked only in the three *Richmond Times-Dispatch* polls. Only one of the coefficients in table 5.1 operating on the place-of-residence variables is statistically significant. In poll 3, city-dwellers were somewhat more likely than residents of suburbs to indicate support for Terry over Allen. Thus, any regional patterns in support for Terry and Allen that exist are captured by the other independent variables included in the models.

The impact of age on support for the gubernatorial candidates evolved rather dramatically over this two-month period. Younger voters were initially more likely to support Terry than to either support Allen or be undecided. By poll 2, however, Terry's advantage over Allen among younger voters had diminished to statistical insignificance. Still, of those not supporting Allen, a higher proportion of younger voters were supporting Terry rather than being undecided. By the second week in October, the pattern had reversed, and Allen enjoyed a significant advantage over Terry among relatively young voters. The final two polls conducted in October show that the ages of Terry and Allen supporters were not statistically distinguishable. In those polls, the marginals indicate that the slight advantage among older voters that Allen had established by early September had grown to a point more similar to his newly acquired advantage among younger voters. These findings suggest that relative to older voters, younger voters moved first and more dramatically toward Allen.

These conclusions are illustrated in figure 5.5. Allen held an advantage among older voters of about 15 percentage points in the predicted probability of support in early September, but Terry offset that edge with a nearly 30 point advantage among younger voters. By the middle of September, older voters had become more likely to be undecided than to support either Allen or Terry. In contrast, Allen began to close the gap among younger voters. By the second week in October, Terry achieved a slight advantage among older voters. However, Allen regained and held his initial advantage among older voters by the third week in October. Conversely, younger voters shifted dramatically away from Terry and toward Allen between polls 2 and 3. Terry closed the gap slightly by the end of the race, but Allen ultimately enjoyed an advantage among younger voters equal to the size of the advantage Terry had held among this group just two months earlier.

Table 5.1 suggests that in early September, Terry and Allen enjoyed

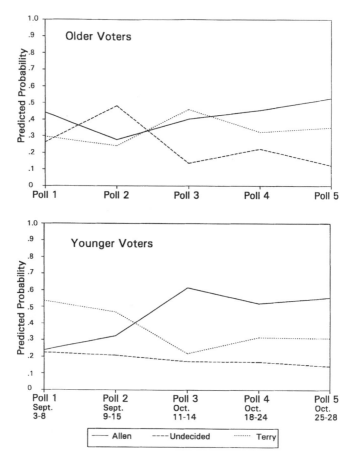

Fig. 5.5.   Predicted level of support for Allen or Terry for governor, by age

roughly equal support across levels of education among respondents. This situation continued until early October, when respondents with higher levels of formal education were likely to support Terry over Allen, holding other factors in the model constant. Among those not supporting Allen, respondents with more formal education were more likely to support Terry than to be undecided. As figure 5.6 illustrates, both patterns are produced by an increase in support for Terry among the well-educated combined with a sharp drop-off in Terry's support among those with less education.

Education level remains a significant predictor of candidate support in polls 4 and 5, although its magnitude declines. Figure 5.6 shows that this de-

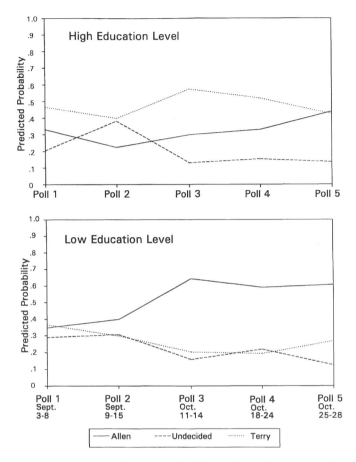

Fig. 5.6.   Predicted level of support for Allen or Terry for governor, by education level

cline appears to result from Allen extending his support late in the race to more respondents with higher levels of education. Again, holding other factors in the model constant, table 5.1 and figure 5.6 suggest that Allen first attracted the support of voters with less education then later attracted voters with higher levels of education. Terry made a slight advance among less-educated voters from poll 4 to poll 5, but that rise was countered by Allen's increased support among the more highly educated.

In table 5.1, poll 1 reports that Terry enjoyed a significant advantage over Allen among respondents with lower levels of family income. The relationship

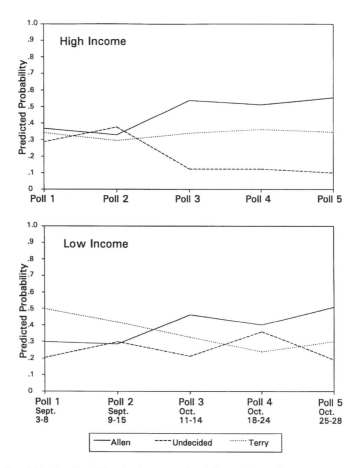

Fig. 5.7.   Predicted level of support for Allen or Terry for governor, by income

between family income and support for Terry over Allen diminished to statistical insignificance by the middle of September, but in the middle and end of October (polls 4 and 5), undecided voters were characterized by significantly lower levels of family income.

Figure 5.7 shows that the significant relationship between income and candidate support at the beginning of this two-month period resulted from Terry's advantage among low-income voters. Indeed, among high-income voters, Terry and Allen had virtually equal levels of predicted support. Income became a statistically insignificant predictor of candidate support over the remaining polls because Allen developed an advantage over Terry among both high- and low-income voters by early October. In polls 1 and 2, high-income voters had a higher predicted probability of being undecided than did low-income voters. However, figure 5.7 implies that when high-income voters made up their minds in October, Allen appears to have benefited. Terry's support among low-income voters declined steadily until late in the race, while Allen's grew almost as steadily.

The change in the relationship between income and being undecided suggests that in early September, upper-income voters who would traditionally be expected to support a Republican candidate were still unsure of Allen and at least in part attracted to Terry's support among business leaders. Thus, upper-income voters had not yet received a clear signal regarding which candidate to support. By the end of the race, lower-income voters became less enchanted with Terry's candidacy, possibly because she distanced herself from working-class concerns while Allen's approach to crime may have attracted these voters. Thus, by the end of the race, lower-income people were more unsure about which candidate would address their concerns. I think the uncertainty among upper-income voters early in the race reflects uncertainty about Allen, while uncertainty among lower-income voters at the end of the race reflects uncertainty about Terry.

Finally, table 5.1 illustrates that African-American respondents were consistently more likely to support Terry than Allen. However, the magnitude of the coefficient changed noticeably across the five polls, increasing noticeably in polls 3 and 4 (the middle of October). This growth was caused not by Terry's increased support among African-Americans but rather by the rapid movement of whites toward Allen. The coefficient diminishes somewhat in the final poll in part because of late movement by some African-Americans toward Allen.

Figure 5.8 illustrates the reaction of African-American voters and non-African-American voters over the course of this time period. In early September, African-American support for Terry was at its peak—fewer blacks were undecided or supporting Allen combined than were supporting Terry. However, figure 5.8 shows that Terry's support among African-Americans gradually declined, first with a shift toward being undecided but ultimately with more blacks supporting Allen by the end of October than had been predicted at the beginning of September.

While Allen and Terry enjoyed roughly equal support among nonblacks in September, by mid-October Allen had opened a substantial advantage by capturing many previously undecided white voters. Thus, at the same time that Allen was clearly gaining the support of whites, Terry's support among blacks, if not shifting completely to Allen, was clearly weakening as higher proportions of blacks than whites found themselves undecided. These findings suggest that Wilder's criticisms of Terry's campaign may have been correct.

To summarize, table 5.1 and figures 5.2 through 5.8 illustrate the shift in

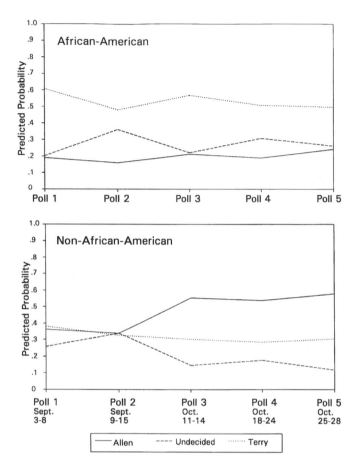

Fig. 5.8.   Predicted level of support for Allen or Terry for governor, by race

Terry's and Allen's support during the final two months of the campaign based on sociodemographic characteristics and party identification. Allen made his largest initial gains among voters who were young, white, politically independent, and male. These are all categories of voters in which Terry entered September either leading or on equal footing with Allen.

At the same time, Terry's support among her base (women, African-Americans, and those with lower incomes) was weakening. In fact, by the end of the race, Terry had lost roughly the same proportion of support among women as among men and nearly the same proportion of support among blacks as among whites—the decline simply happened sooner with whites and with men.

Finally, the movement of undecided respondents regarding several of the independent variables—family income and race in particular—suggests that respondents normally predisposed to vote Republican had some uncertainty about Allen in early September, but voters traditionally inclined to support a Democrat had higher levels of uncertainty about Terry late in the race. Though not captured with this poll data, the weakening of African-American support for Terry suggests that turnout among African-Americans might be expected to be low, which was the case in many areas.

The next step is to examine change in whom voters supported in relation to their attitudes rather than just to sociodemographic characteristics. Several questions measuring voters' evaluations of other political figures, views on crime and abortion, and perceptions of which candidate more represented

TABLE 5.2.   Multinomial Logit Models of Factors Predicting Voter Intentions for the 1993 Virginia Gubernatorial Election, Controlling for Sociodemographic and Partisan Variables

Variable	Comparison	Poll 1	Poll 2	Poll 3	Poll 4
Support five-day	T v A	1.359*	1.266*		1.592*
wait	T v U	1.072*	−0.067		0.527
Yes abolish	T v A		−0.539*		−0.840*
parole	T v U		0.170		−0.334
Yes parental	T v A		−0.490		−1.033*
consent	T v U		0.225		−0.477
Approve of	T v A	0.099	0.502	0.380*	0.738*
Wilder	T v U	−0.400	0.113	0.156	−0.098
Approve of	T v A	1.262*	0.789*	0.647*	0.908*
Clinton	T v U	0.456	0.540*	0.097	1.064*
Approve of	T v A			−0.367*	
Robertson	T v U			−0.160	
Chi-square		284.1*	206.4*	263.1*	413.9*
Percentage correctly predicted		65.3%	62.3%	69.9%	70.3%
Sample size		570	427	498	686

Note: T = Supports Terry for Governor
     U = Undecided
     A = Supports Allen for Governor
Poll 1: *Richmond Times-Dispatch,* September 3–8
Poll 2: Virginia Commonwealth University, September 9–15
Poll 3: *Richmond Times-Dispatch,* October 11–14
Poll 4: Virginia Commonwealth University, October 18–24
*Significant at $p < .05$

change provide an opportunity to examine how Virginians responded to the content of the Terry and Allen campaigns.[14]

Table 5.2 presents the analysis of more extended models using all but the last poll analyzed in table 5.1.[15] The findings presented in table 5.2 control for the influence of the sociodemographic and partisan variables included in table 5.1. Including the additional variables in table 5.2 did not change the basic relationships between these sociodemographic and partisan variables and respondent support for Terry or Allen.

The dependent variable remains unchanged. The additional independent variables to be considered include three dummy variables measuring whether the respondent favors a five-day waiting period for the purchase of a handgun, whether the respondent favors abolishing parole for persons sentenced to prison, and whether the respondent favors a law that would require minors to have permission from a parent or guardian before obtaining an abortion. Also included are measures of attitudes toward Wilder, Clinton, and, in one poll, Robertson.[16]

Table 5.2 shows that in the three polls in which the question was asked, those favoring a five-day waiting period for the purchase of a handgun were more likely to support Terry than Allen. This relationship appears to have held at a reasonably steady rate, increasing slightly in magnitude by the third week in October. In poll 1, those favoring a five-day waiting period were significantly more likely to support Terry than to be undecided. However, by polls 2 and 4, respondents not supporting Allen who favored a five-day waiting period were as likely to be undecided as to support Terry compared with those who did not favor the five-day waiting period. Despite her focus on this issue, Terry apparently did not convince large numbers of undecided voters favoring a five-day waiting period to support her campaign.

Examining the predicted probability of supporting Allen or Terry based on support or opposition to the five-day waiting period shows that Terry lost support to Allen at somewhat similar rates among both supporters and opponents of a five-day waiting period, although opponents moved toward Allen in somewhat larger numbers. In poll 1, five-day waiting period supporters had a predicted probability of supporting Terry of .44, but by poll 4, that number dropped to .37. At the same time, supporters of a five-day waiting period had a predicted probability of supporting Allen in poll 1 of .32, which increased to .41 by poll 4. Thus, Allen actually gained support among those who agreed with Terry on one of the central issues of her campaign. This gain was much less than the average increase of 17 percentage points but is surprising nonetheless. Allen's predicted support among opponents of the five-day waiting period increased from .52 to .73. This tremendous gain in support among opponents of the waiting period produced the continued and somewhat growing relationship between support for the waiting period and support for Terry over Allen reported in table

5.2. This phenomenon might be taken as evidence that Terry's focus on the five-day waiting period failed. However, the heresthetic argument does not guarantee that making an issue more salient will necessarily translate into more votes. Terry's efforts clearly helped maintain the salience of the issue, and her decline in support among advocates of a five-day waiting period might have been more dramatic had she not campaigned on the issue. However, it appears that her campaign may have done more to mobilize opponents of the waiting period on Allen's behalf than to mobilize supporters for Terry herself. This response must have discouraged the Terry campaign, as survey respondents demonstrated high levels of support for a five-day waiting period throughout the campaign. Eighty-six percent of the respondents in poll 1 favored such a policy, and even by late October, 76 percent of the respondents in poll 4 supported the idea.

Only the two polls conducted at Virginia Commonwealth University asked respondents about their attitudes regarding abolishing parole and prior parental consent for minors seeking an abortion. By the second week in September, those voters who favored ending parole were likely to support Allen over Terry. Yet poll 2 also found that only 45 percent of respondents favored such a program, while 35 percent opposed it. By the third week in October, the magnitude of the relationship between support for ending parole and supporting Allen over Terry increased noticeably, and the proportion of voters favoring such a policy grew to 69 percent, with only 16 percent opposing it. The Allen campaign appeared to succeed in making abolishing parole more salient to voters and may have increased the base level of support for such a program. The first finding is predicted by the theory of heresthetic change. The second goes beyond that theory, suggesting that a significant proportion of voters were in fact persuaded or converted on this issue. I argued in chapter 2 that such changes were less likely than simply altering the salience of an issue for voters. Yet conversion, when it occurs, is probably more likely on relatively new issues. To the degree that it even existed, prior opinions on abolishing parole were likely not held as strongly and thus not as difficult to move as, for example, prior views on gun control or abortion.

In mid-September, supporters of a law requiring parental consent for a minor to receive an abortion outnumbered opponents by nearly two to one. However, respondents' views on this issue did not predict whom they supported for governor. This failure cannot be because the candidates did not differ on this issue. Terry had clearly stated her opposition to any changes in Virginia's abortion laws, and Allen indicated his support for a parental-consent law early in his candidacy.[17] The finding of no significant relationship in early September instead reflects the fact that the candidates had not made their positions on abortion an important part of their campaign effort to that point.

That situation changed by late October. Terry had begun attacking Allen's association with Robertson and the conservative wing of the state's Republican

Party while repeatedly mentioning the abortion issue. Allen tried to avoid getting into a debate over abortion, but he did say that his support of parental consent and Terry's opposition to it made her the extremist on abortion. In table 5.2, poll 4 shows that voters reacted. By late October, those favoring parental consent before a minor could receive an abortion were significantly less likely to support Terry. The overall level of support for parental consent did not change from September to October, but table 5.2 makes clear that the issue's salience did change.

An interesting aspect of how voters responded to the campaigns emerges in the degree to which the gubernatorial candidates were viewed as associated with other political figures. Table 5.2 shows that Terry's level of support was significantly lower among those who did not approve of President Clinton, even though Allen did not make an explicit attempt to link Terry with Clinton. This result suggests that Terry was not able to escape the evaluations of a president from her own party (Holbrook-Provow 1987; Simon 1989; Carsey and Wright 1998), even after she repudiated Clinton's policy agenda early in her own campaign.

Instead, Allen linked Terry to unpopular state Democratic political figures Wilder and Robb. Table 5.2 shows that voters had not yet made the link between Wilder and Terry by Labor Day. Poll 1 shows no significant relationship between approval of Wilder and support for Terry. By poll 2, the relationship begins to appear, although it is still statistically insignificant. However, by early October, respondent evaluations of Wilder significantly predicted the probability of supporting Terry or Allen for governor, a relationship that continued into late October. Again, voters appear to have responded to Allen's efforts to make evaluations of Wilder a salient issue in this gubernatorial race.

Finally, poll 3 in table 5.2 shows that by mid-October, those with a favorable view of Robertson were significantly less likely to support Terry for governor. With only one poll asking respondents to evaluate Robertson, any conclusions based on whether the relationship reported in poll 3 emerged in response to the late strategy of the Terry campaign would be tenuous. However, by the end of the campaign, support for both candidates was linked to the images and evaluations of other prominent political figures, which was part of Allen's strategy from the beginning and Terry's plan for the home stretch.

To summarize, table 5.2 provides direct evidence of voters responding to the specific themes stressed by candidates. The salience of each of the three issues presented increased over the final two months of the campaign, as did the role played by evaluations of Wilder. In addition, Allen's efforts to make abolishing parole more salient appear to have extended to conversion on the issue for some voters.

In noting the educational role of campaigns, an Allen staff member said, "We had to teach [voters] about the crime rates of repeat offenders and about how soon many criminals were getting out on parole. We also had to press [Terry] on the five-day waiting period and show that it doesn't work." The two polls conducted at Virginia Commonwealth University asked voters about their positions on a five-day waiting period, abolishing parole, and parental consent for a minor to have an abortion, and they also asked if voters knew whether Terry and/or Allen supported or opposed these policies. Table 5.3 presents the marginal distributions of responses to these questions.

Nearly 50 percent of the respondents in mid-September did not know Allen's stand on any of these issues, and more than 60 percent did not know Terry's position on abolishing parole or parental consent for abortion. In fact, those willing to attribute a position to Allen or Terry on abolishing parole and abortion were split equally as to whether the candidate in question supported or opposed that policy. Only Terry's position on the five-day waiting period was reasonably well known by voters.

By October, the proportion of respondents claiming to know the stands of each candidate on these issues increased by 11 to 42 percentage points.[18] The majority of these increases resulted from respondents who were correct. Thus, table 5.3 shows that voters did in fact learn about the stands both candidates took on these issues. From these data and the information in table 5.2, it seems clear that voters responded to what the candidates said during their campaigns both by learning the positions advocated and by using that information to inform the decision of which candidate to support.

TABLE 5.3. Frequency Distribution of Respondents' Views on the Positions Held by Terry and Allen (by percentages)

	Yes	No	Don't Know
September 9–15			
Does Allen favor a five-day waiting period?	25	26	48
Does Terry favor a five-day waiting period?	58	5	36
Does Allen favor abolishing parole?	19	6	74
Does Terry favor abolishing parole?	13	13	74
Does Allen favor parental consent?	34	5	60
Does Terry favor parental consent?	17	22	60
October 18–24			
Does Allen favor a five-day waiting period?	20	46	33
Does Terry favor a five-day waiting period?	61	7	32
Does Allen favor abolishing parole?	61	6	32
Does Terry favor abolishing parole?	16	33	50
Does Allen favor parental consent?	48	9	42
Does Terry favor parental consent?	16	34	49

Finally, a significant part of the campaign centered on which candidate more represented change and which candidate would do the better job of fighting crime. Terry had an initial advantage in the eyes of many observers on the crime issue. Yet she also used her convention speech to try to sell herself as an agent of change. At the same time, Allen chose crime in general and abolishing parole in particular as the focus of his campaign. Allen's attempts to link Terry with Wilder and Robb were also a part of his effort to depict himself rather than his opponent as an agent of change.

The three *Richmond Times-Dispatch* polls asked respondents which candidate they viewed as better able to fight crime and which candidate they viewed as more representing change. What follows is an analysis of how those evaluations changed over the course of the campaign and which factors predicted whether respondents felt Terry or Allen better fit these two evaluations.[19]

At the beginning of September, Terry was viewed as more representing change by 52.3 percent of those expressing a preference. That percentage slipped to 35.5 percent by the second week in October and bottomed out at 31.7 percent by the end of October. Table 5.4 illustrates which sociodemographic factors predicted evaluations of the candidates in terms of which more represented change. The dependent variable is a dummy variable, coded 1 if the re-

TABLE 5.4.   Logit Models Predicting Whether a Respondent Viewed Terry as More Representing Change

Independent Variable	Poll 1	Poll 3	Poll 5
Constant	0.723	−1.237*	−0.311
Female	0.598*	0.550*	0.693*
Democrat	1.713*	1.419*	1.169*
Republican	−1.015*	−0.538*	−1.113*
City residence	0.016	0.438	0.193
Rural residence	0.121	0.016	0.434
Age	−0.179*	0.062	−0.199*
Education level	−0.040	−0.014	−0.161
Family income	−0.188	−0.147*	−0.094
Black	0.077	1.020*	1.002*
Chi-square	141.30*	98.67*	134.90*
Percentage correctly predicted	73.6%	75.6%	75.6%
Sample size	503	439	558

Note: Poll 1: *Richmond Times-Dispatch,* September 3–8
Poll 3: *Richmond Times-Dispatch,* October 11–14
Poll 5: *Richmond Times-Dispatch,* October 25–28
*Significant at $p < .05$

spondent said Terry more represented change and a 0 if the respondent selected Allen. Each of the independent variables are coded as they were for table 5.1. The dichotomous nature of the dependent variable suggests using a simple logit model.

To summarize table 5.4, we find some clear similarities between it and the analysis presented in table 5.1. The bulk of the shift from Terry to Allen in terms of which candidate more represented change occurred among white men. The coefficients on the Democratic variables also indicate some softening in support for Terry within her base of support. Again, not shown in this table but captured in the constant is the substantial movement that took place among independent voters away from Terry and to Allen.

Table 5.5 presents how sociodemographic variables and party identification influenced respondent evaluations of which candidate would be better at fighting crime. In early September, of those respondents making a choice, Terry was viewed as being better at fighting crime by 57.8 percent of the respondents. In early October, that figure slipped to 45.6 percent, and by the final week in October, only 39.7 percent of those responding felt Terry would be better than Allen at fighting crime. Table 5.5 shows many of the same patterns found in tables 5.1 and 5.4. Terry's support among respondents in terms of general candi-

TABLE 5.5.   Logit Models Predicting Whether a Respondent Viewed Terry as Better Able to Fight Crime

Independent Variable	Poll 1	Poll 3	Poll 5
Constant	0.354	$-1.751*$	-0.462
Female	$0.571*$	$0.575*$	0.329
Democrat	$1.498*$	$1.649*$	$1.488*$
Republican	$-0.987*$	$-1.174*$	$-1.391*$
City residence	0.321	0.189	0.079
Rural residence	0.307	-0.225	-0.366
Age	-0.052	$0.213*$	-0.006
Education level	-0.094	$0.289*$	0.138
Family income	-0.102	$-0.136*$	-0.176
Black	0.166	$1.525*$	0.682
Chi-square	$114.19*$	$150.18*$	$151.42*$
Percentage correctly predicted	72.5%	75.1%	74.7%
Sample size	480	441	557

Note: Poll 1: *Richmond Times-Dispatch,* September 3–8
Poll 3: *Richmond Times-Dispatch,* October 11–14
Poll 5: *Richmond Times-Dispatch,* October 25–28
*Significant at $p < .05$

date preference as well as evaluations of which candidate more represents change and which would be better at fighting crime appears to have declined significantly and first among whites and dramatically among men. Terry's support among Democrats compared to independents along these three dimensions either remained fairly stable or declined, as did her support among those with lower incomes and younger voters. Though men left Terry's camp for Allen earlier than did women, Allen made clear gains among women on the issue of crime—so much so that the gap between men and women regarding which candidate would better fight crime declines to statistical insignificance by the end of October.

Chapters 2 and 3 outline a theory that argues that voters respond to the themes candidates stress during a campaign. This dynamic process unfolds over the course of a campaign as voters learn more about the candidates and candidates learn more about their opponents' strategy. Candidates try to make various issues and/or cleavages more or less salient to voters for that particular election. We saw exactly this process take place in Virginia in 1993.

Terry began the campaign as the clear favorite and ran her campaign that way. She tried to ignore Allen's message, focusing on his inability to raise money during the summer. She hoped to capitalize on her large initial advantage in name recognition and money by keeping the campaign from appearing close. The Terry camp hoped that seven years as attorney general and support of a five-day waiting period for the purchase of handguns would insulate her on the issue of crime. At the same time, she hoped to sell herself as an agent of change. She avoided her record as well as that of Governor Wilder's, and she took early steps to distance herself from President Clinton.

Allen capitalized on Terry's passive summer campaign by gradually defining himself as a conservative but not a right-wing extremist. As one Allen campaign staffer indicated, Allen made himself a candidate that traditional conservatives and moderates could feel safe supporting. He focused on crime, bringing change after twelve years of state Democratic rule, and, in the end, halting what he called the insider politics of the Democratic political machine.

Voters responded to Allen's message, forcing a change in tactics by Terry late in the campaign. She shifted her focus to Allen's connection with Robertson and the candidate's views on abortion. Again, voters responded to these late Terry appeals as the salience of these two factors appeared to grow in October public opinion polls.

The interviews with campaign staff members in Virginia show that their approach to developing campaign strategy corresponds to the heresthetic theory guiding this book. Candidates do not pick issues out of a hat or normally switch their positions on issues for a campaign. In fact, the one switch that did take place—Terry's newfound support for a five-day waiting period—appears to have done nothing to help her campaign. In general, candidates do not try to convert voters on issues that are already meaningful to them. Allen's campaign did generate additional support for abolishing parole, but this phenomenon was more a case of voters learning about and developing views on a relatively new issue rather than a converting on an existing issue. No aggregate conversion was uncovered on the issues of support for a five-day waiting period or parental consent for a minor to have an abortion.

Instead, the candidates worked over the course of the campaign to alter the salience of these issues as well as evaluations of other political figures. As the quotes that open this chapter predicted, the candidate who controlled the agenda and defined the issues of the campaign was more successful. To paraphrase the last of those quotes, the candidate whose views were accepted by more voters won the election.

CHAPTER 6

New Jersey's 1993 Gubernatorial Campaign

"The job of the campaign is to raise the level of emotions of voters by tapping those hot-button issues. A campaign has to hit issues that will stick with voters for sixty days."

New Jersey Democratic Party official

"The decision regarding what strategy to adopt [for a campaign] really depends on the candidates themselves in combination with what matters to the public. I have yet to see a candidate that designed [his or her] policies completely around poll results."

New Jersey state GOP official

"Campaign themes need to come out of reality. They need to be based on the record of the candidate."

Florio campaign staff member

"We need to define [Whitman] more clearly and what she stands for and not let Florio define her."

Whitman campaign staff member

"If [Whitman] is successful, voters will think about the 1990 tax increase and that Florio lied and failed [as governor]. If we are successful, Florio will be viewed as courageous and as a strong leader, and [Whitman] will be viewed as out of touch."

Florio campaign staff member

In 1993, New Jersey witnessed one of the more interesting gubernatorial elections in the United States in recent times. Democratic incumbent Jim Florio won his first term in 1989 by a near record-setting margin after two earlier attempts for the governor's office failed. However, shortly after taking office, he pushed through an unpopular tax increase, leading most observers to conclude that his chances for reelection four years later were already dashed.

His Republican challenger, Christine Todd Whitman, rode the wave of

New Jersey residents' anger toward the Florio tax increase from obscurity to a near upset victory over Democratic incumbent Bill Bradley in the 1990 race for the U.S. Senate. From that point on, Whitman was viewed as the Republican front-runner for the 1993 governor's race. Thus, observers of New Jersey state politics had a pretty good idea three years before the 1993 gubernatorial election of who the candidates would be and that taxes would be at least one of the key issues. However, few would have predicted the path these two candidates would follow during the 1993 campaign, even if many had predicted the ultimate outcome.

New Jersey's statewide elections are generally competitive. Of the two most lopsided gubernatorial elections, one was won by a Republican (Tom Kean in 1985), the other by a Democrat (Florio in 1989). Ironically, the closest gubernatorial race in New Jersey history involved these two record-setters (Kean defeated Florio in 1981 by 1,797 votes). Most successful gubernatorial candidates in New Jersey run near the ideological middle. The state's voters are volatile, with a large segment attached to neither major party. More specifically, both candidates in 1993 thought that the swing voters were white suburban residents. While party organizations remain important, particularly for Democratic get-out-the-vote efforts in urban areas, the campaigns themselves are largely candidate-centered (S. A. Salmore 1986). Campaign staff members in the Whitman and Cary Edwards[1] campaigns before the June primary said they believed GOP voters would focus on the electability of potential GOP challengers to Florio. This observation suggests that even primary voters in New Jersey are viewed as being pragmatic rather than ideological.

Thus, the gubernatorial candidates in 1993 had to demonstrate their ability to do the job. They knew that extreme ideological appeals might push away middle-ground voters, that neither candidate enjoyed an advantage among partisan identifiers, and that even though the stage had been set three years earlier, the volatility of the electorate left the outcome of the 1993 race in doubt. As in Virginia, New Jersey's 1993 gubernatorial election provided the candidates with the opportunity to influence voters through their campaigns.

Florio was well known to New Jersey voters, having served in the state legislature and having represented the state's First District (composed primarily of Camden and Gloucester County residents) in the U.S. House of Representatives. In Congress, Florio developed a strong environmental record. He had run unsuccessfully for governor in 1977 and again in 1981. After finally winning in 1989, Florio's reputation as an environmentalist was quickly overshadowed by his unpopular decision to push a $2.8 billion tax increase through the state legislature early in 1990.

Tax increases rarely endear governors to their citizens (Jewell and Olson 1988), and Florio's approval rating plummeted to only 18 percent in large part because during the 1989 campaign he had said that he did not see the need to raise taxes. The increase spawned a citizens' movement that nearly resulted in Bradley's defeat in 1990 and helped Republicans capture control of both houses of the state legislature in 1991.

Despite the political fallout from the 1990 tax increase, Florio managed to slowly restore some of his support through strong environmental programs and gun-control legislation, so much so that he did not face a primary challenge in 1993. As Aldrich (1980a) points out, candidates who secure their party's nomination early have an advantage over those who must battle opponents in their own party before focusing on the general election. Florio's major weakness clearly centered on the tax increase. He also suffered from a lagging New Jersey economy, with unemployment reaching 9.1 percent in the summer of 1993. In addition, Florio's chief of staff resigned in the face of two federal grand jury investigations into the distribution of state contracts under the Florio administration.

Whitman, the daughter of longtime New Jersey GOP activists, entered the general election campaign in New Jersey much like George Allen did in Virginia—largely unknown to voters. She had served as an elected member of the Board of Freeholders in Somerset County and was appointed to the State Board of Public Utilities by Governor Kean in 1988. Her chief political accomplishment was her near upset win over Bradley in 1990—a race in which Whitman attacked the Florio tax increase while Bradley barely campaigned. Voters were somewhat familiar with her name but had little idea of where she stood on most issues. This ignorance, combined with her lack of experience, meant that Whitman's chief obstacle was voter uncertainty about her. Her chief advantage was that she was running against an incumbent governor who had raised taxes and presided over a declining state economy (Jewell and Olson 1988; Chubb 1988; Howell and Vanderleeuw 1990).

The strategies for both Florio and Whitman were clear. As the quote from the Florio campaign staff member at the beginning of this chapter suggests, Florio would try to avoid the tax and economic issues and focus instead on his leadership abilities while trying to define Whitman as unfit for the job. Whitman planned to focus on taxes and the economy while presenting herself as a reasonable alternative to Florio.

Several campaign insiders on both sides talked about the 1993 race as a referendum on Florio. "The [general election] will not be between two candidates, but, rather, it will be a referendum on Florio. When the question is asked, 'Are you better off than you were four years ago?' nobody in New Jersey will say 'Yes,'" said an Edwards campaign staff member. Even a Florio adviser said, "Whitman's best bet is to run a race that is a yes/no vote on Jim Florio." Finally, a reporter for one of the state's newspapers said that the race was really about whether voters approved of Florio: "Those that liked him voted for him— those that didn't, didn't." The reporter asserted that "absolutely anybody" could have done at least as well against Florio as Whitman did.

This view is too simplistic. Other campaign staff members on both sides knew that, like all challengers, Whitman had to give voters both a reason to vote against the incumbent and a reason to vote for her (Salmore and Salmore 1989). Florio's tax increase, the ailing New Jersey economy, and allegations of wrongdoing by members of the Florio administration provided the means to the first goal, but if Whitman was not viewed as a credible alternative, Florio could still win. One Whitman staff member said, "In the past, people talked about anyone being able to beat Florio because he was so unpopular. Now he has improved his standing enough that it isn't enough to just be 'not Florio.' We need to also tell voters what [Whitman] will do and what she is like." Another GOP insider said early in the race that while Florio was clearly beatable, "the campaign could still be lost if [Whitman's campaign] let Florio define the race."

Most members of the Florio campaign understood this situation as well. Right after the primary, one staff member acknowledged, "We will probably have to go negative." He added, however, "but it is better to be the second one to go negative, not the first." Even before the primary, the Florio campaign had decided to try to paint Whitman as aloof, out of touch with average people, and unable to do the job. A Florio staff member said, "We will contrast Florio with Whitman in terms of making tough decisions, experience, and being in touch with voters."

So, even though voters knew Florio, and many held negative views of him, Whitman's obscurity presented a problem for her and an opportunity for Florio. A Florio campaign staff member said, "Voters that are angry about the tax increases have had three years to make up their minds [about Florio] on that issue. Those that are still undecided are voters that we can still win." Described this way, it may be more accurate to say that the 1993 gubernatorial election in New Jersey was more a referendum on Whitman's fitness for the job than Florio's.

Whitman faced challengers Cary Edwards and James Wallwork in the GOP primary. Edwards served in the state assembly in the 1970s and was attorney general from 1985 to 1989. He sought the nomination for governor in 1989 but finished third in the GOP primary. Wallwork, considered a long shot by most going into the race, had been a member of the state assembly since 1981. Whitman entered the primary as the strong favorite, leading in most polls by 10 to 15 percentage points. Edwards's staff members, however, believed that Whitman's lead was purely a function of the name recognition she had generated among Republicans during her 1990 senate race and that when voters began to focus on the issues, Edwards would prevail.

Edwards attacked Whitman late in the primary campaign in a manner that Florio copied in the general election. Edwards came from a humble background, while Whitman's family had substantial wealth. As a result, Edwards suggested that he was closer to average voters than was Whitman. Whitman avoided engaging her opponents for most of the primary campaign, hoping to ride her advantage in the polls to victory. However, her lead in the polls slipped as Edwards attacked, forcing her to abandon her strategy of nonengagement long enough to claim that Edwards was no different than Florio.[2] Florio, also from humble beginnings, used the same attack as part of his general-election strategy.

Whitman's image was not helped by the revelations that she had employed illegal aliens without paying social security taxes and that she had failed to vote in a recent school board election. She had also made a comment to the effect that a hundred dollars might seem like a lot of money to some people, but it really was not. It was also revealed that Whitman and her husband had claimed substantial tax write-offs on an estate that technically qualified as a working farm. These factors helped Edwards during the primary and Florio during the general election campaign portray Whitman as an out-of-touch aristocrat.

The Whitman campaign obviously did not welcome the attention these issues received, although one staff member did suggest that if these issues were going to be brought up, maybe it was better that it happened early. He argued that early airing allowed these issues to play themselves out in the media well before the general election, which prevented them from having any surprise impact late in the race. In this regard, he compared Whitman's situation to the early troubles of the 1992 Clinton presidential campaign.

Though Florio ran unopposed in the primary, he still spent the maximum allowed for his primary campaign. He focused on building his image as a tough decision maker and calling on the Republicans to say what they would have done in 1990 to solve New Jersey's budgetary problems without raising taxes. Florio's incumbency provided him with additional advantages. New Jersey suffers from a unique media market situation. It has no network-television-affiliated stations, receiving its network news from stations in New York City and Philadelphia. In addition, these two media markets are two of the most expensive in the country. Thus, it costs New Jersey candidates a lot of money to advertise on network television, most of the people that will see the advertisements are not even New Jersey residents, and it is difficult to get free coverage from the local news shows because they focus on Pennsylvania and New York.

This situation is compounded by limits on campaign spending by gubernatorial candidates. New Jersey has a system of public financing for gubernatorial primary and general-election campaigns. Candidates who qualify receive matching funds from the state at a rate of about two dollars for every dollar they raise on their own. However, those accepting public funds (every gubernatorial candidate since the program's inception) must abide by strict spending limits. In 1993, those limits were $2.6 million per candidate for the primary election and $5.9 million for the general election.

The oddities and expense of New Jersey's media markets combined with the limits on spending make coverage in the free local media, both television and print, particularly important. One Democratic Party official reported that some polls show that as many as 88 percent of the state's voters get their information from newspapers. In such a tight media market, the general advantage incumbent governors have over challengers in attracting free media coverage (Salmore and Salmore 1989) is greater.

A Whitman staff member expressed concern about this situation, saying that Florio "can get on TV doing some public service announcement any time he wants. If the governor talks, the press covers it. [The Florio campaign has] the power to create a bunch of free media coverage." He also noted the difficulties of running a mass media campaign under these circumstances. "We are heavily mail-dependent in order to get out our message. We also use radio and some cable TV along with the small weekly newspapers. However, it seems that people don't think you are a real campaign until/unless you are on network TV."[3]

Florio, demonstrating the power of incumbency, held a press conference right after the primary at a new facility built in large part through cooperation between himself and several Republican state legislative leaders. The event was staged as a ribbon-cutting ceremony rather than a simple press conference, which put a GOP legislative leader in front of cameras praising Florio for his part in the project. This ceremony allowed Florio to demonstrate his ability to work with a GOP-controlled legislature and helped divert attention away from Whitman's victory in the GOP primary. Polls immediately following the primary gave Florio a slight lead. The Whitman campaign viewed Florio's early advantage as a combination of a return of Florio's natural constituency and Whitman's lower level of name recognition.

The campaign went largely dormant between the June 8 primary and the beginning of August. Florio spent a lot of time looking and acting like a governor but not really engaging Whitman. Whitman did less—having few campaign events and attracting little free media coverage. Furthermore, virtually the only attention Whitman's campaign attracted came as a result of missteps. For example, she hired and fired several campaign advisers, including Larry McCarthy, the creator of the famous Willie Horton attack ad of the 1988 presidential race.

By the second week in August, several GOP consultants had publicly criticized Whitman's campaign, saying that she was handing the election to Florio. On August 10, Roger Stone, a prominent Republican consultant, released to the press a letter urging Whitman to present a specific tax-cut proposal, to push Florio to take a position on President Clinton's tax proposals, and to attack the Florio administration as corrupt (McClure 1993c, 4). In the same article, a Whitman adviser, Ed Rollins, agreed with much of what Stone said.

Whitman's campaign lacked focus throughout the summer, and most of the blame was placed on her brother and campaign manager, Dan Todd, whose only previous political experience was helping a friend run a local campaign in

Montana. While Whitman's staff members never said to me that Todd was the problem, reports circulated in the press that the Whitman staff lacked confidence in Todd, that his temperament was not suited to the job, and that other advisers felt unable to express their criticisms of Todd to Whitman.

When Florio began to engage Whitman in August, he did so not on specific policies but rather on issues of candidate quality. The Florio campaign focused on Whitman's wealth, suggesting that she could not relate to average voters. On August 11, a Florio campaign film crew went to the Whitman farm to record video for a commercial attacking Whitman for claiming that it was a working farm for tax purposes. Whitman filed a trespassing complaint, the issue got several days of play in the press, and the Whitman camp apparently felt compelled to defend itself by inviting reporters to the farm five days later for a staged media event complete with farm animals, bales of hay, and a cookout (Clarke 1993, 4). Critics of the Whitman campaign said her actions kept the issue in the newspapers and helped Florio put her on the defensive.

Of course, Florio's campaign had problems, too. In an interview well before the June primary, a Whitman campaign staff member suggested that the New Jersey Education Association (NJEA), a teachers' union, might be the most powerful interest group in New Jersey, and that Whitman expected the NJEA to work for Florio. However, newspapers reported on August 15 that the NJEA had decided not to endorse a candidate in the governor's race. Florio had pushed a school refinancing plan in 1990 that called for an end to state funding for teachers' pensions, which had angered the NJEA (*Trentonian* 1993c, 3). The other major event that troubled Florio's campaign was the resignation of his chief of staff, Joe Salema, in the face of a federal investigation into charges of corruption in the awarding of New Jersey state bond issues. While Florio was never directly implicated, the press, particularly the *Trentonian,* kept the issue alive by drawing links between Florio campaign contributors and companies awarded state contracts to manage bonds.

Thus, while Whitman's campaign was either absent from the public eye or stumbling in front of it, Florio also had problems. However, by the middle of August, it was clear that uncertainty and/or negative evaluations of Whitman weighed more heavily with the electorate. The remainder of the campaign would revolve largely around the definition of Whitman and whether she was a reasonable alternative to Florio.

A poll taken by the *Asbury Park Press* on August 12–14 reported that 38 percent of the respondents favored Whitman, while 37 percent preferred Florio. This poll found that creating jobs was the most important issue to respondents, suggesting that if Whitman could show herself as a viable candidate, she could capitalize on Florio's poor record in that area.

Florio's effort to define himself as willing to make tough decisions centered on an assault-weapons ban passed under his guidance. He repeatedly charged that Whitman would weaken the ban and that the National Rifle Association (NRA) was backing the Whitman campaign. Whitman had suggested some modifications but nothing like a repeal of the ban. Still, Florio hoped to use Whitman's proposals to show that she was weaker on crime and unwilling to take on a tough interest group like the NRA.

Both campaign's strategies were captured by the first television advertisements run over Labor Day weekend. The advertisements were sponsored by the state political parties rather than the candidates, so the commercials had to avoid any direct mention of the gubernatorial candidates.[4] Still, it was clear that these commercials were designed to emphasize the themes that the gubernatorial candidates would be using.

The GOP ad focused on taxes and the poor health of the state's economy. It blamed the Democratic Party for tax increases and the loss of about 280,000 jobs. The Democratic Party's ad was a graphic portrayal of assault weapons and violent crime that highlighted GOP opposition to the ban. Both advertisements were covered by the free media as news events, but the Democratic ad received particular attention due to its graphic nature. According to one Democratic Party official, the ad was designed to attract this attention: "Part of the reason for doing such a graphic ad was to attract media coverage of the commercial." As a result, the ad had a broader impact and received more airtime without the campaign having to pay for it.

Though most of September, Florio's campaign focused on Whitman's lack of a formal tax-cut proposal. Florio had been calling for specifics from Whitman, as had many Republicans. On September 9, newspapers reported that Whitman planned to release her tax-cut proposals in a week. Typical of Whitman's campaign to that point, the plan's release was a week late. Furthermore, the plan was only a two-page proposal calling for a 30 percent reduction in state income taxes. Florio blasted the plan as simplistic, favoring the rich, vague on spending cuts, and nothing but a political ploy. In fact, the Florio camp responded the day after the plan's release with a television ad attacking the credibility of Whitman's plan. Many editorial pages followed Florio's lead, calling Whitman's proposal vague and unrealistic. Even the *Trentonian,* a paper with a history of open hostility toward Florio, said that Whitman was failing to defend her proposal well. It took until October 6 for the press to report that any Republican legislators had endorsed Whitman's tax cut plan (McClure 1993b, 4).

Whitman's campaign was still stumbling, and its handling of this proposal did not help. On September 26, political scientist Cliff Zukin was quoted as saying, "I think this race was [Whitman's] to lose, and so far, she has been doing a good job of that" (McClure 1993d, 4). Two days later, a new poll seemed to confirm Zukin's comment. Under a headline in the *Trentonian* saying, "Poll: It May Be All over for Whitman," the results of a CBS/*New York Times* poll reported Florio leading Whitman 51 percent to 30 percent (Plitch and McClure

1993b, 4). The following day, an editorial in the *Trentonian* suggested that Whitman had fallen too far behind to win (*Trentonian* 1993a, 41). The poll reported that only 10 percent of the respondents believed that Whitman could reduce taxes as she proposed. Furthermore, respondents were evenly split on whether or not Florio's 1990 tax increase had been the right or the wrong thing to do. Just two weeks earlier, a poll conducted by the *Hackensack Record* had the race even at 43 percent.

Whitman's response came on September 30. She announced that her brother would step down as campaign manager and that Rollins would take over. Whitman supporters cheered the move, though Whitman herself downplayed its significance, saying the switch had been part of the plan all along. This change, however, signaled an effort to refocus Whitman's campaign.

Florio countered by appointing Edwards, Whitman's leading opponent in the GOP primary, as head of a special study commission on legal gambling in New Jersey. Edwards still claimed to support Whitman, but the move was clearly designed to reemphasize Florio's appeal to moderates and his ability to work with GOP leaders.

Starting October 2, Whitman began airing new television advertisements calling Florio the worst governor in New Jersey history, due in large part to the tax increases. Whitman and the GOP had previously stressed the Florio tax increases and New Jersey's sagging economy, but this ad attacked Florio more personally. Florio continued his attacks on Whitman's stand on the assault-weapons ban and her tax-cut proposal.

Even with the appointment of Rollins as campaign manager and Whitman's new aggressiveness, her campaign continued to stumble. After performing respectably in the first television debate, the Whitman campaign held a rally designed to build on her performance and demonstrate GOP unity. They told reporters that Edwards and popular former governor Tom Kean would attend, but neither man appeared, leading the media to cover the rally as another botched Whitman event. Two days later, the press reported that one of Whitman's attacks of Florio during the debate was a mistake. She claimed that state prisoners were given expensive brand-name athletic shoes, but the inmates actually received low-cost canvas shoes. These two events were not particularly significant in their own right, but the press treated them as additional examples of Whitman's poor campaign. By implication, her inability to run a smooth campaign raised doubts about her ability to be governor, a view the Florio campaign hoped would take root with voters.

On October 13 Whitman launched a new television ad that again attacked Florio for increasing state taxes and spending. However, for the first time, this ad referred to several current and former Florio aides targeted by two grand jury investigations. The tag line of the ad said, "Jim Florio—rising unemployment, corruption, and higher taxes. We can't afford more."

In mid-October, the race still seemed to be firmly in Florio's hands. A poll released on October 18 had Florio ahead by 12 percentage points, and the same poll suggested that more people thought Florio had won the first debate than thought that Whitman had won (*Trentonian* 1993b, 5). The headline in the *Trentonian* following the second debate read, "Newly Relaxed Florio Tightens Grip on Race" (Plitch and McClure 1993a, 3), and the same article cited another poll giving Florio a 15 percentage point lead over Whitman. Even GOP supporters called the second debate no better than a draw.

Stephen Salmore, a political scientist, said in an interview that Whitman "has 13 days to do what should have been done last summer—show that she is competent enough to do the job. By running an awful campaign, she has allowed Governor Florio to portray her as out to lunch" (McClure 1993a, 4). The same day, Whitman announced that she was starting a three-day, fourteen-county bus tour. New television advertisements from both campaigns followed the next day. Florio promoted his ability to make tough decisions to balance the budget and attacked Whitman for not being specific about how she would pay for her proposed tax cuts. Whitman's new ad featured her speaking directly to the camera, denying Florio's charges that she was weak on crime. In the ad, she said, "If he can't tell the truth about raising taxes, how can you trust him to tell the truth about me?" She also began running an ad saying that New Jersey had lost three hundred thousand jobs in the past three and a half years under Florio and that she would work to create jobs.

Whitman's bus tour ended two days before the third and final debate. Reporters and campaign staff members said the tour revitalized Whitman and helped her to hit her stride with a message of cutting taxes and attacking Florio for a failed term as governor. Many commentators on election night cited this tour as a turning point in the campaign.

The third debate saw no major advances or mistakes made by either side, although some analysts did say that Whitman looked credible, which she needed to do (McClure and Plitch 1993, 4). That day, however, she made a critical statement in defense of her tax-cut proposal. She argued that to achieve the 30 percent reduction in income taxes she proposed over three years would only require a reduction in state spending of five cents out of every dollar. With that single statement, she transformed what had been viewed as the nearly impossible task of cutting taxes by 30 percent to the apparently more reasonable goal of cutting spending by 5 percent. The statement was subtle and was not heralded in the press as a huge development, but for the first time, Whitman made her tax-cut proposal sound feasible.

A poll released the same day reported Florio's lead at only 5 percentage points. Whitman aides credited her television advertisements attacking her opponent. The following day, reports citing campaign sources suggested that internal polls in both campaigns had Florio's lead at 3 to 4 points (Superville

1993, 4). In the same article, Whitman revealed her tag line for the final push, asking voters if they were happy with the past four years or if they would dare to dream that New Jersey could do better.

Realizing the shift in support taking place, Florio attacked Whitman on October 26, saying that a vote for her was a vote for the NRA. In contrast, Whitman's camp disclosed a planned mass mailing to swing voters attacking Florio's tax increases. The mailing was entitled "The Big Lie!" Two days later, Florio went to a gun shop that Whitman had visited much earlier in the campaign to again link her with the NRA, while Whitman surrogates continued to attack the Florio administration's ethics.

The final advertising push by the Whitman camp consisted of an ad featuring popular former governor Kean saying that Whitman could do the job and an ad asking voters to give change a chance. Florio shifted his focus at the end away from attacking Whitman and toward promoting his accomplishments while governor and reporting on the number of newspaper endorsements he had received.

The final few days of the campaign saw a wide range of poll results, reflecting the volatility of New Jersey's voters. Whitman ultimately won by a margin of 2 percentage points. As expected, the suburban areas were keys to her victory, but the returns also revealed that Florio did not win in the urban areas by sufficient margins to counter Whitman's rural and suburban gains. In the end, Florio failed to mobilize his base sufficiently and was unable to make the needed gains with white suburban voters.

In the final two weeks of the campaign, Whitman's more direct attacks reminded voters why they had given Florio an 18 percent approval rating back in 1990 and convinced enough of them that she could be governor and that her tax-cut proposal was feasible. Her bus tour helped to counter the perception Florio had worked so hard to create—that Whitman was aloof and out of touch with average voters and that she was not capable of running a campaign, let alone a state. The themes of tax cuts, giving change a chance, and personal attacks on Florio framed her as a populist running against a failed political insider. Finally, her simple explanation of how cutting spending by 5 percent would allow her to achieve her income-tax cuts and Kean's endorsement gave her enough credibility with enough voters for them to give her a chance to be governor.

In retrospect, it seems amazing that Florio ever had a chance, let alone led for most of the final month by as much as 21 percentage points.[5] As an incumbent presiding over a huge tax increase only months after indicating that no tax increase would be necessary, encumbered by the loss of three hundred thousand jobs since taking office, and haunted by charges of political corruption in the form of two grand jury investigations, it is no surprise that most people felt Florio had no chance to hold onto his job. However, no one predicted that Florio would run such a masterful campaign, dominating the agenda until the final week or two, while his opponent would run such a poor campaign. Whitman nearly managed to snatch defeat out of the jaws of victory by allowing Florio to define her as out of touch and unfit for the governorship. She followed one mistake with another, allowing her own events like the release of her tax-cut plan to be turned against her while turning what should have been minor blips into major gaffes.[6] Even after demoting her brother, it took her campaign another two or three weeks to finally focus its message. As mentioned earlier, the issue during this campaign really was not Florio's fitness for the job but Whitman's.

A final aspect of this campaign not yet mentioned was the role played by presidential politics. The results from chapter 5 suggest that in Virginia, Mary Sue Terry did not escape being linked with President Clinton despite her best efforts, even though her opponent did not try to make Clinton an issue. In New Jersey, Florio actively cultivated an association with the Clinton presidency. Several Clinton administration officials visited the state during the gubernatorial campaign, and both the president and his wife made personal visits as well. Late in the race, Republican U.S. Senator Bob Dole of Kansas came to campaign for Whitman, and commentators early in the campaign suggested that this race might be in part a referendum on the Clinton presidency.

The next step is to examine how voters responded to the campaign. As a backdrop, I begin with a brief overview of the electoral coalition Florio mobilized in his 1989 victory over Jim Courter by the second-largest margin of victory in this gubernatorial election in New Jersey history. This discussion is based on the analysis of an exit poll conducted by CBS/*New York Times.* Florio built a coalition that expanded beyond the traditional Democratic base of African-Americans, liberals, and Democrats. He won equally large margins of support from men and women, and even the dominant issue of 1989, abortion, worked in Florio's favor. Entering the 1993 race, his challenge was to maintain such a broad-based coalition in the face of his dramatic decline in popularity.

Table 6.1 illustrates the flow of support among voters for Florio and Whitman over the course of the campaign in terms of a variety of sociodemographic and political variables. The first poll presented in table 6.1 was conducted in February 1993, and the final poll is an exit poll conducted on election day. In between are five polls conducted between the June 8 primary and the closing days of the campaign. The dependent variables for poll 1 and poll 7 are dummy variables. For polls 2 through 6, the dependent variable is a three-category variable indicating whether a respondent supported Florio or Whitman or was undecided. The nature of the dependent variable in polls 1 and 7 suggests that a simple logit or probit model should be used, and a logit model is presented. Polls 2 through 6 are analyzed using multinomial logit. The independent variables include dummy variables for gender, race, political ideology, party iden-

TABLE 6.1. Multinomial Logit Models of Factors Predicting Voter Intentions for the 1993 New Jersey Gubernatorial Election

Variable	Comparison	Poll 1[a]	Poll 2	Poll 3	Poll 4	Poll 5	Poll 6	Poll 7[b]
Constant	F v W	-2.377*	-1.486*	0.211	0.331	-0.777	-0.419	0.083
	F v U		1.625	-0.508	-0.328	1.279	0.063	
Female	F v W	-0.434*	-0.467*	-0.085	-0.062	0.614*	0.163	0.050
	F v U		-0.548	-0.321	-0.531*	0.079	-0.279	
Black	F v W	-0.080	-0.113	0.465	-0.285	0.221	0.435	0.607*
	F v U		-0.845	0.142	-0.893*	1.259	0.431	
Age	F v W	0.396*	0.405*	0.260*	0.235*	0.245*	0.351*	0.015
	F v U		0.056	0.326*	0.311*	0.152	0.148	
Family income	F v W	0.134	-0.141	-0.118	-0.130	-0.116	-0.154	-0.100*
	F v U		-0.019	0.140	0.174	0.135	0.009	
Education level	F v W	0.069	0.334	-0.068	-0.059	0.021	0.024	0.095
	F v U		-0.118	0.010	-0.009	-0.093	0.429	
Liberal	F v W	0.628*	0.104	0.252	0.186	0.340	0.368	0.187
	F v U		0.173	0.416	0.077	0.594	0.719	
Conservative	F v W	-0.301	-0.417	-0.350	-0.567*	-0.456	-0.563*	-0.718*
	F v U		0.037	-0.468	-0.106	-0.115	-0.228	
Democrat	F v W	1.052*	1.764*	1.270*	1.687*	1.306*	1.296*	1.534*
	F v U		1.849*	1.220*	1.013*	0.728	0.896*	
Republican	F v W	-0.711*	-1.367*	-1.502*	-1.152*	-0.985*	-1.783*	-1.244*
	F v U		-0.192	0.023	-0.209	-0.418	-0.435	
Catholic	F v W	0.016	0.147	-0.452	-0.418*	0.242	-0.002	-0.316*
	F v U		0.149	-0.201	-0.068	0.408	0.079	
Jew	F v W	0.229	0.241	-0.019	0.219	1.156	0.132	0.038
	F v U		0.423	1.126	0.291	-0.096	-0.707	

		Poll 1	Poll 2	Poll 3	Poll 4	Poll 5	Poll 6	Poll 7
Rural	F v W	0.286	−0.282	0.295	0.209	0.316	0.324	—
	F v U		−0.490	0.248	0.098	1.767	0.444	—
City	F v W	−0.373	0.182	0.072	0.129	0.133	−0.149	—
	F v U		−0.565	−0.521	0.227	−0.898	−0.603	—
City-sub	F v W	0.202	−0.380	0.593	—	−0.016	−0.046	—
	F v U		−0.999*	0.918*	—	0.544	−0.394	—
North	F v W	0.183	0.402	0.073	0.366	0.309	0.155	—
	F v U		0.557	0.259	0.199	−0.683	−0.236	—
South	F v W	0.498*	0.514	0.097	0.825*	0.125	0.388	—
	F v U		0.188	0.124	0.182	−0.813	−0.327	—
Chi-square		118.2*	208.9*	170.8*	207.2*	146.4*	232.0*	601.5*
Percentage correctly predicted		70.2%	67.1%	64.4%	60.4%	67.4%	65.6%	76.3%
N size		714	626	525	717	497	672	1,711

Note: F = Supports Florio for Governor

U = Undecided

W = Supports Whitman for Governor

Poll 1: *Star-Ledger*/Eagleton Poll, February 17–24

Poll 2: *Star-Ledger*/Eagleton Poll, June 11–17

Poll 3: *Star-Ledger*/Eagleton Poll, September 10–15

Poll 4: WCBS-TV News/*New York Times* Poll, September 20–26

Poll 5: *Star-Ledger*/Eagleton Poll, October 11–14

Poll 6: *Star-Ledger*/Eagleton Poll, October 27–30

Poll 7: Voter Research and Surveys Exit Poll, November 2

[a]The dependent variable used in Poll 1 is a dichotomous measure of Governor Florio's job approval, coded 1 for those who approved and 0 for those who did not.

[b]The dependent variable used in Poll 7 is a dichotomous measure of reported voter behavior, coded 1 for those reporting having voted for Florio and a 0 for those who chose Whitman.

*Significant at $p < .05$

tification, religious affiliation, and place of residence.[7] Categorical variables are also included, measuring age, family income, and education level.

Poll 1 provides a glimpse of the base of support with which Florio started the 1993 campaign. The dependent variable records whether the respondent approves or disapproves of the job Florio is doing as governor, coded as a 1 for those who approve. The findings from poll 1 point to early weaknesses in Florio's base of support compared to his 1989 electoral coalition, as only 38 percent of the respondents approved of his job performance.

Comparing the analysis of poll 1 in table 6.1 with the analysis of the 1989 exit poll described earlier shows that while Florio lost support across all categories, women, African-Americans, ideological moderates, and young voters in particular had moved away. Even his support among Democrats and liberals had weakened. Poll 1 makes it clear that Florio was vulnerable.

Polls 2 through 6 were taken over the course of the campaign, poll 2 right after the June 8 primary and poll 6 just before the November 2 election. In each poll, voters were asked for whom they would vote if the election were held that day. The dependent variable is trichotomous, allowing voters to indicate supporting Whitman or Florio or still being undecided. Table 6.1 allows us to examine the changing coalitions of support enjoyed by each candidate over the course of the campaign as well as characterize undecided voters. This is an important factor because, as will be shown subsequently, those voters who did not decide until late in the campaign whom they would support had a significant impact on the election's outcome.

Figure 6.1 presents the predicted probability that a respondent in each poll would support Florio or Whitman or be undecided. These probabilities are produced by holding each variable in the models in table 6.1 constant at its mean. As was the case in chapter 5, figures based on predicted probabilities serve to illustrate the pattern of responses among those surveyed. It is important to remember that for each of the figures presented in this chapter, the first poll represents simple approval or disapproval of Florio and the final poll is an exit poll. In particular, the first poll presents support for Florio versus potential support for any opponent rather than actual support for Whitman.

Figure 6.1 closely tracks the aggregate levels of candidate support reported in the press over the course of the campaign. The predicted probabilities plotted in figure 6.1 also closely match the marginal distribution of support for each candidate in each poll.

Figure 6.1 shows that while Florio's job approval ratings in February provided an early opportunity for Whitman, by the start of the general-election campaign, Florio had the advantage. Florio's support rose gradually from the beginning of the campaign, peaking in late September and early October. Whitman's support went in the other direction. From mid-June to late September, the predicted probability that a respondent would support Whitman slipped

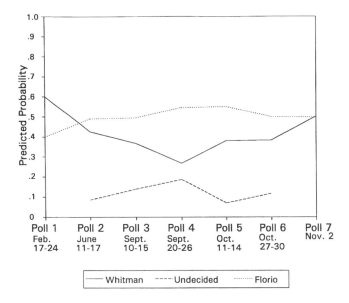

Fig. 6.1. Mean predicted level of support for Whitman or Florio for governor

from .43 to .27. Much of this drop-off in Whitman's support was captured by an increasing proportion of the electorate being undecided. This reflects voters' level of uncertainty about Whitman.

In the last two weeks of October, this pattern changed. Florio saw a slight drop-off in support from poll 5 to poll 6 at the expense of a jump in the probability that a respondent was undecided. Finally, Whitman's support jumped between poll 6 and the exit poll, poll 7, suggesting that she captured the lion's share of those voters who were undecided a week before the election.

Looking first at the effect of gender, among voters who had a preference in June, Whitman enjoyed a statistically significant advantage over Florio among women compared to men, controlling for other factors. While Whitman's gender may have been partly responsible for this gap, Florio already had significantly lower job evaluations in February—before Whitman had won the GOP primary—among women relative to men.[8]

The Florio campaign believed it would have difficulties attracting women voters while running against Whitman. His campaign hoped that focusing on violent crime, paying particular attention to its impact on children, would help. The Democratic Party's first television ad run over Labor Day weekend superimposed the image of a firing assault rifle on the image of a young girl.

By the second week in September, poll 3 shows that Whitman's advantage over Florio with female voters had vanished. By late September, poll 4 shows that women still did not differ significantly from men regarding which candidate they supported, but women were more likely than men to be undecided. I believe the indecision among women at this stage of the campaign results from dissatisfaction with both candidates. Florio had gained ground with the crime issue, but he may have hurt himself with women voters in early September by adopting a tough stance on welfare recipients. As noted earlier, Florio also failed to gain the endorsement of the NJEA, signaling some weakness in his record on education.

Many observers thought that Whitman's gender put her in position in June to take advantage of Florio's weak rating among women. Yet by mid-September, voters in many categories had a high level of uncertainty about Whitman. Finally, both candidates were prochoice on abortion, preventing that issue from serving more generally as an information shortcut for gender-related issues.[9]

In early October, Florio reclaimed a relative advantage over Whitman among women compared to men. However, by the end of the race, Florio could do no better than eliminate the statistically significant advantage among women that Whitman held early on.

Figure 6.2 presents the predicted probabilities regarding candidate support among men and women based on the findings presented in table 6.1. The figure shows Florio with an early advantage over Whitman in the predicted level of support given the two candidates by men. By late September, Florio's advantage among men was paralleled by an advantage over Whitman among female voters as well. Both male and female voters took a sharp turn during the first two weeks of October. Men shifted their support from Florio toward Whitman. Women increased their level of support for each candidate, although slightly more so for Florio, as they moved out of the undecided group. The end of the race actually saw Whitman closing a late gap in support among women.

Looking next at the question of race, table 6.1 shows that throughout the course of the general-election campaign, African-Americans were no more likely to indicate support for Florio than they were for Whitman, controlling for other factors. Furthermore, in late September, poll 4 shows that blacks were significantly more likely to be undecided than to have chosen Florio or Whitman, compared to nonblacks. Poll 7, the exit poll, shows that on election day, blacks who voted were significantly more likely to support Florio over Whitman.

The findings in the earlier polls regarding race hint at a problem many commentators say resulted in Florio's ultimate loss—his campaign failed to energize African-Americans. Polls 1 through 6 suggest that blacks may have been ambivalent regarding the election. While Democratic Party officials said to me that they hoped Florio's focus on crime might signal a broader concern for urban problems, thereby attracting African-American support, neither candidate made direct appeals to minority concerns a central part of their campaigns.

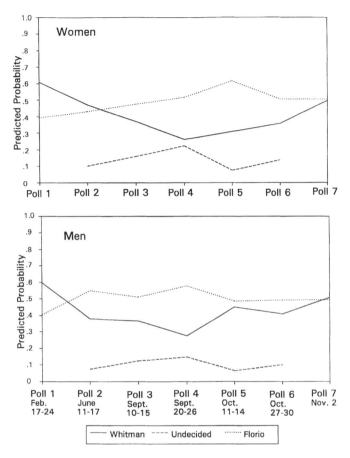

Fig. 6.2.   Predicted level of support for Whitman or Florio for governor, by gender

Figure 6.3 illustrates these findings. In February, African-Americans were just as likely as non-African-Americans to give Florio a negative job evaluation. Over the course of the campaign, Florio enjoyed an advantage over Whitman among both black and nonblack voters, although the level of black support was more volatile. In the end, figure 6.3 shows that Florio maintained an advantage among African-Americans on election day, although they had a predicted probability of supporting Whitman of .38, indicating that she made meaningful inroads in the black community. Figure 6.3 shows that the appearance of a significant difference between black and nonblack voters on election day was the result of Whitman's late gains among nonblacks.

Polls 1 through 6 in table 6.1 show that older voters were consistently more

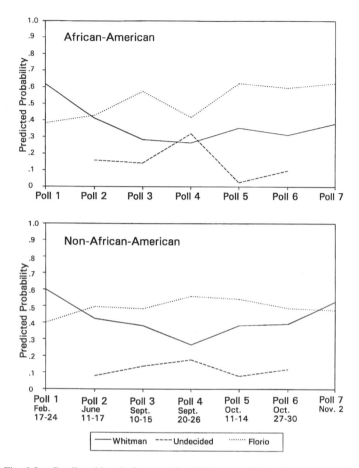

Fig. 6.3.   Predicted level of support for Whitman or Florio for governor, by race

likely than younger voters to support Florio over Whitman. Florio had worked to garner the support of senior-citizens' groups during his tenure as governor, and he received several endorsements from such organizations during the campaign. It may also be the case that younger voters were quicker to support a change. Poll 7 shows that Florio ultimately lost the statistically significant advantage he had with older voters on election day.

Figure 6.4 illustrates the relationship between age and candidate support. Florio's advantage with older voters began in February and grew over the course of the campaign. Among younger voters, Florio started at a tremendous disadvantage that diminished as support for Whitman among younger voters

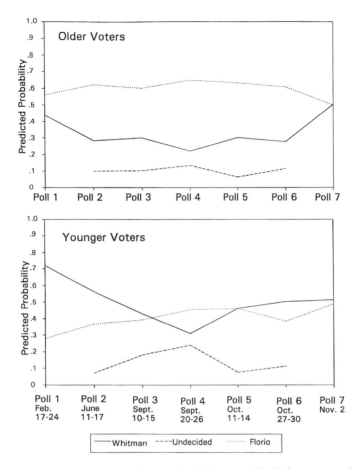

Fig. 6.4. Predicted level of support for Whitman or Florio for governor, by age

dropped dramatically from June to late September. Figure 6.4 shows that Florio gained support among younger voters in the closing days of the campaign, but those gains were more than offset by the tremendous swing from Florio to Whitman among older voters. An advantage among older voters that Florio had held for months apparently evaporated at the close of the campaign.

The findings in table 6.1 regarding family income suggest that Florio's attempt to portray Whitman as an aristocrat and himself a friend of working people failed. At no point during the campaign were low-income respondents significantly more likely than wealthier respondents to support Florio over Whitman.[10] By election day, a moderate relationship between income and vot-

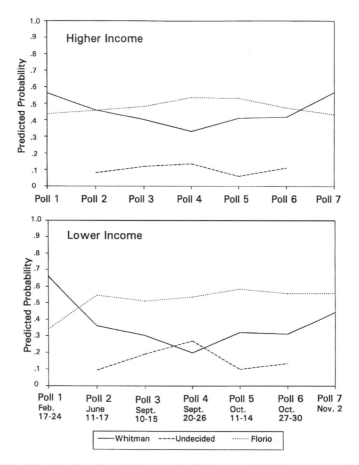

Fig. 6.5.   Predicted level of support for Whitman or Florio for governor, by income

ing behavior developed, but the more general conclusion based on the polls taken over the course of the campaign is that Florio's appeals to a class-based division among voters did not have a major impact on voter behavior. Further-more, the other measure of socioeconomic status included in the analysis of these polls—education—never achieved statistical significance.

Figure 6.5 suggests that during much of the campaign, Florio had an advantage over Whitman among low-income voters compared to those with higher incomes, though this advantage was generally statistically insignificant. The gap only became significant on election day because the slight advantage Florio had held over Whitman among wealthier voters disappeared. The magnitude of the relationship between income and candidate support, as measured by the size of the coefficients in table 6.1, is smaller in poll 7 than in Polls 2 through 6 and is significant in poll 7 only because there is less variance around that estimate.

Table 6.1 reports that in June, self-identified liberals were more likely than moderates to support Florio than Whitman. However, starting in September and continuing through election day, liberals were no more likely to support Florio over Whitman than were moderates. This change results from two developments. First, as Florio's support increased in September, it increased substantially among moderates. However, Florio's advantage over Whitman decreased in October and on election day among both liberals and moderates, maintaining the statistically insignificant difference between the two.

Conservatives followed a different path. In June they were no less likely than were moderates to disapprove of Florio's performance as governor. More important, in June and again in early September, conservatives were no more likely to support Whitman over Florio than were moderates. Whitman clearly had not yet won the confidence of New Jersey's conservative voters.

By late September and continuing through election day, Whitman began to enjoy significantly higher levels of support among conservatives than among moderates, even as moderates began to move away from Florio and toward Whitman as the campaign drew to a close. Whitman released her tax-cut proposal on the first day poll 4 was conducted, and this is the first poll that produced this significant relationship regarding conservatives' support for her. The effect drops just below statistical significance in poll 5, possibly because of Whitman's problems in defending the plan. Polls 6 and 7 show that by the end of the campaign, Whitman had reduced conservatives' uncertainty enough to win their overwhelming support.

Figure 6.6 illustrates these findings. Florio began with an advantage among liberals, but that advantage peaked by the second week in October. His support among liberals declined at the end of the race as Whitman made substantial gains within this group. Among moderates, Florio also held an advantage, though it was slight by election day. Still, figure 6.6 suggests that Whitman's ultimate success came from mobilizing a sufficiently large advantage among conservative voters late in the race. Had she failed to do so, the figure suggests that Florio's advantage among liberals and moderates would have been large enough to give him the election.

The behavior of the partisanship variables in table 6.1 is more stable. From the beginning, partisans maintained significant differences between themselves and independents regarding support for the two candidates. Most of the movement during the campaign came from political independents. Figure 6.7 shows that while many Democrats were unhappy with Florio in February, over the course of the general election, Florio maintained a strong and consistent level

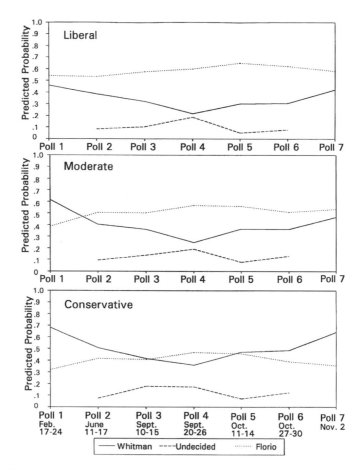

Fig. 6.6.   Predicted level of support for Whitman or Florio for governor, by ideology

of support among his partisans. Whitman, however, struggled to maintain a comparable level of support among Republicans. Figure 6.7 shows that in late September and early October, Florio appeared to be making significant gains among Whitman's own party identifiers. However, by election day, Whitman reclaimed an advantage among Republicans equal to that enjoyed by Florio among Democrats. Not surprisingly, independent voters appear to have been the difference in the final outcome. Florio generated a modest advantage among independents for most of the campaign, but during the last few days of the campaign, independent voters shifted noticeably toward Whitman.

The behavior of the religious-affiliation variable for Catholics in table 6.1

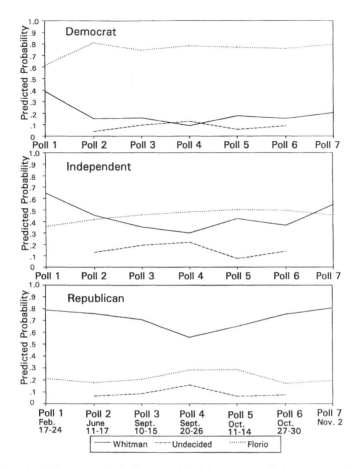

Fig. 6.7.   Predicted level of support for Whitman or Florio for governor, by party identification

is interesting but unclear, while self-identified Jews showed no statistically significant differences from the excluded religious category.[11] For most of the campaign, Catholics were no more likely to support one candidate over the other than were non-Catholics. However, in poll 4 and again in the exit poll, poll 7, Catholics indicated a significantly lower probability of supporting Florio than Whitman. Figure 6.8 shows that the relationship in poll 4 results from a sharp drop in support for Whitman among non-Catholics in this poll. In contrast, the significant relationship found in the exit poll shows that Catholics were less likely to have voted for Florio than for Whitman. These findings are curious given the traditional linkage between Catholics and the Democratic Party

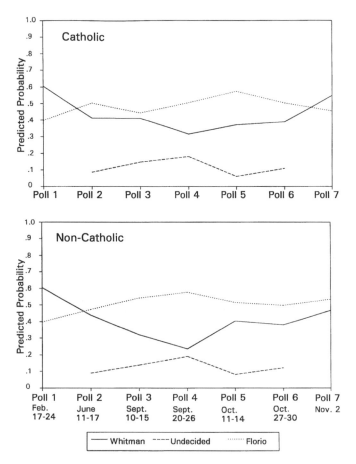

Fig. 6.8.   Predicted level of support for Whitman or Florio for governor, by religion

since the New Deal of the 1930s. Furthermore, though not measured in any of these polls, one might predict that the ethnic identity of many New Jersey Catholics might reinforce any tendency to lean toward supporting Florio.

However, Catholics were no more likely than non-Catholics to support Florio in 1989,[12] and they were neither more nor less likely to give Florio a positive job evaluation in February 1993. Thus, a finding of insignificance throughout most of the campaign is not inconsistent with the past behavior of Catholic voters in New Jersey, but finding a negative relationship is curious. It may be the case that Catholics were attracted to Whitman's education proposals, which included a plan for school choice and the use of vouchers that included private schools. The data available in these polls simply does not permit testing this speculation.

Finally, the behavior of the place-of-residence variables suggests that any reported geographical pattern of voting behavior is produced by other factors in the model. Many observers believed that the battle in this election would be over white suburban voters in the central region of the state. The polls show that neither candidate did any better or worse in the suburbs or in the central part of the state than they did among their geographical bases of support.[13] Only once, in poll 4, taken at the height of Florio's popularity, did any of the regional variables distinguish between supporters of Florio and Whitman, with voters in the southern part of the state being significantly more likely to support Florio. Finally, there was a period early in the race when Florio appeared to be gaining ground in smaller cities and older suburbs. In June, those residents of smaller cities and older suburbs who were not supporting Whitman were more likely to be undecided than to support Florio. By early September, voters living in the same areas who did not support Whitman were more likely to be supporting Florio than to be undecided.

To summarize table 6.1 and figures 6.1 through 6.8, the campaign in 1993 saw Florio starting with a base of support much smaller than his 1989 electoral coalition. He regained some of that support, particularly among women, during the summer and early fall. At the same time, however, he never attracted significant support from liberals relative to moderates or from African-Americans. In October, Whitman finally mobilized her base of support while chipping away at Florio's. She appears to have convinced conservatives to support her at about the same time she released her tax-cut proposal. She countered Florio's early October advantage with female voters, and by election day, Florio's significantly higher support among older voters had evaporated and Catholic voters were more likely to support Whitman. Lost in the analysis presented in table 6.1 but available by looking at the predicted probabilities used to produce figures 6.6 and 6.7 is the movement of moderates and independents. They produced a large portion of the swing in support over the course of the campaign.

Table 6.2 builds on what is presented in table 6.1 by adding, where available, attitudes on issues that constituted the main themes of the campaigns. The coefficients reported in table 6.2 are part of larger models that included all the variables presented in table 6.1. The basic findings of table 6.1 remain largely unchanged, with a few exceptions that will be noted. For ease of presentation, only the estimated coefficients for the new variables are presented in table 6.2.

Poll 1 in Table 6.2 shows that Florio's job evaluation among respondents was significantly related to whether respondents approved or disapproved of the job Bill Clinton was doing as president and whether they had a positive evaluation of New Jersey's economy. Thus, well before the general election began, evaluations of the president were related to evaluations of the governor, and he

TABLE 6.2. Multinomial Logit Models of Factors Predicting Voter Intentions for the 1993 New Jersey Gubernatorial Election, Controlling for Sociodemographic Characteristics, Partisan Identification, and Ideological Identification

Variable	Comparison	Poll 1[a]	Poll 2	Poll 3	Poll 4	Poll 5	Poll 6	Poll 7[b]
Clinton job approval	F v W	1.580*	0.735*	—	1.101*	1.647*	—	—
	F v U		1.033*		0.801*	1.117*		
NJ Economic evaluation	F v W	0.716*	1.529*	1.402*	0.824*	—	—	—
	F v U		0.993	0.581	0.397			
Tax issue	F v W	−0.162	−0.711	—	—	—	—	−1.408*
	F v U		−0.390					
Crime issue	F v W	0.001	1.000*	—	—	—	—	0.558*
	F v U		1.836					
Jobs issue	F v W	−0.050	0.057	—	—	—	—	−0.447*
	F v U		0.229					
Economy issue	F v W	−0.316	−0.079	—	—	—	—	—
	F v U		0.524					
Chi-square		190.3*	265.7*	187.8*	258.7*	185.8*	—	714.4*
Percent correctly predicted		75%	69.3%	65.9%	64.7%	69.6%	—	79.8%
N size		640	626	525	717	496	—	1,494

Note: F = Supports Florio for Governor
    U = Undecided
    W = Supports Whitman for Governor

Poll 1: Star-Ledger/Eagleton Poll, February 17–24
Poll 2: Star-Ledger/Eagleton Poll, June 11–17
Poll 3: Star-Ledger/Eagleton Poll, September 10–15
Poll 4: WCBS-TV News/New York Times Poll, September 20–26
Poll 5: Star-Ledger/Eagleton Poll, October 11–14
Poll 6: Star-Ledger/Eagleton Poll, October 27–30
Poll 7: Voter Research and Surveys Exit Poll, November 2

[a]The dependent variable used in Poll 1 is a dichotomous measure of Governor Florio's job approval, coded 1 for those who approved and 0 for those who did not.
[b]The dependent variable used in Poll 7 is a dichotomous measure of reported voter behavior, coded 1 for those reporting having voted for Florio and a 0 for those who chose Whitman.
*Significant at $p < .05$

was also being rewarded by those who believed New Jersey's economy was doing well, even after controlling for all factors present in table 6.1.

However, approval of Florio was not related to whether respondents thought taxes, jobs, or the economy were the most important issues in the upcoming election. Approval was also unrelated to whether respondents felt that crime was a very serious problem in New Jersey. These findings are interesting given Florio's tremendously unpopular tax increase in 1990, his much-discussed battle with the NRA over a ban on assault weapons, and the concern for the loss of jobs in New Jersey in recent years. In February support for Florio was influenced by presidential politics and evaluations of the state economy, as Chubb (1988), Carsey and Wright (1998), and others would predict. However, specific issues were not yet a part of how voters viewed Florio.

The coefficients operating on the dummy variables for liberal, Republican, and residing in the southern part of the state dropped just below the level of statistical significance for poll 1 when these additional variables were added. This development suggests that these relationships, reported as significant in table 6.1, were so in part because of a correlation with presidential approval and evaluations of New Jersey's economy. This suggests that Republicans per se had not yet developed any firm opposition to Florio that went beyond these evaluations. It also means that Florio did not hold an advantage among liberals or among residents of the southern part of the state beyond that produced by these two evaluations.

Poll 2 in table 6.2 demonstrates that voters began to respond to some of the themes the candidates expressed during the campaign. First, evaluations of Clinton and the New Jersey economy continued to remain important, operating in the expected direction. The salience of the tax issue began to increase, as the magnitude of the coefficient suggests, though it had not yet reached statistical significance. Yet by the end of the primaries, Florio's focus on crime had begun to pay off. Those who felt crime was the most important issue in the election were significantly more likely to support Florio than Whitman. Furthermore, among those who did not support Whitman, respondents saying crime was the most important issue were more likely to support Florio than to be undecided.

In contrast, the GOP message of attacking Florio on taxes and the economy had not enjoyed a similar response, possibly because of the contested GOP primary. Three candidates were busy debating their relative ability to defeat Florio in the general election, preventing a focus on Florio himself. At the same time, Florio ran unopposed, allowing him the advantage of focusing sooner on the issues he wanted to stress during the general election (Aldrich 1980a).

Polls 3 through 5 contain limited information regarding respondent views on issues and evaluations of the president and the economy. Poll 6 does not contain any of these variables. Thus, evaluating empirically the effects of the campaign on increasing the salience of these factors over the course of the campaign is difficult. The size of the coefficients in polls 2, 4, and 5 suggests that evaluations of Clinton became increasingly salient predictors of support for Florio. As members of the Clinton administration and the president himself made public appearances in New Jersey on Florio's behalf, support for Florio's reelection bid seems to have been increasingly tied to evaluations of Clinton. In contrast, the size of the coefficients in polls 2, 3, and 4 suggests that respondent evaluations of New Jersey's economy became less salient to voters during this period. To this point, Whitman had failed to link voters' evaluations of the economy with their feelings about Florio.

The salience of specific issues is critical to the broader argument being put forth in this book. Table 6.2 shows that specific issue positions had no direct effect on evaluations of Governor Florio in February and that by June, only the issue stressed by Florio himself—crime—had a significant effect on predicting candidate support. However, poll 7 in table 6.2 shows that specific issue positions structured voter behavior by election day.[14] Voters reporting that taxes or jobs were one of the two most important issues that mattered to them in the gubernatorial election were significantly more likely to have voted for Whitman. At the same time, those who stated that crime was one of the two most important issues remained significantly more likely to have voted for Florio. Thus, the issues stressed by both campaigns reached a significant level of salience among voters by election day. However, the size of the coefficient operating on the crime issue dropped from poll 2 to poll 7, possibly indicating a diminished effect in the face of the increasing salience of issues like taxes and jobs.

The limited nature of the data contained in polls 1 through 7 regarding respondent evaluations of President Clinton and the health of New Jersey's economy and the large gaps in the data regarding the issues considered important by voters make conclusions based on table 6.2 necessarily cautious. However, it does appear that voters responded to the themes stressed by Florio and Whitman over the course of the campaign. That the crime issue became salient before issues related to taxes, jobs, and the economy suggests that Florio's message reached voters first.

It is interesting that adding the issue position variables in poll 7 reduced the size of the coefficients on race, income, and whether a voter was Catholic to statistical insignificance. Thus, these sociodemographic divisions reported in table 6.1 for poll 7 appear to be in part an artifact of the more specific issue positions held by respondents. The result is that the anomaly of the effect of being Catholic uncovered in table 6.1 in poll 7 is eliminated. More important, the reduction in significance of race and income as predictors of voting behavior shows that once specific issue positions are included, Florio's traditional base of support among African-Americans and the expected support of lower-income groups failed to materialize.

A final analysis helps to illustrate the effects of the campaign on voter behavior in this election. Poll 7, the exit poll, asked voters when they made their decisions about for whom to vote. In analysis not shown, those waiting until the end of the campaign to make their decisions were significantly more likely to vote for Whitman over Florio, controlling for all factors included in tables 6.1 and 6.2. This finding holds true whether "late" deciders are defined as having made their decision in the final two weeks of the campaign or in the final few days.[15]

Table 6.3 illustrates which voters waited until the end of the campaign to decide whether to support Florio or Whitman. The dependent variable is a dichotomous measure coded 1 for those reporting having decided for whom to vote in the final two weeks of the campaign and a 0 otherwise. The independent variables are coded the same as for poll 7 in tables 6.1 and 6.2.

Table 6.3 shows that women, nonblacks, younger voters, those with less education, and political independents were overrepresented among the voters who waited until the last two weeks of the campaign to make up their minds.

TABLE 6.3.   Logit Model of Factors Predicting Which Voters Waited until the Final Two Weeks of the Campaign to Decide Whom to Support in the 1993 New Jersey Gubernatorial Election

Variable	Coefficient	T-Value	Significance
Constant	0.620	1.965	0.050
Female	0.525	4.499	0.000
Black	−0.485	−2.288	0.022
Age	−0.277	−4.533	0.000
Family income	−0.019	−0.403	0.687
Education level	−0.139	−2.466	0.014
Liberal	−0.220	−1.425	0.154
Conservative	−0.136	−0.973	0.331
Democrat	−0.580	−3.968	0.000
Republican	−0.581	−3.984	0.000
Catholic	−0.025	−0.200	0.841
Jew	−0.198	−0.740	0.459
Tax issue	0.091	0.737	0.461
Crime issue	−0.101	−0.638	0.524
Jobs issue	−0.030	−0.243	0.808

Chi-square = 75.17 ($p < 0.000$)
Percentage correctly predicted = 70%
$N = 1,526$

Source: Poll 7, exit poll conducted by Voter Surveys and Research in New Jersey in 1993.

These late deciders were significantly more likely to have voted for Whitman than for Florio, and figures 6.1 through 6.8 have highlighted these groups of voters as having moved to Whitman near the end of the campaign. Whitman's late push apparently persuaded enough of these voters that she was a credible alternative to Florio. That the specific issues voters felt were most important were not associated with when voters made up their minds suggests that these voters waited for some other reason. I suspect that it was their level of uncertainty regarding Whitman combined with their unfavorable evaluations of Florio. As a result, the real battle of the campaign, as mentioned earlier, concerned defining Whitman to the voters.

Table 6.4 illustrates voters' level of uncertainty regarding Whitman relative to Florio. Immediately after the June 8 primaries, poll 2 shows that only 63 percent of respondents could name Whitman as the GOP candidate for governor. More than half of respondents said they knew very little or nothing about her, and when asked whether they had a favorable or unfavorable impression of Whitman, 49 percent said they did not know. The corresponding figures for knowledge of and opinions about Florio show that voters felt they had much more information about him. This fact is not surprising since Florio was the incumbent governor and had been involved in a number of high-profile policy disputes. This finding illustrates, however, that even after the coverage given to the primary election, and after spending more than $2.5 million, many people did not yet know who Whitman was, and half felt they did not have enough information to form an opinion regarding her.

The remaining polls in table 6.4 show little shift in voters' level of information regarding Florio. However, voters became increasingly able to name Whitman as the GOP candidate and became more willing to form an impres-

TABLE 6.4. Percentage of Respondents Knowing and Holding Opinions of the Candidates in the 1993 New Jersey Gubernatorial Election

	Poll 2	Poll 3	Poll 4	Poll 5	Poll 6
Names Whitman as GOP candidate	63	57	—	72	—
Knows little or nothing about Whitman	56	47	—	—	—
Has no impression of Whitman	49	46	26	29	26
Names Florio as Democratic candidate	83	80	—	89	—
Knows little or nothing about Florio	18	14	—	—	—
Has no impression of Florio	19	18	5	16	14

Note: Poll 2: *Star-Ledger*/Eagleton Poll, June 11–17

Poll 3: *Star-Ledger*/Eagleton Poll, September 10–15

Poll 4: WCBS-TV News/*New York Times* Poll, September 20–26

Poll 5: *Star-Ledger*/Eagleton Poll, October 11–14

Poll 6: *Star-Ledger*/Eagleton Poll, October 27–30

sion. By late October, voters still knew more about Florio than Whitman, but the gap had decreased dramatically. Much of this chapter has been devoted to describing the nature of the information about Whitman that the candidates tried to provide to voters during the campaign.

To summarize, the 1993 gubernatorial campaign in New Jersey, like its counterpart in Virginia, witnessed dramatic shifts among voters in part because of the nature of the choice being offered to them. That choice was defined by who the candidates were and the themes they stressed during their campaigns. In this particular race, the battle was waged on two fronts. First, Florio and Whitman worked to stress particular issues on which they believed they held a comparative advantage. Second, underlying the debate on issues was a battle of personal characteristics designed by both candidates to influence whether voters would be willing to take a chance on an unknown challenger or would prefer to stick with Florio.

In this election, the campaigns were more responsive to each other than they had been in Virginia, possibly because of the different styles associated with the chief political consultants hired in New Jersey, James Carville and Ed Rollins. However, I also believe that the conflictual nature of the campaign and its focus on the character of the candidates in New Jersey required such an approach. Mary Sue Terry's initial strategy in Virginia was to ignore George Allen. Later, Allen remained focused on his issue agenda despite a round of attacks by Terry. In contrast, the Florio campaign set out early to define Whitman as unable to do the job of governor, trying to make her, rather than a particular policy, the central issue of the campaign. Florio took every opportunity to quickly respond to every questionable step Whitman took on the campaign trail. Florio's campaign even went so far as to send a crew with a video camera and a cellular phone to every public Whitman event that they knew about. This tactic allowed the Florio campaign to know what Whitman was doing and saying, letting them respond the same day if they chose. It was clear from the beginning that Whitman's camp would attack Florio's record, but this strategy shifted later in the race to attacks on Florio's credibility and fitness for the job. These personal attacks used by both sides in New Jersey forced each campaign to be highly responsive to the other.

Finally, as in Virginia, voters in New Jersey knew little about the GOP challenger. A critical component in both races was voters' level of uncertainty regarding these less well-known candidates. In Virginia, Allen ran an efficient, focused, and well-organized campaign, while his opponent refused to attack. This situation allowed Allen to overcome most of his early disadvantage by Labor Day. In contrast, Whitman ran a stumbling campaign plagued by internal disagreement and a lack of focus, while Florio attacked early and often. Whitman was able to overcome this disadvantage only in the final days of the campaign.

Overall, these two case studies reveal that the strategic thinking and actions of candidates and their campaign staffs conform nicely to the predictions of the heresthetic theory presented in chapters 2 and 3. Candidates battle to provide information to voters while trying to change the salience of various issues and cleavages within the electorate. The analysis of the opinion polls for each case study indicates that these efforts appear to meet with some success.

CHAPTER 7

Abortion and the 1990 Gubernatorial Elections

This and the next two chapters shift the focus of the analysis away from specific case studies toward a more general test of the theory of campaigns and voting behavior outlined in chapters 2 and 3. In so doing, attention also shifts from the dynamics of campaigns to the impact of campaign themes on election-day voting behavior. Each of these three chapters pools a set of election-day exit polls and adds to the data measures of the themes stressed by the candidates during their campaigns. While the analysis examines the final outcome of an election, readers should keep in mind that every one of these campaigns is characterized by the same sorts of dynamic events and strategic decision making that took place in Virginia and New Jersey in 1993.

This chapter examines the role played by the abortion issue in gubernatorial elections in 1990. I show that the salience of the abortion issue to voters as well as the importance of gender and being Catholic in predicting voting behavior responded to whether abortion was stressed during the campaign. I show that these responses varied depending on which candidate campaigned on abortion. I conclude with a discussion of the implications of these findings for the theory of electoral politics presented in this book.

Several scholars have written about the historical and contemporary nature of the politics of abortion in the United States.[1] According to Luker (1984), the abortion debate is not about facts but about their interpretation. Activists on both sides often point to the same historical and religious sources to support their claims. Ultimately, the discussion centers on definitions of personhood and the allocation of scarce resources. Is the embryo human? At what point does it become human? Does the embryo have rights? These questions relate to the relative value placed on the childbearing role of women and the rights of women to control their reproductive lives relative to the interests of the embryo. Preventing a pregnancy is contraception: killing a baby is murder. The abortion debate is about locating the status of the fetus on this continuum.

Prior to the 1960s, abortion was treated primarily as a medical issue in the United States. Efforts in the 1850s to restrict abortion were advocated on medical grounds and in practice did little to limit the number of abortions. Movements beginning in the 1950s to loosen legal restrictions were driven largely by the desire to bring the law into closer conformity with medical practice. Not until the 1960s in California were efforts to liberalize abortion laws linked with a broader conception of the rights of women. The efforts of those whom we would currently label prochoice[2] on abortion produced a major liberalization of abortion laws in California, signed into law by Governor Ronald Reagan. Many states witnessed similar struggles in the late 1960s and early 1970s. However, with its landmark decisions in *Roe v. Wade* and *Doe v. Bolton,* the U.S. Supreme Court fundamentally changed the nature of abortion politics.[3] With these two decisions, handed down in January 1973, the Supreme Court simultaneously activated a prolife mobilization (Staggenborg 1991) and rendered the debate over abortion policy a moot point at the state level just as it was becoming an important issue in many states. Sixteen years later, the Supreme Court put the abortion issue back on the state political agenda.

In the summer of 1989, in *Webster v. Reproductive Health Services,* the U.S. Supreme Court upheld a variety of legal restrictions on abortion imposed by the state of Missouri. While not overturning *Roe v. Wade,* the *Webster* decision clearly signaled the Court's willingness to accept state restrictions on abortion. Between 1973 and 1989, the abortion battle had been waged largely in the court system. With the *Webster* decision, however, the battle shifted almost instantly to state electoral politics (Cook, Jelen, and Wilcox 1992; Blanchard 1994; Staggenborg 1991). For the first time in sixteen years, political rhetoric on abortion from state-level politicians could be followed up by significant policy shifts.

Politicians and activists in many states responded swiftly to the *Webster* decision. Interest groups from both sides mobilized for gubernatorial elections being held in New Jersey and Virginia that fall, with the National Abortion Rights Action League (NARAL) providing resources and conducting focus groups to determine how best to frame the issue (Staggenborg 1991). As a result, the press devoted more coverage to abortion than to any other issue in these elections (Yale 1993). In Florida, Governor Bob Martinez called a special session of the state legislature to consider restrictions on abortion. In a number of other states, the abortion issue changed the electoral landscape (see Segers and Byrnes 1995; Cook, Jelen, and Wilcox 1992; Howell and Sims 1993).[4] However, the *Webster* decision did not force every subsequent gubernatorial election to be a referendum on abortion. Instead, it gave candidates an option: should they focus voter attention on the abortion issue?

To produce heresthetic change, candidates do not have to make an issue more or less important to voters in general. Instead, they simply need to change the salience of that issue for that specific election. By 1990, I assume that most voters who cared enough to consider casting their votes based on abortion had already formed an opinion on the issue. In other words, I do not expect that any candidates for governor converted a large number of voters' positions on abortion. From my review of the newspaper coverage, I saw that candidates did not attempt any significant relocation on the abortion issue during the course of their campaigns. Some attempted to downplay its importance, but most appeared to believe that holding what they thought might be a detrimental position on abortion was less damaging than publicly waffling on such an emotional issue.

In chapter 4, I presented a statistical model that tests for heresthetic change by including a multiplicative interaction term linking whether candidates stressed abortion during the campaign and individual attitudes on abortion. A more general model is presented in appendix B.[5] In this chapter, three types of multiplicative interaction terms were created. Whether abortion was stressed during the campaign was multiplied by attitudes on abortion, gender, and whether the respondent was Catholic.

The data analyzed in this chapter consist of exit polls conducted in thirty-four states and newly developed measures of campaign strategy. The measures of campaign strategy are based on a review of the newspaper coverage of each campaign from October 1 through election day (November 6). Table 7.1 reports that of the thirty-four elections, fourteen saw no candidates or other groups making substantial appeals to voters on the basis of abortion.[6] This fact does not mean that views on abortion should not or could not be predictors of individual voting behavior in those fourteen states. However, it does imply that the influence of abortion-related factors in these states occurred without a candidate, the media, or a major interest group focusing attention on the topic. In six states, abortion was stressed primarily by the Republican candidate, while in six other states, the Democrat was the only candidate focusing on the issue. The remainder of the states saw abortion stressed by either a third party (interest groups or the media) and/or by both candidates.

The traditional alignment between candidates of the two major political parties and views on abortion was clearly reversed in four of these thirty-four elections. The Republican candidates in Kansas, Minnesota, Nevada, and Pennsylvania were all substantially more prochoice than were their Democratic rivals.[7]

Before estimating a model that tests for heresthetic change on abortion, it is helpful to demonstrate that the salience of gender, religious affiliation, and attitudes on abortion did vary across these elections. Table 7.2 presents the results of a state-by-state analysis of voting behavior in these thirty-four gubernatorial elections. For each state, I estimated a model predicting voting behavior as a function of whether a respondent was female, Catholic, and held a prochoice or prolife position. Each variable was measured as a dummy variable.[8] The dependent variable for each model in table 7.2 is a dummy variable

TABLE 7.1.   States in Which Abortion Was Stressed and by Whom, 1990 Gubernatorial Elections

State	Democrat	Republican	Other	Both/All	No One
AL					X
AZ					X
AR		X			
CA	X				
CO		X			
FL				X	
GA					X
HI					X
ID					X
IL					X
IA	X				
KS[a]		X			
ME					X
MD					X
MA				X	
MI			X		
MN[a]			X		
NE					X
NV[a]		X			
NH	X				
NM					X
NY			X		
OH	X				
OK				X	
OR			X		
PA[a]		X			
RI					X
SC	X				
SD					X
TN		X			
TX				X	
VT					X
WI	X				
WY					X

[a]Republican was prochoice, Democrat was prolife.

coded as 1 if the respondent indicated voting for the Democratic candidate for governor and 0 otherwise. Logit is used to estimate the models.

Table 7.2 shows that voters' positions on abortion were consistently more salient predictors of voting for the Democratic candidate than were voters' gender or Catholicism. Fully 60 percent of the coefficients operating on abortion

TABLE 7.2. Logit Coefficients Measuring Effects of Gender, Religion, and Position on Abortion on the Probability of Voting for Democratic Gubernatorial Candidate, 1990

State	Female	Catholic	Prochoice	Prolife
AL	.0337	.4718	.1724	−.4158*
AZ	.1805	.4112*	.2688*	−1.060*
AR	.1874	.0945	.4916*	−.2236
CA	.5501*	.1242	.6057*	−.6176*
CO	.1516	.2019	.3528*	−.3994*
FL	−.0469	−.0307	1.0085*	−.2763
GA	.0483	.1258	.1075	−.8041*
HI	.0387	−.1088	−.1863	−.3915*
ID	.2612*	.2552	.8022*	−.7259*
IL	−.1751*	.0830	.2392*	.0565
IA	−.1558	−.3442*	.5136*	−.9446*
KS[a]	−.1228	.1706	−.8000*	.9884*
ME	−.0131	.3517*	.1339	.0254
MD	.0599	−.0166	.5081*	−.1917
MA	−.0954	.4514*	−.3108*	.1481
MI	.2912*	.1583	.6147	−.6331
MN[a]	−.1755	.0859	−.5148*	.9169
NE	−.2452*	−.2790	.2341	−.2693
NV[a]	.1836	−.1241	−.6696*	.4775*
NH	.0858	−.0066	.8492*	−.4565
NM	.1226	.5597	−.1382	−.2911
NY	.3515*	.2253*	.4854*	−.0786
OH	.0965	−.0015	.7824*	−.5644*
OK	.1575	−.0020	.7980*	−.5383*
OR	.6040*	−.0539	.8388*	−.7273*
PA[a]	−.1474	.2889*	−1.1574*	.9448*
RI	.0075	.2375*	.2744*	−.1366
SC	−.0872	.0898	.5385*	−.1072
SD	−.2547	−.0007	.3435	.0877
TN	.2167	.1214	.0978	−.5119*
TX	.5677*	.3504*	.8815*	−.6051*
VT	.3257*	.1479	.6597*	.1018
WI	.0704	−.2367*	.9454*	−.0631
WY	−.2100	−.1578	.0454	.5695*

Note: Controlling for party identification, race, income, and religion

[a]Republican was prochoice, Democrat was prolife.

*p < .05

attitudes are statistically significant, while only 26 percent of the coefficients for gender and being Catholic are significant. Furthermore, four of the eighteen significant coefficients on gender and Catholicism are unexpectedly negative. Thus, table 7.2 shows that the salience of these factors in predicting voting behavior varied across these elections.[9]

Table 7.2 also shows that prochoice and prolife supporters successfully recognized and responded to the reversal of traditional party positions on abortion adopted by candidates in Kansas, Minnesota, Nevada, and Pennsylvania.[10] Abortion was stressed during the campaign in each of these four states, which may be why voters had sufficient information with which to determine their preferred candidate on abortion despite the reversal of the traditional party-label cue.

Stonecash (1989) argues that a more polarized choice between gubernatorial candidates produces a more polarized electorate along demographic lines. My theory predicts a somewhat similar result: as candidates focus on a particular issue, demographic characteristics associated with that issue should become more salient to voters and thus stronger predictors of their voting behavior. I examine this hypothesis by considering the influence of gender and Catholicism on voting behavior and its response to abortion being stressed during the campaign.

The presence of those four states in which the traditional party positions on abortion taken by candidates are reversed makes the analysis more interesting but more complicated. Because this chapter focuses on abortion, the dependent variable for the remainder of the analysis is the vote choice of each individual voter, coded 1 if the respondent reported voting for the prochoice candidate and 0 otherwise. Except in those four reversal states, the Democratic candidates are treated as prochoice relative to their Republican opponents.

The individual-level independent variables included in this analysis are party identification, race, gender, religious affiliation, family income, urbanity of residence, presidential approval, evaluations of the state economy, and voters' positions on abortion. Party identification is measured using two dummy variables: one indicating whether the voter shares the party identification of the prochoice candidate and one showing whether the voter identifies with the party of the prolife candidate. Race is measured with a dummy variable indicating whether the voter is African-American. Gender is measured using a dummy variable indicating whether the voter is female. Religious affiliation is measured with two dummy variables: one indicating whether a person is Catholic and the other reporting whether the person is Jewish.[11] Family income and urbanity of residence are categorical variables. Income ranges from 1 to 5, with higher values indicating higher income categories. Urbanity ranges from 1 to 6, with higher values indicating a less urban residence. Evaluations of President Bush are based on the question "Do you approve or disapprove of the way

George Bush is handling his job as president?" measured with a dummy variable coded 1 if the voter disapproved. A second dummy indicates whether the voter believed the state economy was in good condition. It is coded as 1 if the voter responded "Excellent" or "Good" to the question, "These days, do you think the condition of [name of state's] economy is: excellent, good, not so good, or poor?"

A voter's position on abortion is determined by their response to the question "Which of these statements comes CLOSEST to your view about abortion? (1) It should be legal in all circumstances, (2) It should be legal only in some circumstances, (3) It should not be legal in any circumstances." Respondents selecting statement 1 or 3 were coded as being prochoice or prolife, respectively. The complexity of attitudes on abortion certainly are not fully captured by a question with such limited possible responses (Cook, Jelen, and Wilcox 1992). However, these two dummy variables do capture those respondents who hold contrasting views on abortion.

To compensate for the four states with candidates whose party positions on abortion are reversed, I include a dummy variable for those four reversal states and interaction terms between it and family income; urbanity of residence; whether the voter is black, Catholic, Jewish, or female; and whether the voter disapproves of President Bush.

At the election level, I include two indicators for whether either candidate in a particular race is an incumbent. One is coded as a 1 if the prochoice candidate running is an incumbent and 0 otherwise. The other is coded similarly for the prolife candidate. I also include measures of candidate spending, adjusted for population and inflation. Because the effect of campaign spending is expected to vary as a function of the incumbency status of the candidates, I include additional interaction terms created by multiplying the incumbency and spending variables together.[12]

The influence of two of the individual-level variables likely depends on the incumbency status of the candidates running. Voter evaluations of the state economy should be particularly important when an incumbent is running for reelection, and disapproval of President Bush, while likely to reflect on all Republican candidates, may be more important when a Republican incumbent is running. Thus, interaction terms are included to account for these potential relationships as well.

Finally, I use a series of dummy variables to record whether abortion was stressed during each campaign and, if so, by whom. I then include a series of interaction terms based on multiplying these dummy variables by the abortion attitude, gender, and Catholic variables outlined previously. The coefficient estimates operating on these interaction terms provide the tests of the heresthetic argument.

As noted in chapter 4, the nature of the dependent variable suggests using a logit or probit model, and logit is used here. Readers should also remember that the clustered nature of the data produced from pooling several polls together into a single data set makes traditional estimates of coefficient standard errors suspect. Thus, robust standard errors based on Huber (1967) and White (1980) are estimated that account for this clustering.[13]

Table 7.3 demonstrates the salience of gender, being Catholic, and the views held by voters on the abortion issue for the elections covered in this analysis.[14] This model does not include any measure of whether the abortion issue was stressed. The cell entries report the difference in the predicted probability of voting for the prochoice candidate for each comparison. These gaps represent the deviation from a base probability of voting for the prochoice candidate of .5 for each individual characteristic. For example, assuming that men have a .5 probability of voting for the prochoice candidate, women would have a predicted probability of .518 of voting for the prochoice candidate.[15]

Table 7.3 shows that women were slightly more likely to vote for the prochoice candidate than were men. Catholics were also somewhat more likely to support the prochoice candidate (Democrat) than were non-Catholics (excluding Jews), but this difference was not statistically significant. Finally, table 7.3 shows that prochoice voters were almost 10 percentage points more likely to have voted for the prochoice candidate than were voters holding an intermediate view on abortion. Similarly, prolife voters were 10 percentage points less likely to vote for the prochoice candidate than were voters in the middle on abortion. Combined, the gap between prochoice and prolife voters in the predicted probability that each would vote for the prochoice candidate for governor is nearly 20 percentage points. Thus, before any controls for whether the abortion issue is stressed are included, there is a slight but significant gender

TABLE 7.3.   Difference in the Probability of Voting for the Prochoice Gubernatorial Candidate, 1990

	Women vs. Men	Catholics vs. Non-Catholics	Prochoice vs. Intermediate	Prolife vs. Intermediate
Gaps in predicted probability	.018*	.022	.096***	−.100***

Note: Entries are deviations in the predicted probability of supporting the prochoice candidate away from a base probability of .5. The full model on which these entries are based is included in appendix C. This table does not present findings for those four elections in which the candidates' traditional partisan positions on abortion were reversed. However, the findings presented are based on models that do include those four elections.

*Underlying coefficient significant at $p < .1$
**Underlying coefficient significant at $p < .05$
***Underlying coefficient significant at $p < .01$

gap, Catholics did not remain significantly more loyal to the Democratic pro-choice candidates than did non-Catholics, and voters' views on abortion dramatically influenced which candidate they supported.

Table 7.4 expands the analysis to explore how the salience of these factors responded to whether anyone stressed the abortion issue in these gubernatorial campaigns.[16] This analysis is done by including a dummy variable coded 1 if anyone stressed abortion during the campaign and a series of interaction terms—whether abortion was stressed multiplied by the gender, Catholic, and abortion-attitude variables. The coefficients operating on these interaction terms measure the change in the salience of being female, Catholic, prochoice, or prolife and its significance.

Table 7.4 shows that when abortion was not stressed, the gap between men and women dropped to near zero and was not statistically significant. However, in elections where abortion was stressed, women were significantly more likely to vote for the prochoice candidate than were men. The difference amounts to almost 4 percentage points. Thus, it appears that the salience of gender responded significantly when the abortion issue was stressed.

Table 7.4 shows that the response of Catholics was different. When abortion was not stressed, Catholics were not significantly more or less likely to

TABLE 7.4.   Abortion Issue and Difference in the Probability of Voting for the Prochoice Gubernatorial Candidate, 1990

	Women vs. Men	Catholics vs. Non-Catholics	Prochoice vs. Intermediate	Prolife vs. Intermediate
Gap in predicted probability when not stressed	−.006	.009	.034*	−.073***
Gap in predicted probability when stressed[a]	.037**	.030	.131***	−.118***
Change in gap (based on the interaction term)	.043**	.021	.090***	−.045

Note: Entries are deviations in the predicted probability of supporting the prochoice candidate away from a base probability of .5. The full model on which these entries are based is included in appendix C. This table does not present findings for those four elections in which the candidates' traditional partisan positions on abortion were reversed. However, the findings presented are based on models that do include those four elections.

[a]Significance levels computed using process described by Jaccard, Turrisi, and Wan (1990, 25–28)

*Underlying coefficient significant at $p < .1$

**Underlying coefficient significant at $p < .05$

***Underlying coefficient significant at $p < .01$

support the prochoice candidate for governor. When abortion was stressed, Catholics were about 3 percentage points more likely to support the prochoice Democratic candidate, but again, this difference is not statistically significant. Thus, even when abortion was a central part of a gubernatorial campaign, the salience of being Catholic was not significantly altered.

Voters' attitudes on abortion significantly influenced their voting behavior even in elections in which abortion was not stressed. However, the magnitude of the effect reported in table 7.4 was reduced compared to table 7.3. Table 7.4 shows that prochoice voters were 3.4 percentage points more likely to vote for the Democratic candidate than were those voters in the middle on abortion when the abortion issue was not stressed during the campaign. Prolife voters remained significantly less likely to support the prochoice Democrat in these races, being more than 7 percentage points less likely to vote for the prochoice candidate than were voters holding the middle position on abortion. Together, the gap in the predicted voting behavior of prochoice and prolife voters was nearly 11 percentage points even in elections when the abortion issue was not a part of the campaign. This figure is about half the size of the predicted gap between prolife and prochoice voters reported in table 7.3.

When the abortion issue was stressed, table 7.4 shows that prochoice voters were about 13 percentage points more likely to vote for the prochoice candidate than were voters holding intermediate views on abortion. This marks an increase of nearly 10 percentage points in the gap in the predicted probability of voting for the prochoice candidate between prochoice and intermediate voters when abortion was stressed. The response of prolife voters was less dramatic and did not quite reach statistical significance. When abortion was stressed, prolife voters were about 12 percentage points less likely to vote for the prochoice Democrat than were voters holding the middle position on abortion. That figure represents a change of 4.5 percentage points from when abortion was not stressed during the campaign. Overall, the gap between prochoice and prolife voters in the predicted probability of which candidate they supported increased from about 11 percent when abortion was not stressed to a substantial 25 percentage points when the abortion issue became a prominent part of the campaign.

Both prochoice and prolife voters responded to appeals made on the basis of the abortion issue, but the difference in the response of each group is worth noting. When abortion was not stressed, both prochoice and prolife voters continued to allow their views on abortion to structure their voting behavior. However, the larger gap for prolife voters reported in table 7.4 suggests that their views on abortion may have been more salient to them than to their prochoice counterparts when the issue was not stressed. In contrast, when abortion was stressed, prochoice voters responded much more dramatically than did prolife voters. In fact, the size of the gap between prochoice voters and those with an intermediate view on abortion surpassed the size of the gap for prolife voters when abortion was stressed. Thus, about 71 percent of the increase in the gap between prochoice and prolife voters that occurred when abortion was stressed resulted from the behavior of prochoice voters. Thus, it appears that in the wake of the 1989 *Webster* decision, prochoice voters were much more volatile regarding the influence their views on abortion had on their voting behavior than were prolife voters.

Without knowing who stressed the issue, table 7.4 shows that voters in 1990 appeared to respond when abortion was a visible part of the race for governor. Next, I explore whether voters responded differently to which candidate stressed abortion during the campaign.

Table 7.5 reports the impact of whether the prochoice or the prolife candidate stressed abortion during the campaign. Looking first at the gender gap, it again seems clear that when neither candidate stressed abortion, the probability that women voted for the prochoice candidate was virtually identical to the probability that men voted for the prochoice candidate. The predicted probabilities for each group differ by less than a single percentage point, which is

TABLE 7.5.   Candidates' Stressing of Abortion Issue and Difference in the Probability of Voting for the Prochoice Gubernatorial Candidate, 1990

	Women vs. Men	Catholics vs. Non-Catholics	Prochoice vs. Intermediate	Prolife vs. Intermediate
Gap in predicted probability when not stressed	.003	.013	.067***	−.101***
Gap in predicted probability when stressed by prochoice[a]	.032	.008	.156***	−.115***
Change in gap	.029	−.005	.089***	−.014
Gap in predicted probability when stressed by prolife[a]	.024	.049*	.015	−.085***
Change in gap	.021	.036	−.052	.016

Note: Entries are deviations in the predicted probability of supporting the prochoice candidate away from a base probability of .5. The full model on which these entries are based is included in appendix C. This table does not present findings for those four elections in which the candidates' traditional partisan positions on abortion were reversed. However, the findings presented are based on models that do include those four elections.

[a]Significance levels computed using process described by Jaccard, Turrisi, and Wan (1990, 25–28)
*Underlying coefficient significant at $p < .1$
**Underlying coefficient significant at $p < .05$
***Underlying coefficient significant at $p < .01$

not statistically significant. When either the prochoice or the prolife candidate alone stressed the abortion issue, the gap between men and women in the probability of voting for the prochoice candidate increased to about 3 percentage points, but neither gap by itself achieved statistical significance. When both candidates stressed abortion during their campaigns, however, the gap between women and men in the probability of supporting the prochoice candidate increased to more than 5 percentage points. Thus, the significant gap between men and women uncovered in table 7.4 when abortion was stressed by anyone appears to be at least in part dependent on both candidates stressing the issue.

The behavior of Catholics differs. When neither candidate stressed abortion, there remains no significant gap between Catholics and non-Catholics regarding their predicted probability of voting for the prochoice Democrat. When the prochoice Democrat stressed abortion, there was virtually no differences in the responses of Catholics and non-Catholics. However, when the prolife candidate stressed abortion, the gap between Catholics and non-Catholics increased to a statistically significant 5 percentage points. This suggests that prolife Republicans had little success in attracting Catholic support when they stressed abortion as part of their campaigns and in fact may have pushed Catholics away. The net effect when both candidates stressed abortion is a slight increase in the gap between the predicted probabilities of Catholics and non-Catholics voting for the prochoice Democrat. Table 7.5 suggests that the abortion issue is essentially a wash regarding the response of Catholics when both a prochoice Democrat and a prolife Republican run and stress their stands on abortion. I will return to this question in chapter 9.

Table 7.5 shows that prochoice candidates who stressed abortion mobilized significant support among prochoice voters. As has been the pattern, both prochoice and prolife voters differ significantly from voters in the middle regarding the predicted probability of supporting a prochoice Democrat when the issue is not stressed by either candidate. However, when the prochoice candidate stresses the abortion issue, the gap between prochoice voters and voters holding intermediate views on abortion increased from nearly 7 to almost 16 percentage points. In an interesting contrast, prolife voters do not become significantly less likely to support the prochoice candidate when that candidate alone stressed abortion during the campaign. In these elections, prochoice candidates apparently increased the salience of the abortion issue for their supporters without mobilizing additional opposition among prolife voters.

When prolife Republican candidates stressed abortion, the gap between prochoice voters and intermediate voters declined to statistical insignificance. However, the magnitude of the shift itself, though substantively large at 5 percentage points, was itself not statistically significant. At the same time, the gap between prolife voters and voters holding an intermediate position on abortion also decreased slightly when the prolife candidate stressed abortion. In this case, the gap remained significant, while the magnitude of the actual shift was not. In short, prolife candidates did not increase the salience of abortion for prochoice or prolife voters when these candidates alone stressed it as part of their campaign. Rather, the salience appears to have diminished somewhat, although the observed changes were not statistically significant. The dampening effects of the prolife candidate stressing abortion combined with the only response to prochoice candidates' focusing on abortion coming from prochoice voters to produce a limited response when both candidates stressed abortion.

The findings in table 7.5 do not tell the whole story of the relationship between voting behavior and abortion being stressed as part of the campaign. Table 7.6 reports the shift in the base probability of voting for the prochoice candidate away from .5 when either candidate stressed abortion. These shifts are based only on the shift in the constant term captured by the dummy variables measuring whether abortion was stressed by either candidate included in the same model that produced table 7.5.

Again, the effects are dramatic. The direct effect of prochoice candidates stressing abortion on the probability that voters will support them is a reduction in that probability of 11 percentage points.. In contrast, when the prolife candidate stressed abortion, the probability that voters would support the prochoice candidate increased by approximately 13 percentage points. In regression terms, these shifts constitute a shift in the intercept, or constant, compared

TABLE 7.6. Candidates' Stressing of Abortion Issue and Difference in the Base Probability of Voting for the Prochoice Gubernatorial Candidate, 1990

	Abortion Not Stressed	Abortion Stressed by Prochoice Candidate	Abortion Stressed by Prolife Candidate
Probability of voting for the prochoice candidate	.5	.388	.63
Change in predicted probability from .5 base		−.112***	.13***

Note: This table includes all thirty-four elections because it is based only on the dummy variables for whether the prochoice or prolife candidate stressed the issue. The inclusion of the four reversal states does not alter these findings or complicate their presentation because this table does not include any of the interaction terms.

Entries are deviations in the predicted probability of supporting the prochoice candidate away from a base probability of .5. The full model on which these entries are based is included in appendix C.

*Underlying coefficient significant at $p < .1$

**Underlying coefficient significant at $p < .05$

***Underlying coefficient significant at $p < .01$

to when neither candidate stressed abortion. Intercept shifts are difficult to interpret because they represent the combined behavior of those individuals who make up the excluded categories for all the dummy variables in the model, a short list of which includes men, nonblacks, non-Catholics, voters with moderate views on abortion, nonpartisans, and races that lack incumbents. Since all of these factors are captured in the intercept term, it is difficult to tell which element is responsible for the shift when abortion is stressed compared to when it is not. There are two related interpretations.

First, most of those groups that make up the excluded categories are those not expected to respond dramatically to appeals made based on abortion. By definition, they are political independents who hold middle-of-the-road views on abortion. It may be that strong appeals made based on abortion push some of these moderates away from a candidate making the appeal. It may be that such candidates appear too extreme and/or hard-line on the abortion issue to attract the support of moderates. If true, it might mean that a focus on abortion is a losing strategy for candidates on either side of this issue.

The second interpretation concerns the larger context within which candidates find themselves when deciding whether to stress abortion as part of their campaign. Abortion is an emotional and divisive political issue that many candidates would probably like to avoid if they could. In particular, widely popular candidates have little reason to campaign on any issue, abortion or otherwise, that is particularly divisive among voters. Candidates going into a campaign as strong favorites with big leads may have little to gain—and maybe something to lose—by campaigning on an issue like abortion. Conversely, candidates entering their races as clear underdogs might use an emotional issue like abortion to try to cut into their opponents' big leads. Finally, candidates in close elections may also be more willing to focus on an issue like abortion in an attempt to mobilize just enough voters to win. If such is the case, then the relationships reported in table 7.6 may be an artifact of the candidates' strategic decision making. If candidates with big leads avoid talking about abortion while only those in close races or who are far behind risk focusing on such a divisive issue, and if candidates with big early leads tend to win by larger margins than candidates who do not start with big leads, then the differences in probabilities reported in table 7.6 based on intercept shifts result from candidates' decisions, not necessarily voters' reactions to those themes. Thus, stressing abortion may not hurt a particular candidate with intermediate voters. Rather, candidates who believe they cannot otherwise win may stress abortion.

It is likely that both phenomena combine to produce the effects shown in table 7.6. Sorting out their relative magnitudes with only two coefficients to examine is problematic. However, my reading of the newspaper coverage of these elections, along with the analysis of the 1993 gubernatorial election in Virginia reported in chapter 5, supports the idea that candidates with comfortable leads avoid divisive issues like abortion. For example, Pennsylvania incumbent Robert Casey entered the 1990 election as the clear favorite. He maintained a broad base of support in public-opinion polls and ran as a safe incumbent would be expected to—avoiding controversy and ignoring his opponent. Casey is pro-life, but he made no effort to publicize that fact. His little-known opponent was Barbara Hafer, a prochoice Republican who had served as state auditor general. She made abortion a major part of her campaign in an effort to pull away pro-choice Democrats and independents who supported Casey. Although she was soundly defeated, table 7.2 shows that prochoice and prolife voters responded to the views held by the two candidates. Still, the overall outcome of the race was a smashing victory for Casey. Casey did not stress abortion because he did not have to. Hafer stressed abortion because she needed a wedge issue with the potential to crack Casey's broad base of support.

For another example, the incumbent running for reelection in Kansas in 1990, Mike Hayden, was anything but safe. He presided over a property-tax revision that caused increases for many voters, and he had also failed to return to voters a windfall in state taxes after the 1986 reform of the federal tax system. He ran against a populist former Republican now running as a Democrat, Joan Finney. Hayden was prochoice, and Finney was prolife. Hayden stressed abortion in part to try to cut into Finney's populist base of support and in part to try to divert attention away from his record on taxes. This race ended up much closer than the one in Pennsylvania, but again, the candidate who stressed abortion lost.

In both of these examples, abortion was selected as a campaign issue almost as a last resort. Candidates who see themselves losing without appealing to abortion do so, and they are successful at raising the salience of the issue and attracting supporters of their position. In fact, because prochoice voters outnumbered prolife voters in both Pennsylvania and Kansas, Hafer and Hayden probably did better than they would have had they not campaigned on abortion. However, the dummy variable measuring whether the prochoice candidate stressed abortion captures the overall failure of candidates like these two to win, which is what produces in large part the negative effects found in table 7.6.

Finally, I will present some discussion of the behavior of gender and Catholic/non-Catholic divisions in those four elections in which the Democratic candidates took the prolife position on abortion while their GOP counterparts were prochoice. First, table 7.1 shows that in each of these four states, someone stressed abortion as part of the campaign. However, the prolife Democrat never did so. This lack of variation limits assessment of the impact of stressing abortion in these four states. The only measures of the change in the level of salience of gender and Catholicism in these four states that can be estimated are those relating to whether the prochoice Republican stressed abortion. As table 7.1 reports, the prochoice Republican campaigned on abortion in three of these four states, Kansas, Nevada, and Pennsylvania. Only in Minnesota did the prochoice GOP nominee choose not to focus on abortion. Thus, the comparisons of the salience of gender and being Catholic in these four states as it responds to whether the prochoice candidate stressed abortion depend on comparing Kansas, Nevada, and Pennsylvania to Minnesota.

Table C1 in appendix C shows that the probability of Catholics and non-Catholics voting for the prochoice candidate differed significantly in the three states where the prochoice Republican stressed abortion, with Catholics being significantly less likely to support that candidate. In these circumstances, Catholics were not caught between their traditional support for the Democratic Party and their religion's official stance against abortion. This situation may explain the significant move away from prochoice Republicans who campaigned on abortion.

Women were more likely to vote for the prochoice Republican candidate when abortion was not stressed (in Minnesota). However, in the three states where the prochoice GOP candidates did stress abortion, women were significantly less likely to vote for them. This result appears to be an artifact produced by the overwhelming popularity of the prolife Democratic incumbent running in Pennsylvania. This suspicion is supported by noting that when Pennsylvania is dropped from the analysis, the relationship between gender and voting for the prochoice GOP candidate in the two remaining states, Kansas and Nevada, becomes insignificant.

Table 7.2 illustrates that in each of these races, prochoice and prolife voters responded correctly to the reversed positions on abortion advocated by the candidates. In seven out of eight cases, prolife and prochoice voters' responses marked a statistically significant difference between themselves and voters holding intermediate views. Since abortion was stressed by someone in each of these elections, it seems reasonable to assume that the response of voters in these four races resulted at least in part from the information provided during the campaign. Furthermore, tables 7.4 and 7.5 demonstrate that in the other thirty elections, prochoice and prolife voters responded when the abortion issue was stressed.

Overall, the findings presented in this chapter lend support to a theory of electoral politics that focuses on the role campaigns play in producing heresthetic change within the electorate. The salience to voters of two demographic cleavages, gender and religion, and an issue-based cleavage, abortion attitudes, varies as a function of whether the abortion issue was a prominent part of the campaign. Furthermore, as much as two-thirds of the gap in the probability that prochoice and prolife voters would vote for the prochoice candidate can be attributed to whether abortion was stressed.

Comparing table 7.3 to tables 7.4 and 7.5 suggests that the gender gap in gubernatorial voting in these elections only appeared in a significant way when the abortion issue was stressed. Yet even with attitudes on abortion controlled, the basic gender cleavage responded to appeals on abortion. This finding suggests that abortion may lie on a similar dimension to other issues related to gender. Those issues may cluster into a more general dimension and/or campaign strategy designed to tap a gender cleavage captured in these models simply by knowing whether abortion is part of the campaign. In other words, because controlling for individual-level attitudes on abortion does not eliminate the response of gender to appeals based on abortion, either abortion appeals are tapping a more general gender-based dimension than just attitudes on abortion, or additional issues coexist with abortion as part of a broader gender-based campaign strategy. Such a situation might be expected to mobilize a response by women (or men) beyond simply how they feel about abortion. Because the gender gap does not appear when abortion is not stressed, it may be that other issues that are capable of contributing to a gender gap are not commonly stressed without also stressing abortion.

The responses of prochoice and prolife voters to varying sets of appeals on abortion are quite interesting. Table 7.4 shows that when someone stresses abortion, both prochoice and prolife voters respond, though the response is clearly more dramatic for prochoice voters. However, table 7.5 showed that when the prochoice candidate stressed abortion, only prochoice voters responded. At the same time, when the prolife candidate stressed the issue, neither prochoice nor prolife voters responded in a statistically significant way. In addition, when abortion was not stressed, the predicted voting behavior of prolife voters differed more from that of those in the middle on abortion than did the behavior of prochoice voters. This finding suggests that prolife voters may be more stable than are prochoice voters in the commitment to voting for like-minded candidates. Prolife voters may more closely fit the definition of single-issue voters than voters holding prochoice views on abortion, even for a set of elections held in the wake of the *Webster* decision. Prochoice voters were activated by appeals on the abortion issue, and it is interesting that prochoice candidates were able to increase the salience of abortion for prochoice voters without producing a significant response among their prolife counterparts.

Again, this analysis of the abortion issue in 1990 provides support for the theory of heresthetic change guiding this book. The salience of individual-level cleavages related to abortion changed when abortion was a prominent part of the informational context within which voters found themselves. Voters responded correctly when the traditional party positions on abortion were reversed for the gubernatorial candidates in four of these elections. In addition, evidence reported in table 7.6 is consistent with the idea that the choice of whether to stress the abortion issue was a strategic decision made by candidates operating under different conditions at the beginning of their campaigns.

CHAPTER 8

Presidential Approval in Gubernatorial Elections

In chapter 1, I noted that there is some disagreement regarding the factors that predict voting behavior in gubernatorial elections. In particular, there remains debate regarding the influence of national politics on how voters cast their ballots for the governorship. While the disagreements often center on empirical issues (see the interchange between Carsey and Wright 1998 and Atkeson and Partin 1998), the question is one of theoretical importance. Political parties provide voters with an important informational cue that links candidates across different political offices. Voters attribute some functional responsibility to candidates holding different offices (Carsey and Wright 1998), suggesting a degree of independence between candidates for governor and their national party leaders. However, the centrality of presidential politics in defining what the two political parties represent cannot be denied. As a result, voters' evaluations of the president should influence how voters evaluate candidates for lower political offices. The analysis presented in this chapter confirms this prediction. However, the real question to be answered in this short chapter is whether the impact of presidential politics varies as a function of the campaigns gubernatorial candidates wage.

Stein (1990) finds that voters do not hold sitting governors accountable for states' economic health unless those governors are of the same party as the sitting president. Peltzman (1987) argues that voters blame or reward candidates from the president's party rather than governors for economic conditions.

In contrast, Howell and Vanderleeuw (1990) and Carsey and Wright (1998) report that how voters evaluate the health of their state's economy influences how they vote in gubernatorial elections and/or how they evaluate gubernatorial job performance independent of presidential politics. Chubb (1988) also notes that state-level changes in the economy significantly impact voting in gubernatorial elections, although in the same study, he reports a much stronger effect for changes in the national economy. Holbrook-Provow (1987) also finds a strong effect on gubernatorial elections resulting from changes in the national economy. Yet Howell and Vanderleeuw do not find an effect of evaluations of the national economy on gubernatorial job performance evaluations. Kenney (1983) finds no consistent relationship between state-level changes in unemployment and the cost of living and gubernatorial voting.

A number of studies indicate that gubernatorial elections are becoming increasingly independent of presidential politics. The correlation between state-level presidential voting returns and gubernatorial voting returns has declined from 1900 to 1969, both in the South and elsewhere (Turett 1971). More recent studies (Tompkins 1984, 1988; Chubb 1988; Jewell and Olson 1988) find a continued decline in the importance of presidential coattails, and Cohen (1983) links gubernatorial popularity rather than presidential popularity to evaluations of state government. Still, Simon (1989) shows that presidential popularity particularly influences the voting behavior of independents and those who lean toward a particular party in gubernatorial elections.

The central question that emerges out of this mix of contrasting findings remains the degree to which gubernatorial elections depend on state-specific versus national factors. Typically, the question becomes to what degree gubernatorial politics is linked with presidential politics in terms of party labels. Stein (1990) and Carsey and Wright (1998) find that such a link exists. There appears to be no way to completely isolate gubernatorial elections from the influence of national politics. Yet these findings do not deny the potential importance of state-specific factors. More relevant for the study presented here, these studies, by their designs, assume that the degree to which gubernatorial voting behavior responds to national presidential politics is constant across elections.

In this chapter, I explore the relationship between evaluations of presidential performance and voting behavior in gubernatorial elections using exit-poll data from twenty-nine states that held gubernatorial elections in both 1990 and 1994.[1] There are more than seventy-seven thousand usable respondents from the fifty-eight election-day exit polls included in this analysis. To my knowledge, this is the single largest set of data mobilized to explore the effect of presidential approval on voting for governor. In that regard, the results of this analysis should contribute to settling the disagreement surrounding this question.

The key feature of this chapter, however, is in identifying voter responses to the changing nature of campaigns regarding the role played by presidential politics. The elections held in 1990 and 1994 took place in the middle of the first terms of the presidential administrations of George Bush and Bill Clinton, respectively. However, these two years witnessed a distinct contrast in the extent to which presidential evaluations were brought into gubernatorial campaigns.

Heading into the 1990 election season, President Bush had enjoyed a reasonably popular first two years in office. The Berlin Wall had come down, and the Cold War as the world had known it for forty-five years had ended. The domestic economy was not expanding at the time, though widespread belief in an economic recession also had not taken hold. There were no major domestic achievements toward which the Bush administration could point. Overall, the domestic political environment at the beginning of 1990 could be characterized as reasonably stable.

Two important events took place in the late summer of 1990, however, that defined the Bush presidency. However, it is not clear that either of these events played a major role in the 1990 elections, particularly those for governorships. First, in August 1990, Iraq invaded Kuwait, prompting the United States to send nearly two hundred thousand troops to Saudi Arabia and into the Persian Gulf by election day, November 6.[2] However, the bulk of the troop buildup, the United Nations resolution authorizing the use of force, the resulting political debate in Congress over the prospect of a massive use of military force, the war itself, and the surge in popularity enjoyed by Bush following the war all took place after the 1990 elections. In the early weeks of the military buildup before the November election, public opinion was split, and elected officials were divided on the subject. The prospect of Iraqi control of the Persian Gulf alarmed most people, but many felt equally uneasy about direct military involvement in the distant and politically unstable Middle East. The action raised the public's level of attention, but a solid public opinion had not yet formed. Add to this situation the fact that the issue concerned foreign policy, and it is obvious why most gubernatorial candidates avoided the topic entirely during their campaigns.

The second event of the late summer occurred when President Bush, along with congressional leaders from both parties, announced in September a budget deal that involved both a series of spending cuts and a number of tax increases. With Bush's "Read my lips—no new taxes" campaign pledge still ringing in the public's ears, this turnaround drew a lot of attention. However, because leaders of both parties were involved, it was difficult for Democrats to make Bush's support of this deal a campaign issue in 1990. Some gubernatorial candidates pointed to the deal, but most did not make it a part of their election campaigns. With the bipartisan support for the budget agreement, the uncertainty of Bush's political future as it related to the crisis in the Middle East, and the fact that the dominant issues defining the Bush presidency to date had largely concerned foreign policy, it appears that most gubernatorial candidates found little to be gained by making the Bush presidency an issue in their campaigns. Thus, despite these two important events just prior to the November election, there is little reason to expect that voter evaluations of the president would be abnormally strongly associated with voting in gubernatorial elections in 1990, though voters certainly were paying attention to the president's actions.

An article in *Congressional Quarterly* from early September opens by noting the Gulf crisis and other national events but argues that the gubernatorial races being held that year would not turn on national factors: "No presidential election or conspicuous national current exists to carry gubernatorial hopes" (Idelson 1990, 2840). Instead, the article reports, "These races are the stuff of property tax classifications, management overhauls, state lotteries and, of course, abortion" (2840). Even the savings-and-loan crisis, an important issue in many congressional races that year, was described as "a minor feature in most gubernatorial contests" (2840).

In contrast, President Clinton was on center stage as the 1994 campaign season hit full swing. Unlike Bush, Clinton's major efforts early in his first term centered on domestic policies. The Cold War had long since passed in the minds of voters, the Gulf War had ended, and Clinton himself had defined his candidacy in terms of a domestic agenda. Clinton's connection to subpresidential elections in 1994 is obvious in the case of congressional elections, as House Republican candidates rallied around Newt Gingrich's "Contract with America." The GOP actively sought to make the midterm congressional elections a national referendum on Clinton's performance. While the economy was improving, Clinton's stand on gays in the military and his failed attempt at health-care reform, among other things, had left his popularity among voters sagging.[3] This campaign theme spilled over into gubernatorial elections as well. The national media reported how GOP candidates in Florida, Texas, and New York worked to link their Democratic incumbent opponents to President Clinton. However, this phenomenon was much more widespread. The postelection summary of gubernatorial elections published in *Congressional Quarterly* (Groppe and Babson 1994), for example, mentioned Clinton as a direct factor in gubernatorial elections in Kansas, Georgia, Arkansas, Wyoming, Idaho, Alaska, and Arizona. Indiana Governor Evan Bayh, chair of the Democratic Governor's Association at the time, was quoted as saying, "It's apparent that there was a tidal wave running across the country and it hit the statehouse just as it hit the U.S. House" (Groppe and Babson 1994, 3247).

Thus, partly because of the efforts of GOP congressional candidates pushing the "Contract with America," but also because of a conscious effort by nearly all the Republican candidates for governor, we should expect to see that voters' evaluations of President Clinton's job performance were more salient predictors of voting behavior in 1994 than were voters' evaluations of President Bush in the same states four years earlier. By focusing on President Clinton, GOP candidates were attempting to introduce heresthetic change in the electorate's issue space. They believed that their chances of winning in November increased if voters more willingly allowed their evaluations of President Clinton to influence their evaluations of the gubernatorial candidates. In the language of the theory outlined in chapters 2 and 3, GOP candidates were trying to increase the salience of presidential politics to voters in gubernatorial elections in 1994.

The model to be estimated here should be familiar by now. It includes a measure of presidential job approval, a dummy variable to indicate the year of the election, and a multiplicative interaction term between the two. The dependent variable is a dummy variable indicating whether the respondent voted for the Democratic candidate for governor. The measure of presidential approval is the voter's response to the question, "Do you approve or disapprove of the way [George Bush or Bill Clinton] is handling his job as president?" Voters were allowed only to approve or disapprove—there was no middle category. As a result, this variable is coded as a dummy variable. To simplify the analysis, this variable is coded to produce a positive coefficient if presidential approval of Bush is positively related to supporting GOP candidates in 1990 and if presidential approval of Clinton is positively linked to voting for Democratic candidates in 1994. The year dummy variable is coded as a 1 for elections taking place in 1994 and as a 0 for those held in 1990. The interaction term is created by multiplying the presidential approval variable by the year dummy variable. As in the previous chapter, because of the dichotomous nature of the dependent variable and the pooled nature of the data, the model is estimated using logit with robust standard errors.

Readers might be concerned that the particularly poor showing of the Democratic Party's candidates in 1994 might confound this analysis. To the degree that 1994 was a bad year for Democrats in general, that effect will be captured by the coefficient operating directly on the year dummy variable. Such is the case even if the general problems faced by Democrats in 1994 were the result of voter attitudes toward the Clinton administration. In other words, the unpopularity of the Clinton administration may have worked to mobilized strong GOP challengers, prompted strong Democrats not to run, or have in some way hurt the Democratic Party's chances in these twenty-nine gubernatorial races without voters necessarily making a direct link between their attitudes toward Clinton and their choice of gubernatorial candidate.

The test of whether presidential job evaluations were more salient to voters in the 1994 gubernatorial elections than to voters in the same states in 1990 centers on the coefficient operating on the interaction term. If positive and significant, we can conclude that President Clinton's job performance mattered more to voters casting ballots in gubernatorial elections in 1994 than did voters opinions about Bush four years earlier. Table 8.1 presents the results. The analysis controls for individual-level income, party identification, and race as well as the incumbency status of the candidates involved in these elections.

Table 8.1 shows that the coefficients operating on the presidential approval variable, the 1994 year dummy variable, and the multiplicative interaction term are all statistically significant. What does this information mean? First, the coefficient operating directly on the presidential-approval variable captures the relationship between voters' evaluations of President Bush's job performance and their vote for governor in 1990. Because of the way the variable is coded,

TABLE 8.1.   The Effect of Presidential Approval on the Probability of Voting
in Gubernatorial Elections, 1990–94

Variable	Coefficient (Standard Error)
Presidential job approval	0.726 (0.106)**
1994 year dummy	−0.673 (0.166)**
Presidential job approval/1994 dummy interaction term	0.658 (0.180)**
Family income	−0.028 (0.017)
Democratic Party identification dummy	1.190 (0.038)**
Republican Party identification dummy	−0.859 (0.062)**
African-American	0.974 (0.115)**
Female	0.094 (0.031)**
Democratic incumbent running	0.535 (0.149)**
Republican incumbent running	−0.302 (0.168)*
Constant	−0.526 (0.097)**

$N = 77,272$
*$p < .05$ (one-tailed)   **$p < .01$ (one-tailed)

the positive coefficient indicates that voters who approved of Bush's performance were significantly more likely to vote for the Republican candidate for governor than were those who disapproved of the way Bush handled his job. Holding the control variables in the model constant at their means,[4] including presidential job approval, the baseline predicted probability of voting for the Democratic candidate for governor in 1990 was .524. That predicted probability increases to .623 for those who indicated that they disapproved of how Bush was handling his job, still holding the other variables constant at their means. Those who approved of Bush's performance had a predicted probability of voting for the Democratic candidate of just .444. Overall, the gap in the predicted probability that a voter would support the Democratic gubernatorial candidate between those who approved of Bush's job performance and those who did not is .623 − .444 = .179, or 17.9 percentage points. The magnitude of this gap rivals that presented in the previous chapter regarding the gap between prochoice and prolife voters. This gap of nearly 18 percentage points represents the impact of presidential approval ratings on voting behavior in gubernatorial elections when the candidates running do not stress presidential politics during their campaigns.

The predicted probability of voting for the Democratic candidate for governor in 1994 holding all variables including presidential approval constant at their means was .392. This figure differs from the base level of .524 observed for 1990 and demonstrates the across-the-board drop in support for Democratic Party candidates that was witnessed in 1994. This drop is a function of the significant negative coefficient operating on the 1994 year dummy variable. For whatever reason, 1994 was a bad year for Democratic candidates compared to 1990.

However, the significant coefficient operating on the interaction term shows that presidential approval was a more salient predictor of voting behavior in gubernatorial elections in 1994 than in 1990. The predicted probability that voters who approved of the way President Clinton was performing voted for the Democratic candidate for governor, holding the control variables constant at their means, is .619. In contrast, those who did not approve of President Clinton's job performance had a predicted probability of supporting the Democratic gubernatorial candidate of only .290. Thus, the gap between those who approved and those who disapproved of Clinton's job performance is .619 − .290 = .329, or 32.9 percentage points. This figure represents an increase of 15 percentage points from 1990. In other words, the gap in predicted voting behavior between those who approved versus those who disapproved of President Clinton's job performance in 1994 was nearly twice as large as the same gap regarding evaluations of President Bush's job performance in 1990. This evidence supports the idea that voters responded to the GOP effort to make President Clinton a more salient issue in gubernatorial elections in 1994.

All told, Democratic candidates faced an uphill climb in 1994 for two reasons. First, 1994 was a bad year for Democratic candidates across the board. Even after controlling for how voters evaluated President Clinton's performance, they were simply less likely to support Democratic gubernatorial candidates in 1994 than in 1990. Second, voters linked their vote in gubernatorial races with how they felt about the president more strongly than they had four years earlier, and the majority of voters surveyed in these exit polls (54 percent) disapproved of the job Clinton was doing. Republicans capitalized on this disapproval by successfully making evaluations of President Clinton a more salient issue in 1994 than such evaluations of Clinton's predecessor were four years earlier. Thus, Republican candidates as a group appear to have induced the sort of heresthetic change in 1994 described in chapters 2 and 3.

I will make one final observation regarding the differential impact of presidential evaluations on voting behavior in these two election years. In 1990 exit polls revealed that 57 percent of the voters approved of the way Bush was handling his job as president, while the comparable figure for Clinton in 1994 was only 46 percent. This discrepance raises the question of whether the overall level of presidential support influences whether gubernatorial candidates try to make presidential approval ratings more salient and/or whether voters rely more heavily on their feelings about the president. If voters are risk averse, negative evaluations of the president might be more prominent than positive evaluations would be. In this sense, if the president's performance does not present a problem, voters are more free to consider other factors when deciding whom to support for governor. Similarly, candidates may find it easier to campaign against an unpopular president rather than with a more popular president. Because presidential approval is measured here as a dichotomous variable, there is no way to test whether those with negative evaluations of the president were more influenced by those opinions than were those with positive evaluations of the president. I return to this issue of responding to positive versus negative campaign themes in the concluding chapter.

CHAPTER 9

Voter Response to Gubernatorial Campaigns, 1982–1992

Chapters 7 and 8 demonstrated that voters in gubernatorial elections responded in 1990 to appeals made on the abortion issue and in 1994 to appeals based on evaluations of President Clinton. These two chapters provided support for the theory of electoral politics outlined in chapters 2 and 3 by showing that the salience of various demographic cleavages, as well as the salience of opinions on abortion and presidential evaluations, responded to what candidates said during their campaigns. This final empirical chapter expands the analysis to incorporate more issues, more cleavages, and more gubernatorial campaigns.

In this chapter, I explore how the salience to voters of gender, race, religion, income, and partisanship responded to campaign themes in seventy-one gubernatorial elections held between 1982 and 1992.[1] This is not a random sample of elections. Large states and competitive races tend to be somewhat overrepresented. Still, races from thirty-seven states from every region in the country including usable responses from more than ninety-three thousand voters are included in this chapter. To my knowledge, this chapter analyzes the largest single pool of voters in gubernatorial elections ever assembled. The theory described in chapters 2 and 3 predicts that candidates strive to induce heresthetic change as a general campaign strategy. This chapter tests that prediction under more general circumstances.

To begin, table 9.1 presents a list of the seventy-one elections included in this analysis along with the main issues stressed by the two main candidates. I coded up to four issue-based themes for each candidate, although as table 9.1 makes clear, most of the campaigns covered in this analysis focused on fewer than four main issues. The process of coding the content of campaign themes was described in detail in chapter 4.

The theory of electoral politics guiding this book assumes that the salience of individual-level characteristics to voters varies across elections. Of course, the key assumption is that this variation results in part from the themes candidates stress during their campaigns. However, before estimating a model designed to explain this variation in how voters behave across elections, I first demonstrate the existence of that variation.

For each election, I estimate a logit model predicting the probability of voting for the Democratic candidate for governor. Table 9.2 presents the logit coefficients operating on the independent variables gender, race, income, party identification, and Catholicism for each election. Whether a voter is female, African-American, Catholic, a Democrat, or a Republican is measured using dummy variables for each, coded a 1 if the voter has that characteristic and a 0 otherwise. Income refers to the total income of the respondent's family and is coded on a 1 to 5 scale, with higher values indicating higher incomes. The dependent variable for each model is whether the respondent reported voting for the Democratic candidate for governor. The dichotomous nature of the dependent variables suggests using logit to estimate the models.[2]

The findings presented in table 9.2 demonstrate that the salience of these factors varied substantially across these elections. Both partisanship variables achieved statistical significance in all but one case, and all are in the expected direction. Still, the magnitude of the logit coefficients operating on the two party-identification variables varied from election to election from those with an absolute value of less than .7 to several with an absolute value above 2.0.

The four demographic variables show equal volatility, occasionally achieving statistically significant relationships in the opposite direction from what would normally be expected. Comparing coefficient estimates from models applied to different data sets should be done with caution. However, table 9.2 does illustrate in a straightforward manner that the importance of particular individual-level characteristics in predicting voting behavior varied across these elections.

Table 9.3 begins the search for the role played by campaign themes in structuring gubernatorial voting behavior by laying out the expected relationships between several campaign themes and sociodemographic characteristics. It shows that I expect the gender cleavage to respond when candidates stress environmental issues, crime, and/or abortion as part of their campaign themes. The gap between blacks and nonblacks should respond to campaign themes targeting education and/or crime issues. The salience of personal family income should respond to candidates' appeals based on income differences among voters (i.e., "I am for working people; my opponent is for the rich"). Chapter 7 suggests that the difference between Catholics and non-Catholics might respond to whether abortion is stressed during the campaign.[3] Finally, I expect individual party identification to become more salient when someone during the election makes direct party-based appeals.

The expectations regarding which issues might tap which dimensions developed out of several considerations, though this process was complicated by

TABLE 9.1. Issues Stressed during Gubernatorial Campaigns, 1982–92

Election	Gun Control	Taxes	Education	Environment	Economy/ Jobs	Budget/ Spending	Crime	Abortion	Class-based Appeals	"Stay the Course"
1982										
AL					D, R				D	
AR			D		D, R		R		D	
CA				D	D		R		D	
CT					D					D
IL					D					R
IA			D				D		D	R
ME		D, R								D
MA		R				R	R		D	
MI					D	R			D, R	
MN					D	D, R				R
NE					D	D				
NV		D, R			D					
NM					R				D, R	
NY		D, R				D, R	R		D	
OH		D, R			D, R					
RI					R					
TN			D, R		D	R	D		D	D
TX			R			R	R			R
VT				D	R				D	
WY				D, R	D, R					R

1984						
NH	R			D		R
NC	R				R	
VT	R		R		D, R	R
1986						
CA	D, R	R	D		R	D
CO	D, R				R	R
FL	D, R	D		D	R	
GA	D				R	D
IL	D	D			R	R
MD						D
NV	R				R	D
NY	R				R	D
OR	R	D, R			D	R
PA		D, R				D
TX	R	R				
1988						
IN	D			D, R	R	
MO	R			R		R
NC	D		D	D	D	R
WA	D, R	D		R	R	

(continued)

TABLE 9.1.—Continued

Election	Gun Control	Taxes	Education	Environment	Economy/Jobs	Budget/Spending	Crime	Abortion	Class-based Appeals	"Stay the Course"
1990										
AL			D			R				R
AZ	D, R	D, R	D	D,R		D		R	D, R	D
AR	R	R						D		
CA		R	D	D	R		D, R	R		
CO		D, R	D, R							D
FL		D						D, R		
GA		R	D							
ID		R			D	D				D
IL		D, R	D, R							
IA			D		R	D	R		D	R
ME		D, R					R	D		
MD		R		D	D	D				D
MA		D, R	D				R	D, R		
MI		R	D				R			D
NE		D	D		R	D				
NH						D		D		R
NM		D, R	D, R	D	D, R					R

NY			D,R		D,R	D
OH	D,R	R		D	D	D
OK	D,R	D			D,R	
OR	D	D,R		D		
RI	D	R				R
SC		R				R
SD	D	R		D		R
TN	R	D,R		R		D
TX			D,R	R	D	
VT	D,R	R		D	D,R	D
WI	R	D,R		D	D	D
WY		R		D		R
						D

1992

MO	R	D		D,R		D
NH	D,R	D				D
NC	R	D			D,R	
WA	R	D	D	R		

D = Democratic candidate
R = Republican candidate

TABLE 9.2. Logit Coefficients Measuring the Effect of Various Factors on the Probability of Voting for the Democratic Candidate for Governor, 1982–92

Election	Democrat	Republican	Family Income	African-American	Catholic	Female
1982						
AL	1.812*	−0.891*	−0.467*	0.811*	−0.853*	−0.285*
AR	0.894*	−1.733*	−0.082	1.203*	−0.117	0.202
CA	1.161*	−1.427*	−0.059	1.865*	−0.188	0.158
CT	1.022*	−1.404*	−0.170*	0.247	0.399*	0.252*
IL	1.190*	−1.643*	−0.132*	0.601*	−0.066	−0.234
IA	1.217*	−1.481*	0.024	−0.042	−0.392*	0.151
ME	1.225*	−1.108*	−0.221*	−0.785	0.396*	0.191
MA	1.369*	−1.695*	−0.228*	1.874*	−0.108	0.251*
MI	1.849*	−1.448*	−0.110	1.021*	0.116	0.265
MN	1.503*	−1.339*	−0.147*	−0.212	0.401*	0.000
NE	1.078*	−1.331*	−0.183*	0.151	0.087	0.001
NV	0.940*	−1.031*	−0.179*	0.062	−0.207	0.002
NM	1.065*	−1.318*	−0.111	0.887*	1.365*	−0.052
NY	1.170*	−1.171*	−0.064	1.385*	−0.032	0.058
OH	1.518*	−1.519*	−0.033	0.920*	0.181	0.131
RI	1.113*	−0.876*	0.126	−0.227	0.638*	0.416*
TN	2.010*	−1.093*	−0.181*	1.362*	−0.192	0.138
TX	2.046*	−1.385*	−0.250*	0.758*	0.073	0.249*
VT	0.789*	−1.941*	−0.237*	−0.526	0.132	0.342*
WY	1.527*	−1.273*	−0.227*	0.267	−0.042	0.025
1984						
NH	1.527*	−1.273*	−0.227*	0.267	−0.042	0.025
NC	1.375*	−1.063*	−0.205*	1.168*	0.530*	0.041
VT	0.801*	−1.607*	−0.088	0.530	−0.369*	0.432*
1986						
CA	1.146*	−2.138*	−0.050	1.239*	−0.434*	0.402*
CO	1.486*	−1.446*	0.153*	0.640*	0.041	0.176
FL	1.314*	−1.754*	−0.172*	0.527*	0.085	0.116
GA	1.355*	−0.302	−0.154	0.240	−0.884*	0.266
IL	1.491*	−1.509*	−0.011	0.670*	−0.281	0.030
MD	1.560*	−1.072*	−0.028	−0.114	—	−0.153
NV	1.385*	−0.681*	0.037	−0.143	0.209	0.348*
NY	1.308*	−0.747*	0.016	0.609*	−0.350*	0.188
OR	1.412*	−0.670*	0.136*	−0.220	0.073	−0.392*
PA	1.159*	−1.149*	−0.073	0.821*	0.557*	−0.046
TX	1.837*	−1.440*	0.032	0.887*	0.487*	0.281*

(continued)

TABLE 9.2.—*Continued*

Election	Democrat	Republican	Family Income	African-American	Catholic	Female
1988						
IN	1.645*	−1.283*	−0.217*	0.256	0.142	0.038
MO	0.807*	−1.708*	−0.373*	1.346*	−0.203	0.035
NC	1.566*	−1.445*	−0.122	1.067*	0.019	0.049
WA	0.849*	−0.948*	0.059	0.564*	0.249	−0.192
1990						
AL	1.592*	−1.357*	0.144	2.125*	0.476	0.005
AZ	1.707*	−1.180*	−0.027	0.729*	0.340*	0.199
AR	1.426*	−0.756*	−0.004	1.104*	0.141	0.159
CA	1.532*	−1.679*	−0.049	1.499*	0.020	0.550*
CO	1.620*	−0.623*	0.209*	0.007	0.096	0.144
FL	1.382*	−1.339*	−0.056	0.954*	−0.145	−0.006
GA	1.522*	−1.220*	−0.223*	1.389*	0.110	0.006
ID	1.748*	−0.902*	0.202*	−0.751	0.216	0.150
IL	1.231*	−1.273*	0.134*	0.332*	0.028	−0.164
IA	1.537*	−1.676*	−0.114	0.063	−0.539*	−0.147
ME	1.588*	−1.473*	−0.141*	0.134	0.343*	0.000
MD	0.776*	−0.884*	0.066	0.810*	−0.120	0.057
MA	0.883*	−0.828*	0.082	0.344	0.541*	−0.113
MI	1.449*	−1.127*	−0.014	1.318*	0.087	0.303*
NE	1.218*	−1.100*	−0.255*	−0.153	−0.408*	−0.248
NH	1.553*	−1.592*	−0.006	0.612	−0.255	0.149
NM	1.320*	−0.984*	−0.053	0.694	0.612*	0.130
NY	1.609*	−0.855*	−0.020	0.905*	0.204	0.345*
OH	1.627*	−1.254*	−0.205*	0.898*	−0.162	0.091
OK	1.234*	−1.402*	−0.166*	0.551	−0.123	0.130
OR	0.886*	−1.877*	0.070	0.567	−0.057	0.670*
RI	0.830*	−0.534*	−0.062	0.041	0.185	0.022
SC	1.118*	−1.539*	−0.154*	2.635*	0.205	−0.085
SD	0.729*	−1.019*	−0.023	1.067	−0.010	−0.233
TN	1.533*	−0.826*	0.028	1.008*	0.180	0.195
TX	1.628*	−1.431*	−0.008	1.948*	0.279*	0.599*
VT	0.962*	−2.026*	−0.157*	−0.737	0.028	0.354*
WI	1.401*	−2.001*	−0.114	−0.027	−0.366*	0.090
WY	0.538*	−0.657*	0.208*	−0.484	−0.068	−0.210
1992						
MO	1.771*	−1.019*	0.186*	1.111*	0.144	−0.124
NH	1.219*	−1.288*	0.062	0.691	−0.520*	0.238
NC	1.187*	−1.411*	0.001	1.781*	−0.401	−0.083
WA	1.599*	−1.727*	−0.069	0.036	0.350	0.077

*p < .05

TABLE 9.3.   Index of Issues/Themes Stressed during a Campaign and the
Individual-Level Characteristic with Which They Are Expected to Be Associated

	Individual-Level Characteristic				
Issues Stressed	Female	Black	Income	Catholic	Party Identification
Education		X			
Environment	X				
Class-based appeals			X		
Crime	X	X			
Abortion	X			X	
Partisanship					X

the lack of research on how various subsets of voters respond to different types
of appeals. Two sources of information provided the basis for the expected relationships presented in table 9.3. The first is a body of public-opinion research
showing that different groups of voters hold different views on issues as well
as different priorities regarding the focus of government. This research is characterized by Flanigan and Zingale (1994). They show, for example, that mi-
norities support the provision of government services more than do whites. Because public education is the single largest government service provided at the
state level, campaign appeals focusing on education issues might tap this racial
division, whether the appeals are made by Democrats wanting more spending
on education or by Republicans wanting a private-school voucher system.

The expected response of women and Catholics to abortion is based on the
tenets of Catholic teaching on the one hand and the ideals of the women's movement on the other. These assumed relationships are so noncontroversial chapter 7 probably failed to elicit any questions about why a researcher would look
for a response among Catholics and women to appeals based on abortion.

The expected response of gender to environmental issues may be the most
controversial assumption in table 9.3. It is based, in part, on the general liberal
tendency among women relative to men on domestic policy issues (Flanigan
and Zingale 1994). However, further justification comes from the review of the
newspaper coverage of the races in which candidates made environmental appeals. Early in many of these races, either a reporter or someone quoted in an
article often described a candidate's stance on environmental questions as being related to a broader strategy targeting the gender cleavage.

As for the expectation that a focus on crime might make race more salient,
any public-opinion poll regarding the O. J. Simpson murder trial or the trial
of the Los Angeles police officers who beat Rodney King shows that African-
Americans and white people as groups have very different feelings about the
criminal-justice system, the police, and the whole issue of crime. The famous

Willie Horton television ad from the 1988 presidential election dealt with the issue of crime but was widely viewed as tapping a racial division among voters. Finally, a number of newspaper accounts of the elections considered here indicated that a focus on the issue of crime was expected to have race-based repercussions among voters.

I created a series of dummy variables that measure whether a candidate stressed one or more of the issues expected to tap each individual-level factor presented in table 9.3. For example, if a candidate focused on crime as a part of the campaign, then a dummy variable coded 1 for those who stressed issues expected to tap the gender cleavage and 0 otherwise would be coded as a 1. In this example, a dummy variable coded 1 for candidates who stressed an issue that might tap the racial cleavage and 0 otherwise would be coded as a 1 if crime policy was stressed. For each of the campaign-issue dummies designed to tap a demographic cleavage, I have coded whether the Democratic candidate stressed the issue and whether the Republican did so. For the stressing of partisanship, I simply coded whether the campaign itself was structured and discussed in partisan terms without regard for whether one candidate focused on partisanship more than did the other.

To produce the necessary interaction terms, I multiplied the issue dummy variables by the individual-level characteristic expected to respond to such appeals as presented in table 9.3. As presented in previous chapters, the coefficients operating on these interaction terms capture any change in the salience of these individual-level characteristics in response to the issue-based appeals made by candidates.

Table 9.4 presents a baseline analysis of the salience of these five individual-level characteristics across the seventy-one elections included in this chapter.[4] The cell entries in table 9.4 measure the difference in the predicted prob-

TABLE 9.4.   Difference in the Probability of Voting
for the Democratic Candidate for Governor, 1982–92

Comparison	Gap in Predicted Probability
Democrat vs. Independent	.287***
Republican vs. Independent	−.269***
Black vs. nonblack	.219***
Catholic vs. non-Catholic	.013
Women vs. men	.028***
Wealthy vs. poor	−.072***

Note: Entries are deviations in the predicted probability of supporting the prochoice candidate away from a base probability of .5. The full model on which these entries are based is included in appendix D.

*Underlying coefficient significant at $p < .1$
**Underlying coefficient significant at $p < .05$
***Underlying coefficient significant at $p < .01$

ability of voting for the Democratic candidate for governor for each comparison indicated. These differences are computed as deviations from a base probability of .5.[5] For example, identifying with the Democratic Party increases the probability of a respondent voting for the Democratic candidate from a base probability of .5 to a probability of .787, producing a gap of 28.7 percentage points.

Table 9.4 shows that, with the exception of being Catholic, each of these individual-level characteristics appears salient on average to voters across these seventy-one gubernatorial elections even prior to controlling for the content of the campaigns. The probability that Democrats voted for the Democratic candidate for governor is nearly 29 percentage points higher than the probability that independent voters did so. Similarly, those identifying with the GOP had a probability of voting for the Democratic candidate that is 27 points lower than that of independents. Taken together, the predicted probability of supporting the Democratic candidate for governor differs between Democratic and Republican Party identifiers by more than 56 percentage points. Party identification is clearly, though certainly not unexpectedly, a highly salient predictor of voting behavior in gubernatorial elections.

The gap between black and nonblack voters is similarly impressive. African-Americans were 22 percentage points more likely to vote for the Democratic candidate for governor than were their nonblack counterparts. The magnitude of the salience of partisanship and race in general leave some question as to how much more salient these factors could be made over the short term of a campaign.

Catholics were only slightly and insignificantly more loyal to Democratic candidates. They were just over 1 percentage point more likely to vote for the Democratic candidate for governor than were non-Catholic respondents.[6]

A moderate gender gap also exists across these seventy-one elections. Women were significantly more likely than were men to have voted for the Democratic candidate. Again, the magnitude of the gap is a modest 2.8 percentage points. However, when approximately half of the electorate falls on either side of this cleavage, a few percentage points can change the outcome of the election.

Finally, the traditional class-based division among voters exists at the gubernatorial level as well. Those with higher incomes were just over 7 percentage points less likely than those with low incomes to vote for the Democratic candidate. More specifically, this gap represents the difference between voters in the lowest income category and those in the highest income category as observed in the data.

To summarize, table 9.4 suggests that the individual characteristics examined here were salient to voters across these gubernatorial elections, even without considering the campaign themes of candidates and after controlling for other variables, except for being Catholic. These findings represent more or less an average of the state-by-state results presented earlier in table 9.2. Of course, we know from table 9.2 that the salience of these factors varied from election to election. The next step is to try to account for some of that variation by incorporating the issues stressed by the candidates into the analysis.

Table 9.5 examines the response of each of these individual-level characteristics to whether either candidate stressed issues expected to tap each particular cleavage. The full model used to produce table 9.5 is presented in appendix D.

Looking first at partisanship, it is no surprise to find that party identification strongly predicts voting behavior even in the absence of overt party-based appeals among the themes stressed by the candidates. The gap between the Democratic and Republican probabilities of voting for the Democratic candidate was estimated to be 53 percentage points.

However, even such a salient cleavage becomes significantly more important when the campaign is structured in part around partisan appeals. Table 9.5 shows that both Democrats and Republicans responded when party appeals were made, though the Democratic response was just below statistical significance. The gap between the Democratic and independents' predicted probabilities of voting for the Democratic candidate increased by about 2 percentage points when partisanship was stressed during the campaign. The increase was nearly 4 percentage points between Republicans and independents. Taken together, the gap in the Democratic and Republican predicted probabilities of voting for the Democratic candidate for governor was nearly 6 percentage points

TABLE 9.5.   Difference in the Probability of Voting for the Democratic Candidate for Governor When Various Issues Are Stressed by Either Candidate, 1982–92

Comparison	Gap in Probability When Not Stressed	Gap in Probability When Stressed[a]	Change in Gap
Democrat vs. Independent	.277***	.296***	.019
Republican vs. Independent	−.253***	−.292***	−.039**
Black vs. nonblack	.177***	.250***	.073**
Catholic vs. non-Catholic	.016	−.003	−.019
Women vs. men	.019**	.034***	.015
Wealthy vs. poor	−.054***	−.116***	−.062**

Note: Entries are deviations in the predicted probability of supporting the prochoice candidate away from a base probability of .5. The full model on which these entries are based is included in appendix D.
[a]Significance levels computed using process described by Jaccard, Turrisi, and Wan (1990, 25–28)
*Underlying coefficient significant at $p < .1$
**Underlying coefficient significant at $p < .05$
***Underlying coefficient significant at $p < .01$

larger when partisan appeals were made than when they were not. Likely the most salient predictor of individual voting behavior in gubernatorial elections, partisanship was made even more so when candidates stressed that cleavage during their campaigns.

When crime and/or education issues were not part of the campaign themes of either gubernatorial candidate, African-Americans continued to support Democratic Party candidates for governor at a much higher rate than did their nonblack counterparts. The gap between the black and nonblack probabilities of voting for the Democratic candidate was about 18 percentage points when these issues were not stressed.

When such issues were stressed, the gap between blacks and nonblacks increased significantly. The probability that African-Americans voted for the Democratic candidate was 25 percentage points higher than the probability that nonblacks cast their ballots for the Democrat, an increase of more than 7 points. Race clearly structures voting behavior regardless of the issues stressed in a campaign. Yet table 9.5 suggests that as much as one-third of the gap between African-Americans' and non-African-Americans' predicted voting behavior can be attributed to a response to appeals made by the candidates.

When abortion was not stressed, Catholic voters remained somewhat loyal to Democratic Party candidates. Catholics were only 1.6 percentage points more likely to vote for the Democrat than were non-Catholics, a gap that was not statistically significant. When the campaign of at least one of the candidates included a focus on abortion, the difference between Catholics and non-Catholics declined to near zero, though the actual shift produced by the coefficient operating on the interaction between stressing abortion and being Catholic is not statistically significant in its own right. However, focusing on abortion reduces the already-small gap between Catholics and non-Catholics even further. Thus, it appears that Catholics may have been slightly pushed away from candidates of the party associated with the prochoice position on abortion when that issue was stressed during the campaign.

The gap between men and women remained statistically significant even when issues expected to tap gender were not stressed as part of the campaign. Women remained about 2 percentage points more likely to vote for the Democratic candidate for governor than were men. The gap expanded to a significant 3.4 points when the environment, crime, and/or abortion were stressed as part of the campaign, though the shift itself was not statistically significant.

The response of the income variable is more clear. Even when neither candidate made class-based appeals during the campaign, voters in the highest income bracket were less likely to vote for the Democratic candidate for governor than were voters in the lowest income category. This difference is more than 5 percentage points and is statistically significant. When class-based appeals were made by either candidate during the election, the salience of personal family income more than doubled, reaching about 12 percentage points. Both the gap itself and its increase in response to candidates' class-based appeals are statistically significant.

To summarize, table 9.5 shows that the salience of several individual-level cleavages among voters responded to what candidates said. The gaps between partisans and independents, African-Americans and non-African-Americans, and high-income voters and their less-well-off counterparts expanded when candidates made appeals on issues that tap these dimensions. The gap between Catholics and non-Catholics diminished to near zero when abortion was stressed, while the gap between men and women expanded slightly when candidates stressed issues related to the gender cleavage. The next step is to examine whether the voters' responses along these various cleavage differ when appeals are made by different candidates.

Table 9.6 repeats the analysis that produced table 9.5, this time measuring the specific effects of whether the Democratic candidate or the Republican candidate stressed any of the issues expected to tap one or more of the individual-level cleavages under consideration. The coding of the variable measuring whether partisan appeals were made during the campaign does not allow for the estimation of the independent effects of each candidate making party-based appeals. Thus, the effects reported for that variable in table 9.6 are based on whether partisanship was stressed by both or either candidate during the campaign. In fact, the findings regarding partisanship presented in table 9.6 are virtually identical to those presented in table 9.5, so I forgo additional discussion of them here.

Table 9.6 reiterates that race remained salient even when issues that tap that dimension were not stressed by either candidate. African-American voters have a predicted probability of voting for the Democratic candidate 18 percentage points higher than the predicted probability of nonblack voters even when neither candidate stressed crime or education as part of the overall campaign theme. When the Democratic candidate stressed these issues, the gap between black and nonblack voters increased by about 2.5 percentage points. However, the magnitude of that increase did not reach statistical significance.

In contrast, when the Democratic candidate stressed abortion, the gap between Catholics and non-Catholics responded dramatically. In races where neither candidate stressed abortion, the gap between Catholics and non-Catholics was a positive, though statistically insignificant, 1.6 percentage points. Thus, the loyalty of Catholics to Democratic candidates when they did not stress abortion was similar to the level reported in table 9.5 and in chapter 7. When the Democratic candidate stressed abortion in a gubernatorial election, table 9.6 shows that the gap reversed direction and became statistically significant. Catholics were nearly 4 percentage points less likely than non-Catholics to vote for Democratic candidates who stressed abortion. The overall shift in the gap between

TABLE 9.6.   Differences in the Probability of Voting for the Democratic Candidate for Governor When Candidates Stressed Various Issues, 1982–92

Both/Either

Comparison	Gap in Probability When Not Stressed	Gap in Probability When Stressed by Both/Either[a]	Change in Gap
Democrat vs. Independent	.282***	.297***	.015
Republican vs. Independent	−.250***	−.292***	−.042**

Democrats

Comparison	Gap in Probability When Not Stressed	Gap in Probability When Stressed by the Democrat[a]	Change in Gap
Black vs. nonblack	.182***	.207***	.025
Catholic vs. non-Catholic	.016	−.038*	−.054**
Women vs. men	.018**	.017	−.001
Wealthy vs. poor	−.053***	−.140***	−.100***

Republicans

Comparison	Gap in Probability When Not Stressed	Gap in Probability When Stressed by the Republican[a]	Change in Gap
Black vs. nonblack	.182***	.248***	.066*
Catholic vs. non-Catholic	.016	.083***	.067***
Women vs. men	.018**	.044***	.026**
Wealthy vs. poor	−.053***	−.006	.047

Note: Entries are deivations in the predicted probability of supporting the prochoice candidate away from a base probability of .5. The full model on which these entries are based is included in appendix D.
   [a]Significance levels computed using process described by Jaccard, Turrisi, and Wan (1990, 25–28)
   *Underlying coefficient significant at $p < .1$
   **Underlying coefficient significant at $p < .05$
   ***Underlying coefficient significant at $p < .01$

Catholics and non-Catholics when the Democratic candidate stressed abortion compared to when neither candidate stressed abortion was 5.4 percentage points. The Democratic candidates in all of these races held a position on abortion that either resembled that of their GOP opponents or was clearly more prochoice. Combined with the historical ties between the two parties and supporters on each side of the abortion issue, it seems clear that Catholic voters moved away from prochoice Democratic candidates in significant numbers relative to non-Catholics when the Democrats campaigned on the abortion issue.

Table 9.6 shows that the gender gap did not respond to gender-based appeals made by Democrats running for governor. Women had a predicted probability about 2 percentage points higher than did men of voting for the Democratic candidate when no gender-based appeals were made. This significant difference was virtually unchanged when the Democratic candidate stressed the environment, crime, and/or abortion.

Finally, income levels predicted the probability of voting for a particular gubernatorial candidate even when class-based appeals were not made. Those in the highest income category were about 5 percentage points less likely to vote for the Democratic candidate than were those in the lowest income group. When Democrats made class-based appeals part of their campaign strategies, the gap between the rich and the poor nearly tripled to 14 percentage points.

The patterns in these relationships were somewhat different when Republican candidates made specific issue-based appeals. First, the gap between black and nonblack voters changed significantly from 18 percentage points when these issues were not stressed to almost 25 percentage points when they were. This response is much larger than was the response of the racial cleavage to appeals made by Democrats and is statistically significant.

The behavior of the Catholic/non-Catholic comparison is difficult to explain. When abortion was not stressed by anyone, Catholics were slightly, though insignificantly, more likely to vote for the Democratic candidate. However, when the GOP nominee stressed abortion, Catholics became significantly more supportive of prochoice Democrats. Thus, when Democrats stressed their prochoice views, Catholics seemed to be somewhat pushed away. Yet when Republicans appealed to voters on abortion, they also seemed to push away Catholic relative to non-Catholic voters. This situation suggests that Catholics respond differently to the appeals of different candidates. Catholics appear to have been turned off when candidates from the party they have traditionally favored, the Democratic Party, focused on prochoice views. Yet when prolife Republicans stressed the issue, Catholics may have reacted negatively, possibly because of a perception that the GOP may be working to undercut the rights of others. In other words, it may be that when Republicans stressed abortion, they created an impression of intolerance. Catholics may also object to the broader religious interpretations prolife Republicans often use to justify a more restrictive abortion policy. Finally, GOP appeals on abortion may have produced a larger gap between Catholics and non-Catholics by attracting additional support from prolife non-Catholics at a higher rate than from prolife Catholics. These speculations are admittedly post hoc, however, and should be read as such.

The gap between men and women, like the gap between blacks and nonblacks, was more sensitive to the issues stressed by Republican candidates than to the same issues when stressed by Democrats. The already significant moderate gap between the predicted voting behavior of men and women more than doubled to 4.4 percentage points when the Republican candidate stressed the environment, crime, and/or abortion.

Finally, the salience of income regarding voting behavior responded to GOP appeals made on a class basis in an interesting way. For the other issues considered thus far, appeals made by either the Democratic candidate or the Republican candidate, if they had an effect at all, were expected to have an impact in the same direction, even if the appeals were directed at different sides of the cleavage. For example, the kinds of appeals made on crime issues by Democrats or Republicans, even though often different in focus, were expected to increase the gap in the predicted voting behavior of blacks and nonblacks.

Such is not the case with class-based appeals. When Democratic candidates made such appeals, the language typically took the form of "I am for the working people in this state, while my Republican opponent just wants to protect the rich." Such appeals should make the gap between the voting behavior of wealthy people and poor people increase, which is what happened.

The expectation regarding the response of the income cleavage to class-based appeals made by the Republican candidate is less clear. Just by raising the issue, one might expect that any such GOP appeals might increase the salience of the income division among voters, thus increasing the gap between rich and poor. However, from reading the coverage of the campaigns, when Republican candidates raised the class issue, they were typically trying to reduce the salience of income differences among voters. When Republicans talked about class in gubernatorial elections, they defended themselves against charges of being a party for the rich only. They claimed to represent middle-class and working-class taxpayers, and they often attacked their Democratic opponents for promoting class warfare. In that sense, Republican candidates openly acknowledged that their Democratic opponents sought to make income differences more salient to voters. Thus, if GOP appeals dealing with income and class-based issues were successful, we should see a decrease in the salience of personal income to voters.

The second part of table 9.6 provides evidence that GOP candidates for governor had some success with this strategy. The significant gap between high-income and low-income voters that existed when class-based appeals were absent from the campaign was reduced to near zero when the Republican candidate made appeals on these issues. While this shift is of equal substantive magnitude to the original division based on income, the variance around the estimated shift is greater. Thus, the actual shift does not achieve statistical significance. Still, the substantive conclusion, though somewhat shaky, remains that Republican candidates had some success at reducing the salience of an income-based cleavage among voters by formulating a campaign theme designed to do so.

Finally, some attention must be given to the direct effects of stressing various issues on voting behavior in these gubernatorial elections. As discussed in chapter 7, when a coefficient on a multiplicative interaction term is significant, it demonstrates that the gap between the two groups in question, for example, men and women, is getting larger (or smaller). The coefficient does not indicate whether the change in the gap results from men, women, or both changing their voting behavior. Looking at the coefficients operating on the simple dummy variables included to mark whether a particular issue was stressed does, however, provide some indication. In regression terms, these variables constitute shifts in the intercept or constant term in the model. They capture the behavior of all the voters that fall into the excluded categories for all the other dummy variables entered into the model. Again, for these models, those excluded categories include men, nonblacks, independents, Protestants, and voters in elections without an incumbent running, as well as others. Thus, it is hard to tell which factor being captured in the intercept term produces a positive or negative shift in the constant. Furthermore, it is worth remembering that any specific shift in the constant measured by any one of these issue dummy variables occurs after controlling for the shifts in the constant induced by all the other issue dummy variables. These coefficients are reported in the full models presented in appendix D.

I bring this issue up because in the model used to produce table 9.6, the constant shifts in a negative direction in elections in which issues that tap the racial dimension are stressed by the Republican candidate or by both candidates. In addition, the intercept shifts in a negative direction when gender-related issues are stressed by the Democrat and in a positive direction when gender-related issues are stressed by the Republican. I suspect that these negative shifts result primarily from white males' reaction to race and gender-based appeals. Why there is a positive shift in the constant when GOP candidates stress gender-related issues is not clear.

To summarize, this chapter has produced more generalized support for the theoretical argument made in chapters 2 and 3 regarding the response of voters along various cleavages to the themes stressed by candidates during the campaign. Candidates appear to create heresthetic change within the electorate through the issues they stress during their campaigns. Voters respond to the choices with which they are presented and learn about those choices through the informational context within which they find themselves. Campaigns help to shape that context by defining for voters the nature of the choice with which they are presented.

Voters also respond differently in some circumstances when appeals designed to tap a particular cleavage are made by either the Democrat or the Republican. Prochoice Democrats may run the risk of diminishing their support among Catholic voters by stressing views on abortion. Democrats appear to be able to increase the gap in voting behavior between high-income and low-income voters, while GOP candidates are somewhat able to mute some of that effect with their campaign appeals. The gap between black and nonblack voters appears to be particularly responsive to Republican candidates tapping that cleavage, and the negative intercept shift when GOP candidates stress issues that tap the racial cleavage suggests that whites may be responding as much as blacks. Finally, the gender gap is much more responsive when Republicans stress themes that tap that dimension.

The response of the racial, gender, and Catholic/non-Catholic divisions among voters to appeals made by specific candidates suggests a pattern. Catholics are pushed away from prochoice Democrats relative to non-Catholics when prochoice Democrats stress abortion but are not attracted to prolife Republicans when they stress the issue. Women are pushed away from GOP candidates relative to men when Republican candidates tap the gender cleavage but are not attracted to Democratic candidates when they do the same. African-Americans are pushed away from the Republican candidate relative to nonblacks when Republicans tap the race-based cleavage but are not attracted to Democratic candidates through their efforts to highlight this dimension.

This pattern suggests that voters may respond to themes advocated by candidates that voters view as hostile to their interests more dramatically than they do to campaigns designed to mobilize their support. Even the ability of Democratic candidates to magnify the salience of income divisions within the electorate more than Republicans are able to dampen the salience of those divisions fits with a pattern of voter behavior characterized as risk averse and responsive to divisive appeals. This finding is consistent with a view of voters placing a higher value on preventing loss rather than on acquiring benefits from the outcome of an election.

This pattern also suggests something about the strategies candidates will and do adopt under different circumstances. In chapter 7, I suggested that only candidates who feel that they cannot otherwise win will risk campaigning on a divisive issue like abortion. Candidates prefer to run safe campaigns that appeal to as many voters as possible and would certainly like to avoid risking the loss of any voter if doing so is possible. The findings of this chapter also suggest that issues that tap politicized cleavages within the electorate may produce a hostile reaction among some voters.

This conclusion does not mean that only losing candidates will try to tap one or more cleavages, particularly if the side of the cleavage on which the candidate is located is in the majority within the electorate. However, failing to respond to the demands of a minority group, if that group constitutes a substantial part of that candidate's traditional constituency, can cost that candidate the race. Several Democratic defeats that occurred in the elections included in this chapter, along with Jim Florio's defeat in New Jersey in 1993, were attributed in part to the failure to mobilize black support. Thus, even if it makes the gap between blacks and whites expand, Democratic candidates may need to try to tap the racial cleavage to turn out their own political base.

So, tapping a divisive cleavage appears to guarantee the loss of support among voters on the other side of the cleavage, which limits the breadth of the coalition a candidate could assemble over the course of a campaign along with the margin of victory that candidate might achieve. Such limits on the size and makeup of the electoral coalition will in turn likely constrain victors in implementing their policy programs. That voters respond to campaign themes in a more negative rather than positive way and that such appeals extenuate divisions within the electorate provides a strong incentive for candidates to avoid when possible themes that might be divisive. It is no wonder that we see popular candidates running on valence issues while underdog challengers attack, trying to create a split in the leader's coalition of support. However, most gubernatorial elections are competitive races in which neither candidate has the luxury of avoiding conflict. Furthermore, the 1993 gubernatorial campaign in Virginia demonstrates that there are risks involved in running a "safe" campaign.

It must encourage many observers of the electoral process in the United States to see that voters respond to the issue content of gubernatorial campaigns. Candidates' policy priorities reach voters, influencing their decision making. Any normative critique of representative democracy must consider this finding as evidence in support of a system in which both voters and candidates pay attention to the policies advocated during the campaign. Chapters 7 through 9 demonstrate that the salience of demographic characteristics, positions voters hold on issues, evaluations of the president, and even party identification vary as a function of the themes stressed by candidates. Candidates do appear to produce heresthetic change through the issues they stress during the campaign.

CHAPTER 10

Conclusions

I began this book by suggesting that political science needs a new way of thinking about electoral politics. The subsequent chapters developed and tested a theory of electoral politics that places the campaign itself more squarely at the center of the electoral process. I conclude in this chapter by suggesting more generally the advances made by this study, a broader set of implications suggested by its findings, and a consideration of its limitations with an eye toward future research.

The evidence presented in this book supports the conclusion that campaigns affect elections by altering the salience of particular issues or cleavages among voters. Campaigns produce heresthetic change. They do so because the campaign process is a learning process for voters. Voters respond to the choices presented to them, and the candidates' campaigns help to define the nature of those choices. Campaigns provide voters with information about the candidates, and this research shows that voters respond to that information. Thus, campaigns produce heresthetic change by helping to shape the informational context in which voters find themselves.

Viewed from this perspective, the strategies and themes adopted by candidates during their campaigns do not have a direct effect on voting behavior. Rather, their effect comes from how campaign themes interact with preexisting divisions among voters on sociodemographic characteristics, evaluations of the president, or even specific issue positions. Thus, any model of electoral politics hoping to capture the influence of campaign themes on voting behavior must be sensitive to this interactive effect. Heresthetic change means changing the shape of the issue space of the electorate, which is exactly what campaigns are designed to do. Campaigns alter the pattern of factors that best predict voting behavior in any particular election by changing their relative salience to voters.

The theory developed and tested in this book is well grounded in social-science theory and the political science literature on campaigns, elections, and voting behavior. It is consistent with the spatial model of voting, and it fits the data well. Equally important is the fact that this way of thinking about electoral

168

politics conforms nicely to the understanding of the process expressed by its practitioners. Not surprisingly, during the hours of interviews with campaign staff members and party officials, they never uttered the phrase "heresthetic change in the electorate"; it also did not appear in any of the thousands of newspaper articles read as part of this research. However, the case studies in particular make clear that campaign strategy is designed to produce exactly the kind of response among voters predicted by the theory in chapters 2 and 3. Campaign staff members describe campaigns in terms of controlling the agenda, tapping hot-button issues to mobilize various segments of the electorate, and defining the nature of the choice presented to voters. The language may differ somewhat, but the process they describe is an effort to induce heresthetic change.

More generally, the comments of campaign staff members suggest a broader understanding of the electoral process that conforms to the theory for which I argue. Campaign staff members realize that their candidates must have some credibility on the issues they stress during their campaigns. They know that candidates are not free to relocate in the issue space of an electorate and that candidates risk alienating current supporters if they attempt such moves. The GOP convention in Virginia certainly demonstrates the pull that party activists can have on a candidate.

Campaign staff members, particularly those involved in developing the overall strategy for a campaign, are keenly aware of these constraints. They adopt a view of campaigns as efforts to control the agenda and to define the choice presented to voters because they realize that this is about all that campaigns can be expected to do.[1] Chapter 2 suggests that rational candidates seeking to win an election, faced with a series of constraints, would choose trying to induce heresthetic change over the course of the campaign as their most reasonable strategy. Campaign practitioners appear to operate with exactly this vision of electoral politics in mind.

As much as the campaign is a learning process for voters, it is also a learning process for the candidates. Candidates seeking to focus the campaign on particular issues struggle to learn as much as they can about how voters might respond to specific appeals. From a theoretical perspective, one might argue that this drive for information about the electorate, assuming sufficient levels of funding and expertise on both sides, leads both campaigns to learn a similar amount about potential voters. In so doing, neither campaign would develop an informational advantage, they would be equally able to test campaign themes and predict their impact, and the campaigns themselves might cancel each other out. This argument is consistent with that put forward by Gelman and King (1993) regarding presidential campaigns. The two case studies conducted for this research suggest that this view is incorrect, at least for gubernatorial elections.

First, we saw in Virginia that both candidates believed that their specific stands on crime issues would help them win the election. In other words, both wanted their stands on crime to be salient to voters. However, the polling done by the Allen campaign found that it actually had the advantage on the crime issue. When respondents were presented with a hypothetical choice between Candidate A, who favored abolishing parole for violent criminals but opposed a five-day waiting period for the purchase of handguns, and Candidate B, who took opposite positions on both issues, Allen's polling determined that voters overwhelmingly preferred Candidate A. Had the Terry campaign had equal information, she would likely have focused her campaign differently.

Second, even if campaigns have similar information about the electorate, they still need to convey their themes adequately to voters. The 1993 gubernatorial election in New Jersey clearly shows that the ability to do so is not equal across campaigns, even when advisers with presidential-campaign experience are involved on both sides. Florio kept the focus of the campaign away from his liabilities and on Whitman's shortcomings for nearly the entire campaign. Only during the final week or two of the campaign was Whitman able to convey her message to voters about the choice they were about to make in a manner that was clear enough to allow her to win. There was nothing inevitable about this last-minute turnaround. Had Whitman continued to struggle on the campaign trail, she would have lost.

Whereas Allen refused to let Terry pull him away from the issue focus of his campaign, Whitman repeatedly responded to Florio's attacks in a manner that defined the day-to-day content of the campaign in terms beneficial to Florio. In the end, instead of responding to the content of Florio's attacks, Whitman characterized them as evidence of Florio's integrity and trustworthiness—for example, the late television ad in which Whitman said, "If you can't trust Florio on taxes, how can you trust him to tell the truth about me?" Campaigns clearly do not always learn equally about voters, and campaigns certainly are not always equally able to convey their messages to voters. Campaigns do not simply cancel each other out, at least in gubernatorial elections.

The learning process of campaigns also incorporates candidates trying to learn about what their opponents will and/or might do. Who candidates run against matters to them. Because Terry and Florio were unopposed in their respective bids for nomination, they had the luxury of preparing for the general election earlier than did their opponents. And while one Terry staff member said that the basic focus of Terry's campaign did not depend on her ultimate opponent, other Terry advisers and several Florio staff members confessed that their strategies would be influenced significantly simply by who their opponent was. In fact, Florio's campaign prepared several different speeches for him to deliver on the night of the primary election, each one designed around a different outcome on the Republican side.

In interviews conducted very early in the campaigns, staff members in each campaign believed that they had a fairly good idea about what their opponents might stress during the election, which is not surprising given that candidates are generally aware of their own strengths and weaknesses as well as those of their opponents. However, this general level of knowledge does not keep candidates from trying to learn more about each other. For example, the Allen campaign, through its Leadership Committee newsletter and several mass meetings held during the early stages of the campaign, coached supporters regarding how to respond to telephone poll questions should they be called. They were told to answer any questions a pollster asked them, and they were encouraged to report that they were undecided about which candidate to support. By asking them to claim to be undecided, Allen staff members were hoping to get the names of Allen supporters added to the phone and mailing lists used by the Terry campaign to learn more about Terry's campaign strategy.

Allen campaign staffers also instructed Allen supporters to write down every question that pollsters asked in as much detail as possible and report it to the Allen campaign immediately. Through this process, the Allen campaign hoped to learn what questions the Terry campaign asked voters. From knowing the questions, the Allen staff believed it could infer what themes Terry might stress either in speeches or through advertising during the campaign. One Allen staff member said that by the fall, his campaign workers believed that they knew most of the questions that Terry pollsters had asked.

Another example of the lengths to which campaigns will go to learn about each other was the Florio campaign's hiring of teams to follow Whitman to every public event with a video camera and a cellular phone. While this strategy was enacted in part to add pressure to a relatively inexperienced candidate, the primary goal was to document the opposing campaign's every public step and to be able to respond the same day to whatever Whitman was saying. The Florio campaign did not want to wait until the following day to respond to whatever the press reported about Whitman. They wanted every press report about what Whitman was doing or saying to contain a response from Florio as well.

That voters respond to the content of political campaigns has important normative implications for democratic government. In particular, this analysis shows that voters respond to the issue content of campaigns. Since *The American Voter* (Campbell et al. 1960), scholars have searched for and struggled to find an issue basis for voting behavior. A common belief is that representative government requires voters to include issue positions in making decisions about candidates. This analysis finds that when candidates stress issues, voters use that information when deciding for whom to vote. Voters respond to campaigns of substance, suggesting that they may not be easily duped by a campaign devoid of ideas. The content analysis of the newspaper coverage of the gubernatorial races covered in this analysis suggests that only truly safe incumbents can successfully avoid presenting specific issue positions to voters during a campaign. Furthermore, voters appear reasonably sophisticated in terms of how they respond to candidate appeals. Not every voter responds the same way to a particular campaign theme, and voters do not respond the same way regardless of who stresses an issue. Specific issues tap specific cleavages within the electorate. Thus, supporters of representative democracy should find good news in this project's findings.

However, the nature of the response may be less heartening to advocates of citizen-controlled government. Chapters 7, 8, and 9 suggest that voters may respond more strongly when they view a candidate as hostile to their interests than when a candidate is supportive. In other words, voters may be more risk averse than they are benefit seeking. In so doing, voters' negative candidate evaluations may be more salient than are positive evaluations. The only exception to this was the positive response of prochoice voters when prochoice candidates stressed abortion, as reported in chapter 7.

At the same time, the two case studies suggest that candidates and their staffs view the task of controlling the campaign agenda as more easily achieved through aggressive attacks on or comparisons with their opponents. Candidates make an issue or cleavage more salient by highlighting a contrast between themselves and their opponents. Doing so necessarily entails casting the opponent in a negative light. Thus, candidates highlight negative aspects of their opponents, and voters seem to respond. In this sense, voters seem motivated more by avoiding a candidate who will do more harm rather than finding a candidate who will do more good for that state's citizens. Such a perspective hardly casts the best light on democratic theories of government, although it does suggest some underlying support among voters for the concept of a limited government.

By its very nature, the process of producing heresthetic change described in this project is largely divisive. Candidates working to make an issue or characteristic more salient to some voters in a positive way often produce a negative response of equal or greater magnitude among those voters who do not share the same issue position or characteristic as the target group. Of course, such need not be the case. Heresthetic change can involve reducing the salience of a division within the electorate. Chapter 9 provides some evidence for this contention by showing that when Republican candidates made appeals designed to reduce the salience of income divisions among voters, the candidates met with some success. Also, chapter 7 found that prochoice candidates were able to mobilize support from prochoice voters by stressing abortion without producing a similar negative response among prolife voters. However, the more general pattern is one of increasing the differences between groups of people in terms of which candidate they support. As long as divisions among voters exist that can be made politically salient, candidates will likely do so.

The strengths of this analysis are many. Chapters 7, 8, and 9 mobilize exit-poll data for well over one hundred thousand voters participating in more than a hundred gubernatorial elections over a twelve-year period. This breadth allowed for factors at the individual level, the election level, and the national level to be included as predictors of voting behavior. The multilevel models designed and tested in this analysis provide a guide for future research that can compare the relative impact of factors like individual party identification, candidate spending, incumbency, and presidential politics in a single model of voting behavior.

This project also presents original data on the themes stressed by candidates during their campaigns, greatly expanding the extent to which campaign-related variables are incorporated into the analysis of voting behavior. Hundreds of hours went into reading about these campaigns and coding the issue content of the candidates' themes. These data made operationalizing a test of the theory of heresthetic change possible in chapters 7 and 9, and these data can serve as a base for further research on the themes that candidates stressed during their campaigns.

This extensive comparative empirical effort is complimented by the two specific studies of Virginia and New Jersey. The case studies allow for a close examination of the dynamics of election campaigns not possible through any other means. In-depth interviews provide insight into how campaign practitioners think about political campaigns. For this analysis, the clear connection between the theory developed in chapters 2 and 3 and the description of the electoral process by those who run campaigns for a living reinforces the validity of the theory.

It may be as important in the understanding of campaign strategy to know something about the choices candidates did not make during the election. While newspaper accounts typically report only what candidates do and say, in-depth interviews shed light on the options candidates chose not to exercise. Candidates make choices that have real implications for the outcome of the election. Knowing something about the options that were discarded highlights this fact.

The in-depth studies also provide an appreciation for the extent to which campaigns seek to learn as much as possible about voters and their opponents and how campaigns work to control as much of the surrounding information as possible. Campaign organizations fear uncertainty. The Allen campaign went to great lengths in its attempt to control everything from the floor of the Republican convention to the content of supporters' letters to the editor.[2] When following the candidates at public appearances, I observed campaign staff members working to plant specific angles on particular stories with news reporters. Campaign staff workers worry about the smallest details, commonly viewing the campaign as a day-by-day battle. The Allen campaign's grassroots effort during the summer rallied around the theme of trying not to lose a single county fair to the Terry camp.

The case studies also illustrate the troubling nature of the relationship between campaigns and the press. They depend on each other—candidates, especially in New Jersey, need press coverage to assist their efforts to communicate with voters, and the press needs access to candidates to get a more complete story for the evening news or the next day's newspaper. This symbiotic relationship raises concerns about the press's ability to maintain its objectivity. Former reporters, editors, and other employees of the private media populate campaign staffs and are sought after for their ability to get their candidate's views into a news report about the campaign. The mutual dependence goes much farther, however. Not only do reporters following candidates to public appearances receive press packets outlining the candidate's views, but the campaigns often provide reporters with transportation to and from the events. In fact, when following the Terry campaign on a western tour after Labor Day, several reporters pushed to get the last event wrapped up in a timely manner so that the campaign could fly them back to Richmond, where they could write and file their stories in time to meet their deadlines. They made it.

For another example, the Florio campaign had a telephone hot line designed mostly for radio stations. Reporters could call the number and copy prerecorded quotes from Florio or campaign spokespeople on a variety of issues. The sound bites could then be played on the radio as part of the news story. By doing so, the news report appeared more complete and the candidate had more control over the content of the clip that was aired. Exploration of this concern about objectivity is not possible without the careful attention to campaigns that can only be gathered through case-study techniques.

Finally, the studies of Virginia and New Jersey present more than just interesting stories about two campaigns. The polling data provide additional empirical support for the various other sources of information mobilized in chapters 5 and 6. The qualitative and quantitative analysis within these two chapters, as well as within the project as a whole, complement each other, providing a more complete test of the theory guiding this book than would have been possible using only one approach or the other.

No research is without limitations. I suppose all scholars hunger for more data. More detailed information about the campaign strategies employed in the hundred-plus elections examined in chapters 7 through 9 would be beneficial. While exit polls provide information about many voters in many elections, these polls do not provide a great deal of depth of information. More specifically, future research would benefit from more detailed information about voters' views on a variety of specific political issues. The analysis would also be improved by estimating a systematic set of starting points for the distribution of public opinion regarding the salience of various issues and cleavages prior to the start of gubernatorial campaigns. Doing so would provide a more direct test of voters' responses to campaign themes given a prior distribution of expected behavior.

The nature of the data that are available raises some questions about causality versus simple correlation. King, Keohane, and Verba (1994) suggest that the problem of demonstrating causality is one from which political scientists can never fully escape. Chapters 7 through 9 assume that the presence of particular campaign themes causes the change in salience of various individual-level characteristics. However, the data cannot prove this predicted causal relationship. These findings are more accurately described as findings consistent with the theory advocated in this book. The measures of the campaign themes stressed by candidates are certainly based on information observed prior to election day. Yet not knowing the salience of various individual-level factors before a campaign begins limits my ability to claim that the observed variance in the salience of these factors on election day is strictly caused by the themes stressed by candidates.

The poll data mobilized in chapters 5 and 6 make some progress in addressing the nature of the causal relationship. The first poll presented in chapter 5 was taken in early September, and the Virginia candidates had already been campaigning for months, but the tables and figures show that much of the movement of voters is captured by the polls presented. In chapter 6, the first poll, measuring Florio's approval ratings, and the second poll, taken after the June primary, provide better baseline measures of public opinion. However, much of the movement in New Jersey took place between the final public-opinion poll and the election-day exit poll.

Furthermore, comparisons between the timing of the polls and of various campaign events provide more assurance that movement among voters occurred in response to the themes candidates stressed. Yet the problem of causality still remains, as many factors not specifically accounted for in the analysis also changed over the course of these two campaigns. Without more rigorous control and/or more frequent measures of campaign activity and public opinion, the question of strict causality cannot be fully answered. Of course, the data necessary to allay entirely these concerns is not available.

Two key aspects of representative government are not part of this analysis yet are directly related to the topic at hand. First, this analysis does not examine directly the role played by campaign themes in mobilizing turnout among various sectors of the electorate. Florio's loss in New Jersey was attributed by many to the lackluster support and mobilization of African-Americans.[3] Accounts in the newspaper coverage of the other campaigns included in this analysis suggest similar situations occurred in other contexts. The case studies of Virginia and New Jersey, along with the poll data analyzed for each race, do shed some light on African-American voters' unenthusiastic embrace of Florio and Terry. The case studies also point to some traditionally Republican groups of voters' early uncertainty regarding Allen and Whitman, which could have potentially become a mobilization problem for their campaigns. Still, a more systematic look at how campaign themes stimulate turnout among various segments of the electorate would expand our understanding of the role played by campaigns and be entirely consistent with the theory developed here.

Second, this analysis ends on election day. The finding that voters respond to the issue content of themes stressed by candidates during the campaign implies that these themes should have some impact on the behavior of candidates while they serve in office. Establishing that relationship is important for scholars concerned about the responsiveness of elected governments to their citizens, but like the question of mobilization, this area is left for further research.

Candidates who want to win use their campaigns to shape the informational context within which voters find themselves, thereby influencing the probability that voters will support or oppose the candidates at the polls. Voters respond to what candidates say, and this analysis shows in particular that voters respond to the issue content of campaign themes. Campaigns do not simply cancel each other out, and voters do not respond only to candidate qualities and appearances. This book provides a new way of thinking about electoral politics that places the campaign itself at the center of the process, and this work provides a wide variety of evidence suggesting the validity of this view of elections. Who wins and who loses depends in part on which candidate's views are accepted by the electorate, which is what campaigns are all about.

Models and Methods for the Case Studies

In chapter 4, I described the campaign process as a dynamic interaction between the candidates and voters, with the media playing a key linking role. Here I presented a model of that process. While presented as a statistical model, the data necessary for an actual empirical analysis exceed what is available in this project. I specify the model as a set of three simultaneous equations:

$$SA_t = \sum_{i=1}^{I} a_{1i} SA_{it-1} + \sum_{i=1}^{I} b_{1i} SB_{it-1} + \sum_{j=1}^{J} c_{1j} SV_{jt-1}$$

$$+ \sum_{k=1}^{K} d_{1k} M_{kt-1} + \varepsilon_{1t} \tag{A.1}$$

$$SB_t = \sum_{i=1}^{I} a_{2i} SA_{it-1} + \sum_{i=1}^{I} b_{2i} SB_{it-1} + \sum_{j=1}^{J} c_{2j} SV_{jt-1}$$

$$+ \sum_{k=1}^{K} d_{2k} M_{kt-1} + \varepsilon_{2t} \tag{A.2}$$

$$SV_t = \sum_{i=1}^{I} a_{3i} SA_{it-1} + \sum_{i=1}^{I} b_{3i} SB_{it-1} + \sum_{j=1}^{J} c_{3j} SV_{jt-1}$$

$$+ \sum_{k=1}^{K} d_{3k} M_{kt-1} + \varepsilon_{3t} \tag{A.3}$$

where SA_t and SB_t are matrices containing i measures of campaign strategies for Candidates A and B, respectively, directed at potentially salient cleavages among voters. SV_{jt} is a matrix containing j measures of the level of salience of these cleavages among voters. M_{jt} is a matrix of k measures of the content of the media coverage of the election. For all three equations, a is an $i \times 1$ vector of coefficients relating the strategy of candidate A at time $t - 1$ to each dependent variable, b is an $i \times 1$ vector of coefficients relating the strategy of candidate B at time $t - 1$ to each dependent variable, c is a $j \times 1$ vector of coefficients expressing the relationship between the salience of each cleavage at time $t - 1$ and each dependent variable, and d is a $k \times 1$ vector of coefficients relating the content of the media at time $t - 1$ to each dependent variable. The subscripts t and $t - 1$ refer to points in time during any one election. Equations A.1 through A.3 essentially model the dynamic process of the campaigns as a first-order vector autoregressive (VAR) process between candidate strategy and the salience of cleavages among voters because each equation includes lagged values of all three of the dependent variables as regressors. The relationship between the strategies of the two candidates along with the salience of issues to voters as modeled here is also consistent with what Finkel (1995) calls a cross-lagged model.

The initial values for the salience of each cleavage within the electorate could be determined by public-opinion polling prior to the beginning of the campaign. Much of the political context within which campaigns take place is exogenous to this system of equations. For example, the partisan makeup of a state defines opportunities and/or obstacles for candidates and provides a backdrop for the formation of public opinion. Such factors remain relatively constant over the short duration of a campaign. Candidate strategy may influence the salience of such factors but not their existence. Exogenous shocks to the system (for example, revelation of a previously unknown scandal) can enter the system through media coverage and/or the error terms of the equations. The error terms of these three equations would likely be contemporaneously correlated with each other.

As mentioned previously, detailed (possibly weekly) measures needed to estimate this model for the two cases included in chapters 5 and 6 do not exist. Instead, I have five polls for Virginia conducted from September 1 through the end of October and six polls for New Jersey conducted from June through election day. I also have a poll conducted in February 1993 in New Jersey that asked a limited number of questions about the popularity of Governor Florio.

Two of the Virginia polls were conducted by the Survey Research Lab at Virginia Commonwealth University, while the other three were conducted for the *Richmond Times-Dispatch* by the research department of Media General. Four of the preelection polls from New Jersey and the February poll measuring the popularity of the governor were conducted by the Eagleton Institute of Politics.[1] One of the preelection polls and the final poll available from New Jersey, an exit poll, were conducted by CBS/*New York Times*.[2] These polls allow me to test the effect of candidate strategy over the course of the campaign and are described in more detail in chapters 5 and 6.

To summarize, the data necessary to fully estimate the model presented in this appendix are not available, but they could be gathered. Candidates' tracking polls might be the most readily available source of the necessary measures of public opinion. However, the presentation and discussion of the statistical model, even if not currently testable, clarifies the structure of the campaign process articulated in this book.

Models and Methods for the Comparative State Analysis

In chapter 4, I presented a brief statistical model of individual voting behavior responding to campaign themes using the example of the abortion issue. In this appendix, I present a more complete version of that model. The model presented here serves as the basis for the analysis carried out in chapters 7, 8, and 9. For any given election:

$$V_{ijt} = \sum_{k=1}^{K} \alpha_k X_{kijt} + \sum_{l=1}^{L} \beta_l Z_{ljt} + \sum_{m=1}^{M} \gamma_m T_{mt} + \sum_{n=1}^{N} \delta_n S_{njt}$$

$$+ \sum_{o=1}^{O} \zeta_o XS_{oijt} + \sum_{p=1}^{P} \eta_p ZS_{pjt} + \sum_{q=1}^{Q} \upsilon_q TS_{qt} + \varepsilon_{ijt} \qquad \text{(B.1)}$$

In this model, V_{ijt} is the vote cast by individual i in election j at time (year) t. X_{kijt} is a matrix of K individual-level voter characteristics expected to influence voting behavior, such as race, party identification, or attitudes on issues. Therefore, α is a $K \times 1$ vector of parameters expressing the relationship between X and voting behavior. Z_{ljt} represents a matrix of L variables that are constant within each j election but vary across elections. These variables might include the incumbency status and/or quality of the candidates, state political ideology, or campaign spending. Thus, β is an $L \times 1$ vector of parameters linking these election-level factors to individual-level voting behavior.[3] T_t is a matrix containing M measures of national factors that vary only across time. Such factors might include the party of the president, whether it is a presidential election year, or the health of the national economy. Thus, γ is an $M \times 1$ vector of parameters linking elements of T to individual voting behavior. S_{jt} is a matrix containing N measures of campaign strategy for each candidate for each election j held at time t. For this study, S would contain the set of dummy variables measuring which themes were stressed by each candidate. Therefore, δ is an $N \times 1$

vector of coefficients measuring the direct relationship between candidate strategy and individual voting behavior. The actual test of the heresthetic argument comes in the remaining elements of the model. XS_{ijt} is a matrix of O multiplicative interaction terms between elements of X and S. ZS_{jt} is a matrix of P multiplicative interaction terms between elements of Z and S. TS_t is a matrix of Q multiplicative interaction terms between elements of T and S. Under this specification, ζ is an $O \times 1$ vector of coefficients measuring how the strategies of candidates influence the salience of individual-level characteristics in X, η is a $P \times 1$ vector of coefficients measuring the change in the salience of election-level factors in Z resulting from candidate strategies, and θ is a $Q \times 1$ vector of coefficients showing how the salience of national factors in T is influenced by the content of the campaign.

The model in equation B.1 guides the empirical analysis undertaken in chapters 7, 8, and 9. The coefficients operating on the series of multiplicative interaction terms will demonstrate whether voters respond to what candidates say during the election. Thus, the model in equation B.1 tests whether candidates create heresthetic change through the content of their campaigns by altering the salience of factors that predict voting behavior.

Equation B.1 includes the key aspects of my theory in a general model of individual-level voting behavior applicable to the study of elections in a variety of contexts beyond gubernatorial elections. Equation B.1 models those factors beyond the candidates' control yet allows strategic candidates to influence their electoral fortunes by shifting the relative salience of potential cleavages. Campaign activity is bounded by the limits of the political environment, but what candidates do and how well they do it can matter in this model.

Complete Models Examining Votes for Prochoice Gubernatorial Candidates

This appendix contains the complete models on which tables 7.3 through 7.6 are based. Each variable name that ends with a 1 indicates that it has been multiplied by the state reversal dummy variable to account for the partisan direction of the expected relationship between that variable and voting behavior in gubernatorial elections. It should be noted again that abortion was stressed by someone in all four of the reversed states but was never stressed by the prolife candidate. As a result, estimates of some of the interaction terms between whether abortion was stressed in these states and gender and Catholicism are impossible to produce because of perfect colinearity.

In general, the control variables in these models behaved as expected. People with higher family incomes were more likely to vote for the Republican candidate for governor than were those with lower family incomes. Residents of large cities were more likely to vote for Democrats, whereas those living in rural areas were increasingly likely to support the GOP contender. Party identification remained a strong and consistent predictor of voting behavior. In addition, African-American voters were relatively more likely to vote for Democratic candidates. Jews were no more or less likely to vote for Democratic candidates than were non-Jews (excluding Catholics).

Higher spending per capita, adjusted for inflation, by the prochoice candidate increased the probability of a respondent voting for the prochoice candidate if that candidate was not an incumbent. If an incumbent, spending by the prochoice candidate led to lower levels of support among voters, a common finding in the literature on candidate spending. In contrast, spending by prolife candidates had no effect whether or not they were incumbents.

Presidential approval was strongly related to voting behavior. Voters who did not approve of the way President Bush, a Republican, was handling his job were significantly more likely to vote for the Democratic candidate for governor. However, Republican incumbent governors running for reelection did not appear to suffer any more than did other GOP candidates when voters disapproved of the president, except as shown in the final table.

The effects of respondents' evaluations of their states' economies on voting behavior worked through incumbency. Both prochoice and prolife incumbents were rewarded with higher levels of support from voters who believed their state's economy was doing well. State economic evaluations did not have a direct effect on voting behavior in open-seat races.

Finally, a dummy variable for the South, coded as a 1 for those states that were part of the Confederacy and 0 otherwise, never achieved statistical significance. It is also worth noting that the dummy variable required to signify those four states in which the candidates reversed the traditional party positions on abortion never approached statistical significance. This finding indicates that there was nothing unique about the voting behavior in those four states that is not captured by other variables in the models.

TABLE C1.   Complete Model Used to Produce Table 7.3

Variable	Coefficient
Constant	−0.7726***
State reversal dummy	−0.1324
Family income	−0.0760***
Family income1	0.2166***
Urbanity of residence	−0.0585***
Urbanity of residence1	0.0599
Prochoice party ID	1.1822***
Prolife party ID	−0.8411***
Black	0.8509***
Black1	−1.5979***
Jewish	0.0901
Jewish1	0.7585
Prochoice candidate spending	0.0318***
Prolife candidate spending	0.0249
Disapprove of Bush	0.7512***
Disapprove of Bush1	−0.8756***
Evaluation of state economy	−0.0303
Prochoice incumbent	0.6397**
Prolife incumbent	−0.0489
Evaluation of state economy × prochoice incumbent	1.0066***
Evaluation of state economy × prolife incumbent	−0.5722***
Disapprove of Bush × Republican incumbent	0.1722
Prochoice incumbent × prochoice candidate spending	−0.0612***
Prolife incumbent × prolife candidate spending	0.0023
South dummy variable	0.0394
Female	0.0737*
Female1	−0.1156
Catholic	0.0867
Catholic1	−0.1541
Voter is prochoice	0.3889***
Voter is prolife	−0.4062***

$N = 41,222$
*$p < .1$ (two-tailed)   **$p < .05$ (two-tailed)   ***$p < .01$ (two-tailed)

TABLE C2.   Complete Model Used to Produce Table 7.4

Variable	Coefficient
Constant	−0.5377**
State reversal dummy	−0.0331
Family income	−0.0736***
Family income1	0.2062***
Urbanity of residence	−0.0602***
Urbanity of residence1	0.0676
Prochoice party ID	1.1852***
Prolife party ID	−0.8567***
Black	0.8571***
Black1	−1.6136***
Jewish	0.0888
Jewish1	0.7261
Prochoice candidate spending	0.0295***
Prolife candidate spending	0.0244
Disapprove of Bush	0.7456***
Disapprove of Bush1	−0.8906***
Evaluation of state economy	−0.0374
Prochoice incumbent	0.6674**
Prolife incumbent	0.0010
Evaluation of state economy × prochoice incumbent	1.0025***
Evaluation of state economy × prolife incumbent	−0.5590***
Disapprove of Bush × Republican incumbent	0.1848
Prochoice incumbent × prochoice candidate spending	−0.0628***
Prolife incumbent × prolife candidate spending	−0.0036
South dummy variable	0.0674
Female	−0.0241
Female1	−0.1924*
Catholic	0.0373
Catholic1	−0.1657
Voter is prochoice	0.1345*
Voter is prolife	−0.2938***
Abortion stressed by anyone	−0.3585**
Abortion stressed by anyone × female	0.1741**
Abortion stressed by anyone × Catholic	0.0819
Abortion stressed by anyone × voter is prochoice	0.4040***
Abortion stressed by anyone × voter is prolife	−0.1859

$N = 41,222$
*$p < .1$ (two-tailed)   **$p < .05$ (two-tailed)   ***$p < .01$ (two-tailed)

TABLE C3.   Complete Model Used to Produce Tables 7.5 and 7.6

Variable	Coefficient
Constant	−0.7415***
State reversal dummy	0.0267
Family income	−0.0661***
Family income1	0.2033***
Urbanity of residence	−0.0496**
Urbanity of residence1	0.0585
Prochoice party ID	1.2203***
Prolife party ID	−0.8355***
Black	0.9467***
Black1	−1.5181***
Jewish	0.0978
Jewish1	0.6864
Prochoice candidate spending	0.0268***
Prolife candidate spending	0.0275
Disapprove of Bush	0.7206***
Disapprove of Bush1	−0.8836***
Evaluation of state economy	0.0553
Prochoice incumbent	0.4703
Prolife incumbent	0.0680
Evaluation of state economy × prochoice incumbent	0.9002***
Evaluation of state economy × prolife incumbent	−0.6642***
Disapprove of Bush × Republican incumbent	0.3344**
Prochoice incumbent × prochoice candidate spending	−0.0478***
Prolife incumbent × prolife candidate spending	−0.0025
South dummy variable	−0.2177
Female	0.0133
Female1	0.4395**
Catholic	0.0532
Catholic1	0.1367
Voter is prochoice	0.2700***
Voter is prolife	−0.4083***
Prochoice candidate stressed abortion	−0.4571***
Stressed by prochoice candidate × female	0.1161
Stressed by prochoice candidate × female1	−0.8220***
Stressed by prochoice candidate × Catholic	−0.0195
Stressed by prochoice candidate × Catholic1	−0.4014**
Stressed by prochoice candidate × voter is prochoice	0.3761***
Stressed by prochoice candidate × voter is prolife	−0.0612

(*continued*)

TABLE C3.—*Continued*

Variable	Coefficient
Prolife candidate stressed abortion	0.5163***
Stressed by prolife candidate × female	0.0822
Stressed by prolife candidate × Catholic	0.1433
Stressed by prolife candidate × voter is prochoice	−0.2085
Stressed by prolife candidate × voter is prolife	0.0644

$N = 41,222$

*$p < .1$ (two-tailed)   **$p < .05$ (two-tailed)   ***$p < .01$ (two-tailed)

Complete Models Examining Votes for Democratic Gubernatorial Candidates

Appendix D includes the three complete models used to produce tables 9.4 through 9.6. They include control measures for whether a voter was Jewish, the age of the respondent, whether the Democrat or the Republican candidate was an incumbent, the amount spent by each candidate during the primary and general-election campaigns, a measure of the electorate's political ideology, three separate dummy variables for the three presidential-election years included in this analysis, and a dummy variable for the South, defined as former Confederate states. Each of these variables is measured as a dummy variable except age, state ideology, and campaign spending. Age is measured as a categorical variable ranging from 1 to 4. The state ideology measure is Erikson, Wright, and McIver's (1993) measure. Its observed range is from −27.93 to −.81, with increasingly negative numbers indicating increasingly more conservative state electorates. Campaign spending is the dollar amount spent, adjusted for inflation and population. In addition, it is expected that the impact of spending will vary with the incumbency status of the candidates involved. Thus, the two campaign-spending variables are multiplied by whether the respective candidate spending the money is an incumbent. The sample size for each model is 93,858.

The behavior of these control variables is largely as would be expected and is consistent across all three models. Jewish voters are more likely to vote for Democratic candidates, controlling for the other factors in the model. Older voters tended to support Republican candidates more than did younger voters. Incumbents of both parties tended to have an advantage over challengers. Spending behaved as predicted—spending more money helped candidates win votes, but that benefit was diminished if the candidates were incumbents. As state electorates become increasingly liberal, Democratic candidates found it harder to get votes. This apparently counterintuitive finding corresponds to that reported by Erikson, Wright, and McIver (1993) and likely results from the same phenomenon they describe. Democratic candidates did significantly less well in 1984 than in presidential off-year elections, not surprising given Reagan's overwhelming presidential victory that year. The Bush election in 1988 and the Clinton victory in 1992 produced coattail effects in the expected direction, but they were not statistically significant. Finally, the South is no longer a safe haven for state-level Democratic candidates. Once other factors, including party identification and race, have been controlled, voters in the South were less likely to cast their ballots for Democratic candidates.

TABLE D1. Complete Model Used to Produce Table 9.4

Variable	Coefficient
Constant	−0.1216
Democrat	1.3094***
Republican	−1.2031***
Family income	−0.0732***
Black	0.9416***
Catholic	0.0520
Jewish	0.5429***
Female	0.1132***
Age of respondent	−0.0558***
Democratic incumbent	0.4072*
Republican incumbent	−0.4307*
Democrat spending	0.511***
Republican spending	−0.0244
Democratic incumbent × Democratic spending	−0.0083
Republican incumbent × Republican spending	0.0198
State ideology	−0.0168**
1984 dummy variable	−0.5069**
1988 dummy variable	−0.3005
1992 dummy variable	0.1467
South dummy variable	−0.3833**

$N = 93,858$

$*p < .1$ $**p < .05$ $***p < .01$

TABLE D2.　Complete Model Used to Produce Table 9.5

Variable	Coefficient
Constant	−0.0363
Democrat	1.2482***
Republican	−1.1168***
Family income	−0.0544***
Black	0.7383***
Catholic	0.0633
Jewish	0.5199***
Female	0.0773**
Age of respondent	−0.0602***
Democratic incumbent	0.2974
Republican incumbent	−0.7486***
Democrat spending	0.0486***
Republican spending	−0.0211
Democratic incumbent × Democratic spending	−0.0091
Republican incumbent × Republican spending	0.0466
State ideology	−0.0163**
1984 dummy variable	−0.5760***
1988 dummy variable	−0.0880
1992 dummy variable	0.0181
South dummy variable	−0.3371**
Gender-related issue(s) stressed	0.3649***
Gender-related issue(s) stressed × female	0.0594
Partisanship stressed	0.1067
Partisanship stressed × Democrat	0.1154
Partisanship stressed × Republican	−0.2223**
Race-related issue(s) stressed	−0.3793***
Race-related issue(s) stressed × black	0.3597**
Abortion stressed	−0.1100
Abortion stressed × Catholic	−0.0767
Class-based issues stressed	−0.0893
Class-based issues stressed × family income	−0.0662**

$N = 93,858$
*$p < .1$　　**$p < .05$　　***$p < .01$

TABLE D3.   Complete Model Used to Produce Table 9.6

Variable	Coefficient
Constant	0.0600
Democrat	1.2772***
Republican	−1.1006***
Family income	−0.0532***
Black	0.7640***
Catholic	0.0645
Jewish	0.5090***
Female	0.0716**
Age of respondent	−0.0554***
Democratic incumbent	0.1210
Republican incumbent	−0.3891
Democrat spending	0.0446***
Republican spending	−0.0194
Democratic incumbent × Democratic spending	−0.0176
Republican incumbent × Republican spending	0.0034
State ideology	−0.0132
1984 dummy variable	−0.3050***
1988 dummy variable	−0.1052
1992 dummy variable	0.1601
South dummy variable	−0.3627**
Partisanship stressed	−0.0178
Partisanship stressed × Democrat	0.0883
Partisanship stressed × Republican	−0.2350**
Factors stressed by the Democrat	
Gender-related issue(s) stressed	−0.1401
Gender-related issue(s) stressed × female	−0.0041
Race-related issue(s) stressed	−0.0140
Race-related issue(s) stressed × black	0.1168
Abortion stressed	0.0109
Abortion stressed × Catholic	−0.2185**
Class-based issues stressed	0.2155
Class-based issues stressed × family income	−0.0947***
Factors stressed by the Republican	
Gender-related issue(s) stressed	0.5155***
Gender-related issue(s) stressed × female	0.1037**
Race-related issue(s) stressed	−0.55078***
Race-related issue(s) stressed × black	0.3217*
Abortion stressed	0.0083
Abortion stressed × Catholic	0.2719***
Class-based issues stressed	−0.6610***
Class-based issues stressed × family income	0.0476

$N = 93{,}858$
$*p < .1$ $**p < .05$ $***p < .01$

Notes

1. Electoral considerations certainly continue to play a role in gubernatorial behavior after the election. Also, voters continue to observe and evaluate candidates after the election is over. However, during the campaign itself both candidates and voters are focused specifically on the election, and that time period serves as the focus of this analysis.

2. This rather simplified discussion assumes voting is costless. Downs deals with the idea that the costs of voting rarely outweigh its direct benefits if you weigh the potential benefits by the probability that any one vote will make the difference in an election. Thus, Downs acknowledges that many voters may not participate. However, this sort of failure to vote differs from my argument regarding activists intentionally not participating in one election because of a long-term focus on the electoral process.

3. This discussion does not ignore those infrequent cases in contemporary U.S. politics that have witnessed the success of independent candidates. These cases, however, do not alter the fundamental institutional structure that the two-party system creates and should not be considered in any way sufficient evidence to reject this theory.

4. This phenomenon opens the possibility for "campaigns" run by people other than the candidates to influence the salience of various factors or cleavages among voters. In particular, the efforts of interest groups can be melded into this theory of voting behavior.

5. In fact, some scholars may criticize the process by which presidential outcomes are predicted based on these models, several of which are cited by Gelman and King. Typically, such models include no more than a dozen previous elections (Gelman and King include eleven in their predictions). The number of independent variables begins to approach the number of elections in the model once dummies for outlier years, candidate home-state advantage, and the proportion of the population that is Catholic (for 1960) are included. To get around this degrees-of-freedom problem, these models disaggregate to the state level, produce predicted outcomes for each state, then reaggregate the state outcomes to produce a national estimate of who will win the election.

6. Such was the case in the 1990 gubernatorial election in Minnesota. The Republican nominee, Jon Grunseth, was eventually forced to withdraw from the race after the publication of charges that he swam nude with minors and had a long-running extra-

marital affair. In 1982 in Vermont, Democratic challenger Madeline Kunin repeatedly attacked Governor Richard Snelling for secretly allowing the transportation of high-level radioactive waste across the state. In 1992 in Missouri, Democrat Mel Carnahan repeatedly accused his Republican counterpart, William Webster, of improper conduct as attorney general while distributing financial awards in workers' compensation cases. Webster lost and later pleaded guilty to federal conspiracy and embezzlement charges.

Chapter 3

1. A number of works are available that provide more complete introductions to spa-tial voting models. Interested readers should begin with Downs 1957 and Black 1958, then explore Enelow and Hinich 1984 and Hinich and Munger 1997. Most of what is presented here has been developed in these works.

2. But see the directional theory developed by Rabinowitz and Macdonald 1989.

3. Using the square of the distance produces a measure of distance that is always positive. Using the absolute value of the distance would produce the same result. I em-ploy the squared distance here because it facilitates later developments in the model.

4. Another common notation in the literature is to treat $\mathbf{X}$ as a vector of voters and use the x_i to indicate the "ith" voter. The basic structure of what follows, however, does not change.

5. Beginning with $(x - P_{xa})^2$, substitute in $p_a + v_{xa}$. This results in:

$$(x - (p_a + v_{xa}))^2$$

This can be rewritten as:

$$(x - p_a - v_{xa})^2$$

Expanding the squared term leads to:

$$x^2 - 2xp_a + p_a^2 - 2xv_{xa} + 2p_a v_{xa} + v_{xa}^2$$

Because the expected value of $v_{xa} = 0$ (see Alvarez 1997; Enelow and Hinich 1984), this expression simplifies to:

$$x^2 - 2xp_a + p_a^2 + v_{xa}^2$$

Collecting terms, the final expression is:

$$(x - p_a)^2 + v_{xa}^2$$

6. See Alvarez 1997 for a more complete elaboration of these points and Alvarez and Franklin 1994 and Franklin 1991 for some empirical treatments of these issues.

7. The discussion of uncertainty due to incomplete information is readily transfer-able into the multidimensional model I explore, as is the term for nonpolicy factors in-troduced earlier. However, to present the issues raised by a multidimensional policy is-

sue space more clearly, I examine the model at this point without regard to uncertainty. I return briefly to the question of uncertainty at the end of this chapter.

8. It is well known that the spatial model predicts unstable outcomes resulting from voting by several voters over two or more dimensions simultaneously because the median voter theorem holds only in very restrictive circumstances in the multidimensional case. There have been a number of attempts to "save" the theorem, most importantly Shepsle (1979) and Shepsle and Weingast's (1981) development of a model of structurally induced equilibrium. I do not want to explore all these issues here, but I agree with Hinich and Munger's (1997) sentiment that the volatility of the median voter theorem in multidimensional voting does not prevent useful insights into the electoral process through the analysis of spatial models.

9. For the multidimensional case, I use boldface type for the location of Voter X and Candidates A and B to indicate that it represents a vector containing the respective locations of each on each dimension.

10. This common configuration (see Enelow and Hinich 1984; Hinich and Munger 1997) labels the weights using subscripts, assuming that the elements come from a weight matrix, which in the two-dimensional case would be:

$$\mathbf{Z} = \begin{bmatrix} z_{11} & z_{12} \\ z_{21} & z_{22} \end{bmatrix}$$

11. If these two dimensions were expressed as spending for health care and spending for education, respectively, when $z_{11} > z_{22}$, the implication is that a difference of one dollar in spending on health care is more important to Voter X than is a difference of one dollar in spending on education.

12. There is substantial empirical evidence that voters' views on specific issues are better predictors of their voting behavior when they report that those issues are more important to them (see RePass 1971 for an early treatment and Abramowitz 1995 for a recent test regarding abortion). Left unexamined until now, however, is the role played by campaigns in making particular issues more or less salient to voters.

13. Specifically, the major (longer) axis of the ellipses representing the indifference curves will be oriented along the less salient dimension—in this case, Dimension 1. The major axis will be tilted away from that dimension at an angle α such that: $\tan 2\alpha = -2z_{12}/(z_{22} - z_{11})$ with $-45° < \alpha < 45°$ (Enelow and Hinich 1984, 17).

Chapter 4

1. I will subsequently return to the subject of coding campaign themes as simple dummy variables.

2. See Jaccard, Turrisi, and Wan 1990 for an extensive discussion of interaction terms.

3. These polls were made available through the Interuniversity Consortium for Political and Social Research.

4. The 1990 ANES Senate Election Study is an exception.

5. Connecticut is dropped because of a confounding independent candidate, and no poll was conducted in Alaska.

6. See Stimson 1985 for a basic overview of the types of problems faced by pooling data. See also Beck and Katz 1995 for further discussion.

7. The summaries from *Congressional Quarterly Weekly Reports* and the *Almanac of American Politics* served primarily as sources of background information and as a check on the coding based on the newspaper coverage. While helpful, I found that relying exclusively on these two sources would have been inadequate. All coding decisions were based primarily on newspaper coverage.

8. My thanks to Charles Franklin, who provided newspaper clippings for a number of the 1990 elections.

9. A paragraph was counted as dealing with the abortion issue if either candidate's views on abortion were mentioned, if activities, other individuals, or interest groups were described as being connected with the abortion issue and/or the candidates' stands on the issue, or if a direct quote mentioned abortion. I did not limit the coding to only those paragraphs that were devoted entirely to abortion or restrict the coding to include only mentions of the issue made directly by the candidates or representatives of their campaigns. In practice, most paragraphs of a newspaper story that made any mention of abortion were in fact devoted to the issue, because most newspaper paragraphs are typically short and concise. The exception would be paragraphs that briefly lay out a summary of a candidate's stands on various issues or preview several issues, including abortion, that are discussed in more detail later in the article.

Chapter 5

1. These two races occurred in the absence of presidential or congressional campaigns, which allowed the media and voters to focus more attention on these races. It is not clear whether this situation increases or decreases the chances for candidates to create heresthetic change. On the one hand, it allows them to send clear messages that are not lost in a sea of political rhetoric from other races. Thus, voters may receive more information in these races than would be expected in other gubernatorial races. On the other hand, Gelman and King (1993) argue that the abundance of information in presidential campaigns coming from both sides results in the specific content of the campaigns canceling each other out. Because these gubernatorial races are isolated, the level of attention they receive may make them operate more like the presidential contests Gelman and King describe rather than typical gubernatorial races.

2. Detailed accounts of recent Virginia and New Jersey politics are provided by Atkinson 1992 and Salmore and Salmore 1993, respectively.

3. Virginia elects the positions of governor, lieutenant governor, and attorney general, and voters vote for each individual office rather than for a party slate. Thus, voters can—and often do—split their tickets among these three offices.

4. In an interview conducted in August, a Terry staff member said that her campaign would be spending that month working on mobilizing its grassroots organization. The campaign worker also indicated that the Terry campaign did not have in place any sort of mechanism (like a newsletter) to keep grassroots leaders informed and interested in the campaign. In contrast, the Allen campaign had leaders in every voting district in place for the convention in June. The Allen campaign also had a weekly newsletter

(which I received) that went out to about two thousand supporters called the Leadership Team.

5. One of the reporters covering the first day of the Democratic convention had earlier in the day said to me that the news of the first day would probably be about Wilder and Robb, in large part, "because there was no other story" at the convention.

6. This phenomenon shows that candidates running for statewide office do not have complete or identical information about voters' preferences. This finding is consistent with the role of learning as the campaign unfolds and contrasts with Gelman and King's (1993) view of presidential elections.

7. At a debate held in front of the Virginia Bar Association on September 30, Terry was asked to endorse or repudiate President Clinton's proposals regarding gays in the military and taxes. She answered immediately, "I repudiate." This event highlighted Terry's attempt to keep a distance not only from Clinton but from other Democrats as well. As a side note, it was reported that the audience at this debate was stunned for a few seconds at Terry's short reply and then laughed.

8. In fact, the Allen camp had prepared for this contingency in advance, responding the following day with a new television ad attacking Terry for being the first to go negative.

9. This second poll was conducted by Mason-Dixon Opinion Research. A senior staff member in the Allen campaign said that the Mason-Dixon polls closely matched their internal polling results. Reported later in this chapter is a figure that shows the marginal levels of candidate support from the internal polling of the Allen campaign that verifies this claim.

10. The analysis used a multinomial logit model to compare straight-Democratic-ticket voters, straight-Republican-ticket voters, and those who voted for the Republican for governor but also for Terry for attorney general. Very few voters split their tickets for these two offices in the opposite direction, so these voters were deleted from the analysis.

11. These polls were conducted by Media General Research, for the *Richmond Times-Dispatch* and Channel 12 News in Richmond, and the Commonwealth Poll conducted by the Survey Research Laboratory at Virginia Commonwealth University. Using polls conducted by different agencies risks having differences in methods and/or design confound the analysis. However, this problem does not appear to have been a major complication in this case.

12. The one clear difference between figures 5.1 and 5.2 is the consistently higher proportion of voters classified as undecided in figure 5.2, particularly in September. This difference is a result of a coding decision. For figure 5.2 and table 5.2, only voters with a clear preference were coded as supporting one candidate or the other. Follow-up questions, designed to tap whether an undecided respondent was leaning one way or the other, were not used to classify additional respondents as supporters of a candidate. Different coding rules for undecided voters were used by the Allen campaign, thereby lowering that figure in their polls. The results of the following analysis are unaffected by this coding decision.

13. The figures that follow based on predicted probabilities are heuristic devices designed to illustrate the predicted differences between two or more groups of voters. They

compare the average predicted level of support among voters of different categories, but they do not reflect the number of respondents that actually fall into those categories. For example, figure 5.3 shows the average predicted difference between women and men regardless of how many women and/or men are surveyed.

14. The number of available attitudinal questions in these polls is limited, and those that are asked deal directly with the themes stressed by candidates. Thus, questions are asked about a five-day waiting period and abolishing parole, but no questions are asked about many other issues, including taxes, economic development, the environment, and so forth. Readers may wonder if the claims that follow regarding the salience to Virginia voters of these crime-related issues are simply a function of these questions being asked instead of others. In other words, just asking these questions instead of others makes it appear that these issues are more salient (see, e.g., Zaller 1992). This sort of priming effect may raise the overall level of salience of these issues to the survey respondents, but since the question is asked of everyone, this effect is constant across respondents. The analysis that follows compares the salience of the same attitudes across two or more points in time. If the same question is asked of everyone in more than one poll, this priming effect is constant for everyone and cannot be the cause of differences in the salience of these crime-related issues to voters between two or more points in time.

15. This final poll, the last one conducted for the *Richmond Times-Dispatch,* is dropped because it did not include any of the questions contained in the other four polls that are part of table 5.2.

16. In polls 1, 2, and 4, these variables are measured as simple dummy variables and are based on whether the respondent generally approves or disapproves of the performance of Wilder and Clinton, coded as a 1 if they approve and a 0 otherwise. The variables in poll 3 are measured somewhat differently. In this poll, respondents were given a list of political figures and asked to indicate if they were viewed favorably or unfavorably or if the respondents had no opinion. Thus, the evaluation is based on a general question about favorability instead of a more specific question about approval of job performance. In addition, substantial portions of voters reported that they had no opinion of Wilder, Clinton, and, in particular, Robertson. To avoid losing those cases or arbitrarily assigning them to either the favorable or unfavorable category, I coded responses to this question for poll 3 as a 1 if the political figure was viewed favorably, -1 if viewed unfavorably, and 0 if the respondent had no opinion. The effect of this coding scheme is to assume that favorable and unfavorable evaluations have equivalent effects on the respondents who hold these opinions. Second, this coding scheme doubles the observed range of this variable compared to the measures in the three polls using dummy variables, meaning that a coefficient operating on a favorability question in poll 3 would only have to be half the magnitude of a coefficient operating on one of the simple approval dummy variables to capture the magnitude of the gap between respondents holding the most extreme views on either question.

17. As noted earlier, prolife activists played a prominent role at the Republican convention, and the Resolutions Committee's video "report" referred to parental consent.

18. The exception is knowledge of Terry's position on the five-day waiting period, which was already relatively high.

19. A more complete model would show the direct effect of respondent evaluations of candidates on these two dimensions of support for each candidate more generally.

Two factors prevent the estimation of such a model in this case. First, the cross-sectional nature of the data prevents distinguishing whether support of a candidate follows the development of attitudes regarding which best represents change and which would better fight crime or whether these attitudes are projected onto the preferred candidate. Given that all three of these polls asked the general candidate-support question before they asked respondents to evaluate the candidates on these two dimensions, the potential for projection effects is substantial. Second, these polls do not provide measures of any variables that could be expected to predict how candidates are evaluated on these two dimensions that do not also predict general candidate support. Thus, the data are not sufficient to estimate something like a two-stage or three-stage least-squares model.

Chapter 6

1. Edwards challenged Whitman for the GOP gubernatorial nomination in 1993. Further discussion of this topic appears later in the chapter.

2. The New Jersey GOP primary race looked similar to the general-election race for governor in Virginia that year. The front-running candidate, leading primarily on name recognition, adopted a cautious strategy, allowing the underdog opponent to cut into that lead by defining the front-runner in negative terms. Whitman's late attacks were enough to allow her to hold on and win in her primary race. Terry's late attacks were not enough in Virginia's general election.

3. This comment resembles the situation Allen faced in the Virginia general election in the summer and early fall. His campaign felt compelled to advertise on television to keep pace with Terry, hoping to demonstrate his credibility as a candidate.

4. Campaign-finance laws in New Jersey require that any spending that specifically addresses the candidates for governor be counted against the spending limits of the candidates. Thus, if a political party, interest group, or some individual citizen spends money on television advertisements, billboards, or even T-shirts that have a gubernatorial candidate's name on them, the cost of that expenditure will be counted against that candidate's limit, even if the spending was not authorized by the candidate's campaign.

5. A GOP consultant reported after the election was over that internal polls had Whitman down by 13 percentage points at the time the CBS/*New York Times* poll had her down by 21 points. It seems unlikely that Florio's lead ever really reached a solid 21 percentage points, but even so, a year earlier almost no one would have predicted a solid double-digit lead over any GOP candidate.

6. For example, in the middle of October, Florio's campaign adviser, James Carville, called a statewide radio talk show to complain that Whitman and her husband had not released their 1990 income tax statements. Whitman said it was an unreasonable request, even though she had released her returns from several other years. She initially refused but later agreed. The story was covered for the next week or so in the press, until she actually did release her 1990 returns. There were no surprises, but the Florio campaign had managed to direct media attention toward something Whitman was failing to do for a week, forcing Whitman to answer questions about it. It also helped to focus attention on Whitman's wealth, which resulted in less time for the press and for Whitman to devote to attacks on Florio.

7. In polls 1, 2, 3, 5, and 6, place of residence was measured using four categories:

central city; city or old suburb; new suburb; and rural. Poll 4, conducted by WCBS-TV and the *New York Times,* did not make such a distinction. It simply recorded whether a voter lived in an urban, suburban, or rural setting. As table 6.2 makes clear, it does not appear that this coding difference significantly influenced the nature of the findings.

8. Those following the GOP primary process in early February certainly knew that Whitman was the front-runner, which may have contributed somewhat to the negative evaluations women gave to Florio at that time. However, the number of respondents with that level of information was certainly limited. As will be discussed below, only 63 percent of respondents right after the June primary could name Whitman as the GOP candidate, and more than half said they knew little or nothing about her at that time.

9. In chapters 7 and 9, I discuss how the abortion issue may serve as an indicator for a broader range of issues tapping the gender cleavage among voters in gubernatorial elections.

10. It is also worth noting that several of the polls asked about union membership. Again, the respondent being a member of a union or living with a family member who belonged to a union produced no significant relationship with the probability of supporting Florio in any of the polls.

11. The bulk of this excluded category consists of Protestants and other Christians. Models were run with additional dummy variables for the other religious affiliations, including those with no religious affiliation, and the results did not differ from those presented in this chapter.

12. This holds true whether or not abortion attitudes are controlled for in the analysis.

13. Florio's base was expected to be the southern part of the state and in central cities. Whitman's base was in the north and in rural areas.

14. As in chapter 5, these findings on the changing salience of an issue from one poll to the next are not simply the result of voters being primed on these issues by the polls asking them about these issues and not others.

15. The corresponding logit coefficients are -0.679 and -0.618, respectively. Both are significant at the $p < .05$ level. The addition of either variable does not change the findings reported in table 6.3.

Chapter 7

1. See, e.g., Luker 1984; Blanchard 1994; Staggenborg 1991; Goggin 1993; Segers and Byrnes 1995; Craig and O'Brien 1993.

2. Labeling groups *prochoice, prolife, proabortion,* or *antiabortion* inevitably offends someone. I employ the labels *prochoice* and *prolife* to identify both sides in the affirmative.

3. The guidelines laid out by the Supreme Court in these two 1973 decisions were well within the historical trend of how the abortion issue had been treated in the United States. *Roe v. Wade* simply codified what had been normal practice in the United States since at least 1800 (Luker 1984). It is also true that while *Roe v. Wade* articulates a woman's right to an abortion during the first trimester based on an implied right to privacy, the decision in *Doe v. Bolton* stated clearly, "a pregnant woman does not have an absolute Constitutional right to an abortion on her demand" (cited in Blanchard 1994).

4. Abortion remains an important issue in national-level politics as well. In fact,

Abramowitz (1995) found that voter attitudes on abortion were at least as important as voter evaluations of the economy in determining voting behavior in the 1992 presidential election.

5. Because all the elections analyzed in this chapter occurred in 1990, all national-level factors are held constant and, thus, that segment of the model presented in appendix B can be omitted.

6. To estimate the model, I must include states in which abortion was stressed as well as states in which it was not a central part of any candidate's campaign. Other studies focus only on states where abortion appeared important after the *Webster* decision (e.g., Cook, Jelen, and Wilcox 1992). Thus, they cannot demonstrate that abortion has become more important because of *Webster* or that it is more or less important in some states rather than others. In short, such studies lack variation at the state level on the importance of abortion, which limits their ability to discuss its causes and consequences.

7. There is also some question about the positions of the two candidates in Massachusetts. Both claimed to support abortion rights, but the Democrat, John Silber, voiced his view that he personally believed that abortion was murder. The Republican, William Weld, tried to focus some attention on the abortion issue as a way of demonstrating a more general concern for women's issues. Cook, Jelen, and Wilcox (1992) suggest that Massachusetts could be treated like the other states in which the Republican was prochoice and the Democrat was prolife. However, after reading the newspaper coverage of the campaign, I concluded that neither candidate focused primarily on abortion during the campaign. It also seemed that the positions held by the two candidates were not as clearly distinct as they were for Kansas, Minnesota, Nevada, and Pennsylvania. Thus, based on the behavior of the campaigns as reported in the newspaper coverage, I did not code Massachusetts with the other four states.

8. The two abortion dummy variables are coded as a 1 for holding either the extreme prochoice or prolife position on abortion and 0 otherwise. This leaves a middle category of those supporting some restrictions on abortion as the excluded group. These models also include control variables for race, income, and party identification and a dummy indicating whether a respondent was Jewish. Race is measured as a dummy variable coded 1 for blacks and 0 otherwise. Income is a categorical variable measuring annual family income. Party identification is controlled with two dummy variables, one coded 1 for Democrats and 0 otherwise, the other coded 1 for Republicans and 0 otherwise.

9. The variation in the salience of abortion is not just an artifact of the question being asked in the absence of other issue questions. Just asking people about abortion might make it more salient to them compared to other issues (Zaller 1992), which may result in a higher overall mean across these exit polls. However, since the same question was asked of everyone in every poll, this sort of priming effect is constant for all respondents and cannot be the cause of the variation in the salience of abortion attitudes to voters that is observed across these elections.

10. Again, there is some question about how to treat Massachusetts. The data in table 7.2 show that prochoice voters were in fact more likely to vote for the Republican candidate than the Democrat. Prolife voters, however, were not more or less likely to vote for the Democrat. Such findings suggest that a model may fit better if Massachusetts was included with the other four reversal states. However, the magnitude of the effect on these prochoice voters is much smaller in Massachusetts than in any of the other four

states, and the prolife segment of the population did not respond at all. Furthermore, researchers run a considerable risk by making any post hoc coding decisions on variables after looking at the data. It is improper simply to change how I coded the content of the Massachusetts campaign just to make it fit the data better. Doing so would constitute nothing short of doctoring the data, and any findings based on later analysis would be suspect. Given conflicting and weak information, along with the dangers of recoding variables to make models fit better, I did not find sufficient evidence to consider Massachusetts a reversal state.

11. Ideally, one would also control for evangelical and/or fundamentalist Protestants. However, a common variable for either group does not exist across these polls. This situation also makes expectations of the response of Catholic voters to the abortion issue being stressed relative to all other non-Catholics and non-Jews unclear because the excluded category includes a diverse group of mainline Protestants, Evangelical Protestants, and those indicating no religious affiliation.

12. Additional variables measured at the state level were also considered, including a measure of candidate quality based on a simplified version of the candidate-quality measures developed by Squire (1992, 1989); state-level partisanship and state ideology taken from Erikson, Wright, and McIver (1993); state unemployment rate; and the strength of state party organizations based on Cotter et al. (1984). These variables' inclusion in the following models did not alter the findings presented and rarely even approached statistical significance. Given the limited number of states in this analysis, I opted for parsimony and dropped these variables.

13. Failure to account for this clustering effect does produce dramatically different standard-error estimates for some variables, particularly those measured at the election level. In particular, variables cited in n.12 as insignificant often appear dramatically significant using traditional standard-error estimates. These variables were likely taking advantage of the nonindependence of respondent selection produced by pooling data along with any election-specific variation not explicitly modeled.

14. The models used to produce tables 7.3 through 7.6 included all thirty-four elections. To simplify the presentation, tables 7.3, 7.4, and 7.5 do not report the findings regarding whether the voter is female or Catholic for those four elections in which the traditional partisan positions held by the candidates on abortion were reversed. The complete models used to produce tables 7.3 through 7.6 are included in appendix C, as is a brief discussion of the behavior of the control variables included.

15. An assumed probability of .5 for the comparison category for each of the cells in these tables is chosen for several reasons. First, looking at deviations from a starting point of .5 simplifies the calculation of predicted probabilities. Using the formula $P = 1/(1 + e^{-L})$ where L equals $\alpha + \beta_1 \times x_1 + \beta_2 \times x_2 \ldots \beta_k \times x_k$ to produce the predicted probability, setting $P = .5$ and simplifying, L equals 0. Thus, to compute the deviation from .5 produced by any one variable, L only needs to contain that specific variable set to its desired level multiplied by the coefficient operating on it. Second, when pooling thirty-four reasonably competitive elections, .5 is a reasonable a priori prediction of the probability that any one voter would vote for one candidate over the other. Besides, the actual mean predicted probabilities for these models are near .5. Thus, making this assumption greatly simplifies the presentation while sacrificing nothing meaningful in precision.

16. Either candidate, both candidates, some third party—for example, an interest group—or any combination of these that stressed abortion are included.

Chapter 8

1. The states included are Alabama, Arizona, Arkansas, California, Colorado, Florida, Georgia, Idaho, Illinois, Indiana, Kansas, Maine, Maryland, Massachusetts, Michigan, Minnesota, Nebraska, Nevada, New Mexico, New York, Ohio, Oklahoma, Oregon, Pennsylvania, South Carolina, Tennessee, Texas, Wisconsin, and Wyoming.

2. On November 8, two days after the election, Bush announced his plan to double the number of troops deployed to more than four hundred thousand.

3. For a more detailed account of the 1994 midterm elections, see Klinkner 1996.

4. The 1994 year dummy and the interaction term, which do not apply to 1990, are set to zero.

Chapter 9

1. A few elections were dropped because of missing data. Also dropped were the four elections in 1990 in which the Democratic candidate was prolife on abortion while the GOP challenger was prochoice. Also, the 1990 Connecticut race was dropped because the victory of an independent candidate complicates the analysis.

2. Each model also includes control variables for whether a respondent was Jewish and a categorical measure of the respondent's age. The Jewish variable is a dummy variable. The age variable ranges from 1 to 4. In some of the states, the Jewish variable drops out because of perfect colinearity with the dependent variable.

3. Such is particularly the case in the analysis presented here because I am unable to control for individual attitudes on abortion as was done in chapter 7.

4. This model includes controls for whether the respondent is Jewish, respondent age, incumbency of the candidates, candidate spending, state ideology, three presidential-year dummy variables, and a dummy variable for the states of the former Confederacy. Their measurement and impact on the probability of voting for the Democratic candidate for governor are outlined in appendix D.

5. The rationale for computing predicted probabilities in this way was outlined in chapter 7.

6. Again, this figure was computed after controlling for whether the respondent was Jewish.

Chapter 10

1. Allen in Virginia did appear to increase the level of support among voters for his relatively new proposal to abolish parole for violent offenders.

2. The Allen campaign provided advice through its Leadership Committee newsletter on when to write letters to newspapers and how such letters should be designed.

3. Reports circulated after the New Jersey election that the GOP had paid ministers in predominantly African-American churches to discourage their parishioners from turning out. Claims made by Whitman consultant Ed Rollins to that regard were investi-

gated, and no evidence of such an effort was uncovered. I also did not hear from any campaign staff members on either side that they suspected Rollins's claims to be true.

Appendixes

1. For their help in making these surveys available, I thank Scott Keeter, director of the Survey Research Lab at Virginia Commonwealth University; Louise Seals, deputy managing editor of the *Richmond Times-Dispatch;* Steve Shaw, director of the research department at Media General; Edwin Artz III, project manager at Media General; and Ken Dautrich, director of the Eagleton Institute of Politics at Rutgers University.

2. These polls were made available through the Interuniversity Consortium for Political and Social Research.

3. At first glance, it may appear that a level of aggregation has been ignored. Much has been made of the influence on voting behavior of contextual factors that may exist at the county or neighborhood level and that appear to have been excluded from both the X and Z matrices. Such is not the case. Contextual factors measured at the substate level can easily be included in X, while similar measures at the state level could be added to Z.

References

Abramowitz, Alan I. 1995. "It's Abortion, Stupid: Policy Voting in the 1992 Presidential Election." *Journal of Politics* 57:176–86.

Aldrich, John H. 1980a. *Before the Convention: Strategies and Choices in Presidential Nomination Campaigns.* Chicago: University of Chicago Press.

Aldrich, John H. 1980b. "A Dynamic Model of Presidential Nomination Campaigns." *American Political Science Review* 74:651–69.

Aldrich, John H., and Michael D. McGinnis. 1989. "A Model of Party Constraints on Optimal Candidate Positions." *Mathematical and Computer Modeling* 12:437–50.

Allen, Mike. 1993a. "Candidates Take Messages on the Road." *Richmond Times-Dispatch,* September 8.

Allen, Mike. 1993b. "New Terry Ads Offer Callers Forty-Page 'Agenda for Action.'" *Richmond Times-Dispatch,* June 8.

Alvarez, R. Michael. 1997. *Information and Elections.* Ann Arbor: University of Michigan Press.

Alvarez, R. Michael, and Charles H. Franklin. 1994. "Uncertainty and Political Perceptions." *Journal of Politics* 56:671–89.

Asher, Herbert B. 1983. "Voting Behavior Research in the 1980s: An Examination of Some Old and New Problem Areas." In *Political Science: The State of the Discipline,* ed. Ada W. Finifter. Washington, D.C.: American Political Science Association.

Atkeson, Lonna Rae, and Randall W. Partin. 1998. "Economic and Referendum Voting and the Problem of Data Choice: A Reply." *American Journal of Political Science* 42:1003–7.

Atkinson, Frank B. 1992. *The Dynamic Dominion: Realignment and the Rise of Virginia's Republican Party since 1945.* Fairfax, Va.: George Mason University Press.

Austen-Smith, David, and Jeffrey Banks. 1989. "Electoral Accountability and Incumbency." In *Models of Strategic Choice in Politics,* ed. Peter Ordeshook. Ann Arbor: University of Michigan Press.

Bartels, Larry M. 1985. "Expectations and Preferences in Presidential Nominating Campaigns." *American Political Science Review* 79:804–15.

Bartels, Larry M. 1987. "Candidate Choice and the Dynamics of the Presidential Nominating Process." *American Journal of Political Science* 31:1–30.

Bartels, Larry M. 1988. *Presidential Primaries and the Dynamics of Public Choice.* Princeton: Princeton University Press.

Bartels, Larry M. 1993. "Messages Received: The Political Impact of Media Exposure." *American Political Science Review* 87:267–85.

Beck, Nathaniel, and Jonathan N. Katz. 1995. "What to Do (and Not to Do) with Time-Series Cross-Section Data." *American Political Science Review* 89:634–47.

Beck, Paul Allen. 1979. "The Electoral Cycle and Patterns of American Politics." *British Journal of Political Science* 9:129–56.

Beck, Paul Allen. 1986. "Choice, Context, and Consequence: Beaten and Unbeaten Paths toward a Science of Electoral Behavior." In *Political Science: The Science of Politics,* ed. Herbert F. Weisberg. New York: Agathon.

Berelson, B., P. Lazarsfeld, and W. McPhee. 1954. *Voting.* Chicago: University of Chicago Press.

Beyle, Thad L. 1990. "Governors." In *Politics in the American States,* ed. Virginia Gray, Herbert Jacob, and Robert B. Albritton. 5th ed. Glenview, Ill.: Scott, Foresman.

Billingsley, Anna Barron. 1993. "From Pews to Polls: Christian Vote Spoke." *Richmond Times-Dispatch,* November 4.

Black, Duncan. 1958. *The Theory of Committees and Elections.* New York: Cambridge University Press. Reprint, Boston: Kluwer Academic, 1987.

Blanchard, Dallas A. 1994. *The Anti-Abortion Movement and the Rise of the Religious Right: From Polite to Fiery Protest.* New York: Twayne.

Box-Steffensmeier, Janet, and Tse-Min Lin. 1992. "A Dynamic Model of Campaign Spending in Congressional Elections." Paper presented at the Ninth Annual Political Methodology Conference, Cambridge, Mass., July 16–19.

Campbell, A., P. Converse, W. Miller, and D. Stokes. 1960. *The American Voter.* New York: Wiley.

Carmines, Edward G., and James A. Stimson. 1989. *Issue Evolution.* Princeton: Princeton University Press.

Carsey, Thomas M. 1995. "The Contextual Effect of Race on White Voter Behavior: The 1989 New York City Mayoral Election." *Journal of Politics* 57:221–28.

Carsey, Thomas M., and Gerald C. Wright. 1998. "State and National Factors in Gubernatorial and Senatorial Elections." *American Journal of Political Science* 42:994–1002.

Chappell, Henry W., Jr., and William Keech. 1986. "Policy Motivation and Party Differences in a Dynamic Spatial Model of Party Competition." *American Political Science Review* 80:881–99.

Chubb, John. 1988. "Institutions, the Economy, and Dynamics of State Elections." *American Political Science Review* 82:133–54.

Clarke, Toni. 1993. "Christie Dons Jeans to Fight Tax Charge." *Trentonian,* August 17.

Cohen, Jeffrey. 1983. "Gubernatorial Popularity in Nine States." *American Politics Quarterly* 11:219–35.

Cohen, Jeffrey E., Michael A. Crassa, and John A. Hamman. 1991. "The Impact of Presidential Campaigns on Midterm U.S. Senate Elections." *American Political Science Review* 85:165–78.

Coleman, James S. 1972. "The Positions of Political Parties in Elections." In *Probability Models of Collective Decision Making,* ed. Richard G. Niemi and Herbert F. Weisberg. Columbus, Ohio: Charles E. Merril.

Conover, P., and S. Feldman. 1984. "The Origins and Meaning of Liberal/Conservative

Self-Identification." In *Controversies in Voting Behavior,* ed. Richard G. Niemi and Herbert F. Weisberg. Washington, D.C.: Congressional Quarterly Press.

Converse, Philip E. 1990. "Popular Representation and the Distribution of Information." In *Information and Democratic Processes,* ed. John A. Ferejohn and James Kuklinski. Urbana: University of Illinois Press.

Cook, Elizabeth Adell, Ted G. Jelen, and Clyde Wilcox. 1992. *Between Two Absolutes: Public Opinion and the Politics of Abortion.* Boulder, Colo.: Westview.

Cooper, Weldon, and Thomas R. Morris. 1976. Introduction to *Virginia Government and Politics,* ed. Cooper and Morris. Charlottesville: University Press of Virginia.

Cotter, Cornelius, James L. Gibson, John F. Bibby, and Robert J. Huckshorn. 1984. *Party Organization in American Politics.* New York: Praeger.

Cowart, Andrew. 1973. "Electoral Choice in the American States: Incumbency Effects, Partisan Forces, and Divergent Partisan Majorities." *American Political Science Review* 67:835–53.

Craig, Barbara, and David O'Brien. 1993. *Abortion and American Politics.* Chatham, N.J.: Chatham House.

Dalton, Russell J., Scott C. Flanagan, and Paul Allen Beck, eds. 1984. *Electoral Change in Advanced Industrial Democracies.* Princeton: Princeton University Press.

Dexter, Lewis Anthony. 1970. *Elite and Specialized Interviewing.* Evanston, Ill.: Northwestern University Press.

Diesing, Paul. 1971. *Patterns of Discovery in the Social Sciences.* New York: Aldine.

Downs, Anthony. 1957. *An Economic Theory of Democracy.* New York: Harper and Row.

Eismeier, Theodore J. 1979. "Budgets and Ballots: The Political Consequences of Fiscal Choice." In *Public Policy and Public Choice,* ed. Douglas W. Rae and Theodore Eismeier. Beverly Hills, Calif.: Sage.

Enelow, James M., and Melvin J. Hinich. 1984. *The Spatial Theory of Voting.* Cambridge: Cambridge University Press.

Erikson, Robert, and Kent L. Tedin. 1981. "The 1928–1932 Partisan Realignment: The Case for the Conversion Hypothesis." *American Political Science Review* 75:951–62.

Erikson, Robert, Gerald Wright, and John McIver. 1993. *Statehouse Democracy.* New York: Cambridge University Press.

Feld, Scott L., and Bernard Grofman. 1988. "Ideological Consistency as a Collective Phenomenon." *American Political Science Review* 82:773–88.

Fenno, Richard F., Jr. 1978. *Home Style: House Members in Their Districts.* Boston: Little, Brown.

Finkel, Steven E. 1995. *Causal Analysis with Panel Data.* Thousand Oaks, Calif.: Sage.

Flanigan, William H., and Nancy H. Zingale. 1994. *Political Behavior of the American Electorate.* 8th ed. Washington, D.C.: Congressional Quarterly Press.

Franklin, Charles H. 1991. "Eschewing Obfuscation? Campaigns and the Perception of U.S. Senate Incumbents." *American Political Science Review* 85:1193–1214.

Gelman, Andrew, and Gary King. 1993. "Why Are American Presidential Election Campaign Polls So Variable When Voters Are So Predictable?" *British Journal of Political Science* 23:409–51.

Goggin, Malcolm. 1993. *Understanding the New Politics of Abortion.* Newbury Park, Calif.: Sage.

Green, Donald P., and Jonathan S. Krasno. 1990. "Rebuttal to Jacobson's 'New Evidence for Old Arguments.'" *American Journal of Political Science* 44:363–72.

Groppe, Maureen, and Jennifer Babson. 1994. "Republican Surge Gives Party Bigger Share of Statehouses." *Congressional Quarterly Weekly Reports,* November 12, 3247–50.

Hammond, Thomas H., and Brian D. Humes. 1993. "'What This Campaign Is All about Is . . .': A Rational Choice Alternative to the Downsian Spatial Model of Elections." In *Information, Participation, and Choice,* ed. Bernard Grofman. Ann Arbor: University of Michigan Press.

Hardy, Michael. 1993. "Wilder Gives Terry, Allen His View on Budget." *Richmond Times-Dispatch.* September 11.

Hershey, Marjorie Randon. 1984. *Running for Office: The Political Education of Campaigners.* Chatham, N.J.: Chatham House.

Hinich, Melvin J., and Michael C. Munger. 1994. *Ideology and the Theory of Political Choice.* Ann Arbor: University of Michigan Press.

Hinich, Melvin J., and Michael C. Munger. 1997. *Analytical Politics.* Cambridge: Cambridge University Press.

Hirschman, Albert O. 1970. *Exit, Voice, and Loyalty.* Cambridge: Harvard University Press.

Holbrook-Provow, Thomas M. 1987. "National Factors in Gubernatorial Elections." *American Politics Quarterly* 15:471–83.

Howell, Susan E., and Robert T. Sims. 1993. "Abortion Attitudes and the Louisiana Governor's Election." *American Politics Quarterly* 21:54–64.

Howell, Susan E., and James M. Vanderleeuw. 1990. "Economic Effects on State Governors." *American Politics Quarterly* 18:158–68.

Huber, P. J. 1967. "The Behavior of Maximum Likelihood Estimates under Non-Standard Conditions." *Proceedings of the Fifth Berkeley Symposium on Mathematical Statistics and Probability* 1:221–33.

Huckfeldt, Robert. 1983. "The Social Contexts of Ethnic Politics: Ethnic Loyalties, Political Loyalties, and Social Support." *American Politics Quarterly* 99:91–123.

Huckfeldt, Robert. 1984. "Political Loyalties and Social Class Ties: The Mechanisms of Contextual Influence." *American Journal of Political Science* 28:399–417.

Huckfeldt, Robert, and Carol Weitzel Kohfeld. 1989. *Race and the Decline of Class in American Politics.* Urbana: University of Illinois Press.

Huckfeldt, Robert, and John Sprague. 1987. "Networks in Context: The Social Flow of Political Information." *American Political Science Review* 81:1197–216.

Huckfeldt, Robert, and John Sprague. 1995. *Citizens, Politics, and Social Communication: Information and Influence in an Election Campaign.* New York: Cambridge University Press.

Idelson, Holly. 1990. "Budgets, Jobs, and Abortion Are Big Issues in States." *Congressional Quarterly Weekly Reports,* September 8, 2840–48.

Inglehart, Ronald. 1985. "Aggregate Stability and Individual-Level Flux in Mass Belief Systems: The Level of Analysis Paradox." *American Political Science Review* 79:97–116.

Jaccard, James, Robert Turrisi, and Choi K. Wan. 1990. *Interaction Effects in Multiple Regression.* Newbury Park, Calif.: Sage.

Jackson, Robert A. 1993. "Voter Mobilization in the 1986 Midterm Election." *Journal of Politics* 55:1081–99.

Jacobson, Gary C. 1980. *Money in Congressional Elections.* New Haven: Yale University Press.

Jacobson, Gary C. 1990. "The Effects of Campaign Spending in House Elections: New Evidence for Old Arguments." *American Journal of Political Science* 34:334–62.

Jacobson, Gary C. 1992. *The Politics of Congressional Elections.* 3d ed. Glenview, Ill.: Scott, Foresman.

Jacobson, Gary C., and Samuel Kernell. 1983. *Strategy and Choice in Congressional Elections.* 2d ed. New Haven: Yale University Press.

Jewell, Malcolm. 1984. *Parties and Primaries: Nominating State Governors.* New York: Praeger.

Jewell, Malcolm, and David Olson. 1988. *Political Parties and Elections in the American States.* 3d ed. Chicago: Dorsey.

Johnson, Mark. 1993. "88% Support Five-Day Waiting Period on Guns." *Richmond Times-Dispatch,* June 16.

Johnston, Richard, Andre Blais, Henry E. Brady, and Jean Crete. 1992. *Letting the People Decide: Dynamics of a Canadian Election.* Stanford, Calif.: Stanford University Press.

Kenney, Patrick J. 1983. "The Effect of State Economic Conditions on the Vote for Governor." *Social Science Quarterly* 64:154–62.

Kenny, Christopher, and Michael McBurrett. 1992. "A Dynamic Model of the Effect of Campaign Spending on Congressional Vote Choice." *American Journal of Political Science* 36:923–37.

Key, V. O. 1949. *Southern Politics in State and Nation.* New York: Knopf. Reprint, Knoxville: University of Tennessee Press, 1984.

King, Gary, Robert O. Keohane, and Sidney Verba. 1994. *Designing Social Inquiry: Scientific Inference in Qualitative Research.* Princeton: Princeton University Press.

Klinkner, Philip A. 1996. *Midterm: Elections of 1994 in Context.* Boulder, Colo.: Westview.

Knight, Kathleen. 1985. "Ideology in the 1980 Election: Ideological Sophistication Does Matter." *Journal of Politics* 47:828–53.

Kone, Susan L., and Richard F. Winters. 1993. "Taxes and Voting: Electoral Retribution in the American States." *Journal of Politics* 55:22–40.

Kuklinski, James H. 1978. "Representativeness and Elections: A Policy Analysis." *American Political Science Review* 72:165–77.

Layman, Geoffrey C., and Thomas M. Carsey. 1998. "Why Do Party Activists Convert? An Analysis of Individual-Level Change on the Abortion Issue." *Political Research Quarterly* 51:723–49.

Lazarsfeld, Paul F., Bernard R. Berelson, and Hazel Gaudet. 1944. *The People's Choice: How the Voter Makes up His Mind in a Presidential Campaign.* New York: Duell, Sloan, and Pearce.

Luker, Kristin. 1984. *Abortion and the Politics of Motherhood.* Berkeley: University of California Press.

McClure, Sandy. 1993a. "Christie Fights for Credibility in Final Days." *Trentonian,* October 21.

McClure, Sandy. 1993b. "GOPers Support Christie's Tax Plan." *Trentonian,* October 6.

McClure, Sandy. 1993c. "GOP Guru Counsels Aimless Christie." *Trentonian,* August 10.

McClure, Sandy. 1993d. "Whitman Tosses in the Sink." *Trentonian,* September 26.

McClure, Sandy, and Phyllis Plitch. 1993. "Christie Looks 'Credible'; Jim Looks over Shoulder." *Trentonian,* October 25.

McKay, David C. 1989. *Domestic Policy and Ideology: Presidents and the American State, 1964–1987.* Cambridge: Cambridge University Press.

Miller, Warren E., and M. Kent Jennings. 1986. *Parties in Transition: A Longitudinal Study of Party Elites and Party Supporters.* New York: Sage.

Niemi, Richard G., and Herbert F. Weisberg. 1984. *Controversies in Voting Behavior.* 2d ed. Washington, D.C.: Congressional Quarterly Press.

Niemi, Richard G., and Herbert F. Weisberg. 1993. *Controversies in Voting Behavior.* 3d ed. Washington, D.C.: Congressional Quarterly Press.

Ordeshook, Peter C. 1986. *Game Theory and Political Theory.* Cambridge: Cambridge University Press.

Ordeshook, Peter C. 1992. *A Political Theory Primer.* New York: Routledge, Chapman, and Hall.

Patterson, Samuel C. 1982. "Campaign Spending in Contests for Governor." *Western Political Quarterly* 35:457–77.

Patterson, Samuel C., and Gregory A. Caldeira. 1983. "Getting out the Vote." *American Political Science Review* 77:675–89.

Peltzman, Sam. 1987. "Economic Conditions and Gubernatorial Elections." *American Economic Review* 77:293–97.

Pieneson, James E. 1977. "Sources of Candidate Success in Gubernatorial Elections, 1910–70." *Journal of Politics* 39:939–58.

Plitch, Phyllis, and Sandy McClure. 1993a. "Newly Relaxed Florio Tightens Grip on Race." *Trentonian,* October 20.

Plitch, Phyllis, and Sandy McClure. 1993b. "Poll: It May Be All over for Whitman." *Trentonian,* September 28.

Pomper, Gerald M. 1968. *Elections in America: Control and Influence in Democratic Politics.* New York: Dodd, Mead.

Popkin, Samuel L. 1991. *The Reasoning Voter: Communication and Persuasion in Presidential Campaigns.* Chicago: University of Chicago Press.

Putnam, Robert. 1966. "Political Attitudes and the Local Community." *American Political Science Review* 60:640–54.

Rabinowitz, George, and Stuart Elaine Macdonald. 1989. "A Directional Theory of Voting." *American Political Science Review* 83:93–122.

RePass, David E. 1971. "Issue Salience and Party Choice." *American Political Science Review* 65:389–400.

Riker, William H. 1982. *Liberalism against Populism.* San Francisco: W. H. Freeman.

Riker, William H. 1990. "Heresthetic and Rhetoric in the Spatial Model." In *Advances in the Spatial Theory of Voting,* ed. James M. Enelow and Melvin J. Hinich. Cambridge: Cambridge University Press.

Sabato, Larry. 1983. *Goodbye to Good-Time Charlies: The American Governorship Transformed.* 2d ed. Washington, D.C.: Congressional Quarterly Press.

Salmore, Barbara G., and Stephen A. Salmore. 1989. *Candidates, Parties, and Campaigns: Electoral Politics in America.* 2d ed. Washington, D.C.: Congressional Quarterly Press.

Salmore, Barbara G., and Stephen A. Salmore. 1993. *New Jersey Politics and Government.* Lincoln: University of Nebraska Press.

Salmore, Stephen A. 1986. "Voting, Elections, and Campaigns." In *The Political State of New Jersey,* ed. Gerald M. Pomper. New Brunswick, N.J.: Rutgers University Press.

Schapiro, Jeff E. 1993a. "Allen Takes Seventeen-Point Lead in Latest Poll." *Richmond Times-Dispatch,* October 17.

Schapiro, Jeff E. 1993b. "'I run better' as Mary Sue than 'Robb-Wilder-Terry.'" *Richmond Times-Dispatch,* November 4.

Schapiro, Jeff E. 1993c. "Poll Gives Seven-Point Lead to Allen." *Richmond Times-Dispatch,* October 19.

Schapiro, Jeff E. 1993d. "Terry, Allen Avoid Talk of Campaign Problems." *Richmond Times-Dispatch,* August 20.

Schapiro, Jeff E. 1993e. "Terry Trying to Retain Women's Vote." *Richmond Times-Dispatch,* October 26.

Schapiro, Jeff E. 1993f. "Terry Urged to Do More Politicking." *Richmond Times-Dispatch,* August 27.

Schapiro, Jeff E., and Michael Hardy. 1993. "State Republicans Turn to the Right." *Richmond Times Dispatch,* June 6.

Segers, Mary C., and Timothy A. Byrnes. 1995. *Abortion Politics in American States.* Armonk, N.Y.: M. E. Sharpe.

Sellers, Patrick J. 1994. "The Dynamics of Credibility in U.S. Congressional Elections." Ph.D diss., Duke University.

Shepsle, Kenneth A. 1979. "Institutional Arrangements and Equilibrium in Multidimensional Voting Models." *American Journal of Political Science* 23:27–59.

Shepsle, Kenneth A., and Barry Weingast. 1981. "Structure Induced Equilibrium and Legislative Choice." *Public Choice* 37:503–19.

Sigelman, Lee. 1989. "Voting in Gubernatorial Succession Referenda: The Incumbency Cue." *Journal of Politics* 51:869–85.

Simon, Dennis M. 1989. "Presidents, Governors, and Electoral Accountability." *Journal of Politics* 51:186–204.

Squire, Peverill. 1989. "Challengers in U.S. Senate Elections." *Legislative Studies Quarterly* 14:531–47.

Squire, Peverill. 1992. "Challenger Profile and Gubernatorial Elections." *Western Political Quarterly* 45:125–42.

Squire, Peverill, and Christina Fastnow. 1992. "Comparing Gubernatorial and Senatorial Elections." Paper presented at the annual meeting of the Midwest Political Science Association, Chicago, April 9–11.

Staggenborg, Suzanne. 1991. *The Pro-Choice Movement: Organization and Activism in the Abortion Conflict.* New York: Oxford University Press.

Stein, Robert M. 1990. "Economic Voting for Governor and U.S. Senator: The Electoral Consequences of Federalism." *Journal of Politics* 52:29–53.

Stimson, James A. 1985. "Regression in Space and Time: A Statistical Essay." *American Journal of Political Science* 29:914–47.

Stonecash, Jeffrey. 1989. "Political Cleavage in Gubernatorial and Legislative Elections: Party Competition in New York, 1970–1982." *Western Political Quarterly* 42:69–81.

Sundquist, James L. 1983. *Dynamics of the Party System.* Rev. ed. Washington, D.C.: Brookings Institution.

Superville, Darlene. 1993. "Whitman Cuts Florio's Lead with Late Rally." *Trentonian,* October 15.

Tingsten, Herbert. 1963. *Political Behavior: Studies in Election Statistics.* Trans. Vilgot Hammarling. Totowa, N.J.: Bedminster.

Tompkins, Mark E. 1984. "The Electoral Fortunes of Gubernatorial Incumbents: 1947–1981." *Journal of Politics* 46:520–43.

Tompkins, Mark E. 1988. "Have Gubernatorial Elections Become More Distinctive Contests?" *Journal of Politics* 50:192–205.

Trentonian. 1993a. "Florio's Victory, N. J.'s Loss." September 29.

Trentonian. 1993b. "Jim's Lead Drops to 6% in Poll of Informed Voters." October 18.

Trentonian. 1993c. "Teachers Spurn Both Gubernatorial Candidates." August 15.

Turett, J. Stephen. 1971. "The Vulnerability of American Governors, 1900–1969." *Midwest Journal of Political Science* 15:108–32.

Weisberg, Herbert F. 1984. "A Multidimensional Conceptualization of Party Identification." In *Controversies in Voting Behavior,* ed. Richard G. Niemi and Herbert F. Weisberg. Washington, D.C.: Congressional Quarterly Press.

White, H. 1980. "A Heteroskedasticity-Consistent Covariance Matrix Estimator and a Direct Test for Heteroskedasticity." *Econometrica* 48:817–30.

Whitley, Tyler. 1993a. "Allen Has Bigger TV Ad Outlay." *Richmond Times-Dispatch,* July 17.

Whitley, Tyler. 1993b. "Allen Seen as Having Difficulty in Raising Money." *Richmond Times-Dispatch,* August 7.

Whitley, Tyler. 1993c. "Allen, Terry Stick to Script." *Richmond Times-Dispatch,* October 8.

Whitley, Tyler. 1993d. "Conservatives Appear to Lead 3 GOP Races." *Richmond Times-Dispatch,* June 3.

Whitley, Tyler. 1993e. "Democrat Suggests 'Buyouts.'" *Richmond Times-Dispatch,* October 2.

Whitley, Tyler. 1993f. "Differing Campaign Plans." *Richmond Times-Dispatch,* November 7.

Whitley, Tyler. 1993g. "GOP Poll Shows Allen, Terry Deadlocked." *Richmond Times-Dispatch,* August 21.

Whitley, Tyler. 1993h. "State FOP Supports Allen." *Richmond Times-Dispatch,* August 31.

Whitley, Tyler. 1993i. "Terry, Allen Trade Charges of Ethics Lapses." *Richmond Times-Dispatch,* September 28.

Whitley, Tyler. 1993j. "Terry Attack: Good or Desperate Move?" *Richmond Times-Dispatch,* October 14.

Whitley, Tyler. 1993k. "Terry Criticizes NRA Ad, Says It's Meant to Boost Allen Effort." *Richmond Times-Dispatch,* September 9.

Whitley, Tyler. 1993l. "Terry Leads Allen in Race, Poll Shows. *Richmond Times-Dispatch,* June 15.

Whitley, Tyler. 1993m. "Terry Proposes Acorn Fund to Aid Small Businesses." *Richmond Times-Dispatch,* September 23.

Whitley, Tyler. 1993n. "Terry Runs First Attack Commercial." *Richmond Times-Dispatch,* September 15.

Whitley, Tyler. 1993o. "Wilder on Robb: Where's the Beef?" *Richmond Times-Dispatch,* May 8.

Whitley, Tyler. 1993p. "Wilder Opposes NAFTA; Robb Undecided." *Richmond Times-Dispatch,* August 28.

Wilkerson, Elizabeth. 1993. "GOP, Democratic Chairmen Go to War." *Richmond Times-Dispatch,* September 30.

Williamson, Richard S. 1990. *Reagan's Federalism: His Efforts to Decentralize Government.* Lanham, Md.: University Press of America.

Wittman, Donald. 1983. "Candidate Motivation: A Synthesis of Alternative Theories." *American Political Science Review* 77:142–57.

Wright, Gerald C. 1974. *Electoral Choice in America.* Chapel Hill, N.C.: Institute for Research in Social Science.

Wright, Gerald C. 1977. "Contextual Models of Electoral Behavior: The Southern Wallace Vote." *American Political Science Review* 71:497–508.

Wright, Gerald C. 1978. "Candidates' Policy Positions and Voting in U.S. Congressional Elections." *Legislative Studies Quarterly* 3:445–64.

Wright, Gerald C. 1993a. "Errors in Measuring Vote Choice in the National Election Studies, 1952–88." *American Journal of Political Science* 37:291–316.

Wright, Gerald C. 1993b. "Representation and the Electoral Cycle in the U.S. Senate." Paper presented at the annual meeting of the Midwest Political Science Association, Chicago, April 15–17.

Wright, Gerald C., and Michael B. Berkman. 1986. "Candidates and Policy in United States Senate Elections." *American Political Science Review* 80:567–90.

Yale, Marilyn. 1993. "Abortion, Elections, and the Media." In *Understanding the New Politics of Abortion,* ed. Malcolm Goggin. Newbury Park, Calif.: Sage.

Zaller, John R. 1992. *The Nature and Origins of Mass Opinion.* New York: Cambridge University Press.

Zuckerman, Alan. 1975. "Political Cleavage: A Conceptual and Theoretical Analysis." *British Journal of Political Science* 5:231–48.

Index